The economics of the American theater

Thomas
Gale
Moore

The economics of
the American theater

Duke University Press, Durham, N.C.   1968

Preface

Like an iceberg, the world of the theater reveals only a small portion of itself to the casual eye—the professional stage. Unnoticed, in small towns, in suburbs, and in rural communities, thousands upon thousands of community playhouses, college theaters, high school plays, and grade school pageants flourish. In churches, in schools, in rented halls, the live drama is brought to millions. The diversity of the effort is overwhelming; its magnitude, awe-inspiring.

To a large extent such theater is divorced from economic considerations; the marketplace has only the remotest connection with most amateur efforts. Primarily for this reason, the present study is restricted to the professional theater. Undoubtedly, more people are exposed to the stage through the efforts of the little theaters than through Broadway; yet, since most community theaters are inspired by the standards set in the professional theater, and since the scripts performed are usually drawn from those done in New York, it seems more important to concentrate on the professional stage.

The purpose of the study has been broad—to discover the present state of the American professional theater. The stage of today has been compared with the stage of the past and projected toward the stage of the future. The factors most essential to an understanding of the forces affecting the American theater have been explored. Economic trends have been charted, underlying forces traced, the theater's problems indicated. However, because the available data are poor, conclusions must be tentative. Notwithstanding these limitations, interesting and hopefully valid conclusions on the plight of the stage in the United States have been drawn.

The work, except in Chapter VIII, is focused on the professional theater, which is taken to be conterminous with the jurisdiction of the Actors' Equity Association, the union for actors and actresses. The work begins with a discussion of the New York stage, then takes a close look at two key theatrical figures—the producer and the playwright. Costs on Broadway, the theatergoer, and supply and demand for seats are then analyzed, and after an exploration of the theater outside Manhattan, the issues of subsidies, taxes, and potential public policies affecting the performing arts are examined.

An attempt has been made to present the report in a fashion comprehensible both to economists and to those whose interests lie primarily in the theater. Consequently, both groups may find certain parts obvious: what seems simple to those familiar with the stage may be unknown to an economist; conversely, techniques and terms used daily by economists may be completely unfamiliar to even the most knowledgeable layman. I hope, therefore, that the reader will tolerate those sections which were written primarily to explain a point to those without his experience. A glossary of terms is included. Since many common words are here used with special meanings the reader is strongly urged to consult it.

This study would never have been made without the financial support of the Rockefeller Foundation and the aid and encouragement of the Carnegie Institute of Technology. I am deeply grateful to both. In particular, I must thank Richard M. Cyert and George Leland Bach, who have been most helpful. Unfortunately, I cannot begin to express my appreciation to the countless individuals who, through interviews, through responses to questionnaires, and by providing me with financial records, have made this work possible. I must especially thank Irving Cheskin at the League of New York Theatres, the Dramatists Guild, Herman Shumlin, Henry Hewes, and the late John Shubert for contributing their time in order to straighten out many of the author's misconceptions; the study would be less complete without their efforts. In addition I must thank William Baumol, Leonard Rapping, and Martin Bronfenbrenner for critically reading various parts of the manuscript and for their suggestions. Finally, I must express my gratitude to James M. Ferguson, who read the entire manuscript and significantly contributed to its clarity and its accuracy with his perceptive comments. Most of all I must thank my wife Sandra, who not only has read and reread this manuscript to ferret out errors and improve its style but has been a constant source of encouragement. Naturally, I am solely responsible for any remaining errors.

Table of contents

List of tables

List of charts

Glossary

Theater terms

box office receipts Income received for tickets sold, excluding federal excise tax and any city or state taxes.

gross receipts Synonymous with **box office receipts.**

ice Strictly speaking, a bribe to the box office for supplying tickets. The term will be used in this book, as it is often used, to describe any and all illegal receipts above box office prices.

musical A show with music, in which song and dance are generally integrated with the plot.

new show A production hitherto unproduced in New York, but which may have been done abroad, or in summer or winter stock.

operating costs Weekly expenses after a show has opened.

play A dramatic effort on stage that has no more than incidental music.

production Any type of live presentation on the stage, be it a play, musical, review, reading, or solo performance; almost all productions are either plays or musicals.

production costs Those expenses incurred prior to opening a show.

repertory company A stock company that alternates its shows every night.

resident company A permanently located stock company that usually operates during the winter months.

revival A show that has been performed previously.

scalping The selling of tickets illegally, either at a price above the legal limit or by a source not licensed to trade in tickets.

season From June 1 to May 31.

show Synonymous with **production.**

stock company A company whose actors are hired for a particular period of time to do several shows.

straight show	Synonymous with **play.**
summer season	From spring to fall.
tent company	A summer stock company that performs in a tent.
winter stock	Synonymous with **resident company.**

Economic and statistical terms

dependent variable	A variable, such as number of shows, whose value depends on the value of one or more other variables.
dummy variable	A variable that takes on the value of zero or one to distinguish between two situations.
elasticity	A measure of the effect one variable has on another. It is the percentage change in the dependent variable divided by the percentage change in the independent.
independent variable	A variable whose value, for the problem being discussed, is determined by forces outside the problem.
logarithm	The power to which ten must be raised to be equal to the original value.
mean	The sum of all observations divided by the number of observations.
median	The middle figure; half are above and half below.
regression	A statistical analysis of the relationship between a dependent variable and one or more independent variables. Quantitative estimates are made of these relationships.

Introduction

At the first recorded theatrical performance in the American colonies, the performers were arrested. From that 1665 performance of the playlet *Ye Bare and Ye Cubb* at Accomac, Virginia, to *Cat on a Hot Tin Roof* is a long road which this book, while not primarily a history, will trace in part.[1] Using the force of the law to stamp out the theater was not unusual: statutes banning the stage were enacted, and puritanical minds attempted to suppress it. It was not until after the Revolution that, with George Washington's patronage, the theater began to be considered respectable— but only to visit, not to play in.

During the nineteenth century many cities and towns cultivated their own resident stock companies. As transportation improved, they were able to lure stars, usually English, to tour and headline their local productions. The dream was sound but the results were sometimes calamitous. The "pear-shaped tones" of resident actors were at best only barely adequate. It was not long before the harassed and weary traveling stars were forced to include capable supporting actors in their entourage. The next step was inevitable: whole shows toured and the road was born. With the spread of the railroad and the consequent rate reduction, mounting a production in New York or Chicago to tour became cheaper than having local companies produce their own shows. More and more touring companies steadily invaded the domain of waning stock.

After that, homegrown theaters suffered a series of blows: audiences deserted the local product in favor of the more professional shows; then motion pictures siphoned off much of the twenty-five-cent gallery; next the automobile carried America to the big cities for recreation. Resident companies virtually disappeared from the American scene until, years later, the Depression furnished the coup de grâce. Since World War II a faint resurrection has been witnessed; under a non-profit format, local stock and repertory companies—generally privately subsidized—have gradually reappeared in major cities.

As the road replaced the stock system, the importance of New York grew. At first, shows were organized in Chicago, but the public preferred productions that had first met the challenge of a New York audience. By World War I, producers were launching shows on Broadway, hoping only

1. John Anderson, *The American Theatre* (New York: Dial Press, 1938), p. 8.

to cover their production costs. Their profits, they expected, would come from the road.

With the further advancement of motion pictures and of high-powered automobiles, the road, so lately flourishing, also began to wither. No longer were plays opened in New York with the expectation of earning profits by touring. Now they were tried out in Hartford, Boston, or Washington to insure the perfection demanded by critical New Yorkers. Only if productions were successful in Manhattan were they sent on tour. While continuing to shrink slowly, the road still remains an important element in the theater.

The New York theater has been least affected by the calamities that have devastated the stage outside Manhattan. Until the advent of sound in motion pictures, Broadway continued to thrive. Subsequently, the New York theater fared better than the stage elsewhere—except for summer stock theater—and with the birth of off-Broadway since the war, it has flourished.

The onset of the Great Depression produced one new form of theater—summer stock. For all practical purposes unknown in the nineteenth century, summer theater was born under the whiplash of hard times. Bread lines and casting lines sent actors in search of places to perform. Deserted barns, abandoned gristmills, and old halls were transformed into country theaters. From these shaky beginnings the "straw-hat" theater has spread and grown until it dwarfs in number and variety all other forms of the stage in the United States.

By the middle of the twentieth century, the Broadway theater, off-Broadway, touring companies, summer stock, winter stock, and repertory companies formed the world of the professional theater. In spite of its being the most discussed, written about, and worried about part, New York is only one aspect of the theater. The giant is summer stock; according to *Equity* editor Dick Moore, twice as many actors are employed during the summer as during the winter.[2] Box office receipts from touring companies totaled almost $40 million in the 1961/62 season.[3] According to the *Census of Business, 1958* eighteen out of twenty of the largest metropolitan areas outside New York had stock or repertory companies in existence.[4] A partial tabulation reveals that in 1962/63 at least 149 new scripts had American premieres outside New York City—not counting Broadway tryouts[5]—almost three times the number opening on Broadway itself.

2. Interview with the author, October, 1961.
3. *Variety,* June 26, 1963, p. 71.
4. Computed from a tabulation of unpublished census data on theatrical establishments in major metropolitan areas. Hereafter these data will be referred to as Special Census Tabulation.
5. *The Best Plays of 1962–1963,* ed. Henry Hewes (New York: Dodd, Mead, 1963), pp. 358–362.

Yet New York remains the heartbeat of theatrical activity. While drama in the rest of the country exceeds in quantity that in Manhattan, Broadway and off-Broadway set the pattern and primarily determine what the rest of the country will see.

The economics of the American theater

I | The New York theater

A few square blocks on Manhattan Island dominate the theater in the United States. There are shown the most polished productions; there congregate the greatest actors; there the largest audiences converge every night. "Why?" might a frustrated theatergoer in Chicago or Washington ask, "Why does New York have so much and the rest of the country so little? Is it just because it is bigger?"

Over half the receipts of legitimate theaters in the United States originate in Manhattan, far more than even the huge population around New York could explain.[1] Moreover, as Table I-1 shows, the number of theatrical organizations, such as theaters, repertory companies, and producing organizations, per capita in New York far exceeds those in other areas. In the metropolitan area of New York there are over 16 establishments for each million of population; Chicago and Los Angeles, the next two largest cities, have 1.9 and 6.8 per million respectively. All other major cities have fewer establishments per million than does Los Angeles. New York, in other words, has considerably more theater than would be expected on the basis of population alone.

Why then should there be so much theater in New York? Perhaps it is cheaper to produce a play in Manhattan than elsewhere. Perhaps some element—such as skilled acting talent—necessary to the production is located or concentrated in New York. Perhaps it is more efficient to bring theatergoers to one locality than to bring the theater to the theatergoers.

If it is cheaper to produce a show in Manhattan than elsewhere, ticket prices should be lower or certainly no higher than ticket prices in other areas. Ticket charges, however, are lower outside New York. In a week drawn at random during the 1961/62 season no city among the fifteen that had visiting touring companies listed prices as high as those in New York. For example, during that week, the average ticket price for a straight show on Broadway was $5.02; in Milwaukee, $4.46; in San Francisco, $4.05; in Boston, $3.75; and in Washington, $3.18. Although the cost of a seat in Milwaukee was higher than anywhere else outside Manhattan, it was still almost sixty cents less than the cost on Broadway. Since ticket prices are higher in New York than elsewhere and since we have good

1. Special Census Tabulation.

Table I-1 Theatrical establishments per one million population in major standard metropolitan statistical areas

Central city	Establishments
New York–Northeastern New Jersey Standard Consolidated Area	16.25
Chicago–Northwestern Indiana Standard Consolidated Area	1.89
Los Angeles Metropolitan Area	6.83
Detroit Metropolitan Area	1.16
Philadelphia Metropolitan Area	4.47
San Francisco Metropolitan Area	2.96
Washington Metropolitan Area	2.86
Pittsburgh Metropolitan Area	5.83
San Diego Metropolitan Area	5.43
Baltimore Metropolitan Area	1.64
Boston Metropolitan Area	4.22
Seattle Metropolitan Area	2.56

Source: Special Census Tabulation.

reason to believe that the Broadway theater is highly competitive,[2] it is probably true that operating and production costs are greater in New York than in other cities.

Is the theater then concentrated in New York because of the availability of an essential factor? Certainly there are many performers living around Manhattan not only because of the theater but because of the employment opportunities in radio, television, and night clubs. Yet, according to the 1960 census, there are more actors in Los Angeles than in New York. The concentration of performers, therefore, cannot be the sole explanation. No other ingredient essential to the theater seems wedded to Manhattan. Therefore it cannot be the localization of some necessary factor which results in a concentration of dramatic activity.

The centralization of the theater must stem from demand. Since it is easier and cheaper for the public to go to the theater than for the theater to go to the public, the bigger the city the more theatrical variety it can offer. Consequently, play-lovers, who wish to be able to select from the largest variety will tend to visit Manhattan. But visitors alone cannot explain the large amount of theatrical activity in New York. Inasmuch as 70 per cent of the audience is from the metropolitan area, the New York audience must be supporting about 70 per cent of the establishments—a rate of about 11.4 theaters per million population. Therefore, even excluding the portion of the stage supported by outsiders, New York contains more theater rel-

2. See Appendix D.

ative to its population than do other cities.[3] From this we must deduce that New Yorkers like the theater more than do people outside the area. Of course, many industries that are related to the performing arts are concentrated in Manhattan. Advertising executives and radio and television personnel would naturally have strong interest in Broadway. Moreover, it seems likely that young men and women who are enthusiastic about the performing arts tend to look for work in New York rather than in other cities.

The net result is that drama enthusiasts tend to congregate in New York. As a consequence the rest of the country is stripped of those who might do the most to encourage local theater. In part, then, the dominance of Manhattan stems from easy transportation—the jet plane and the automobile—which facilitates a movement to the New York area of those interested in the theater and related fields.

The trend in Broadway activity

Since New York and especially Broadway are so important, it is essential that we investigate its past and the forces shaping its future. Was Howard Taubman right when he wrote, "It is later than Broadway thinks"?[4] Articles suggesting the theater is ailing have become commonplace. In fact, its early demise is constantly being predicted. Substantiating the gloomy picture has been the drop in productions launched on Broadway, from a high of 264 in 1927/28 to 67 in 1964/65.[5] Simultaneously, the number of new plays slumped from 183 to 35 and new musicals declined from 53 to 17.[6] The contraction in the theater has not, however, been continuous. Under the impetus of a booming stock market, a pleasure-seeking public, and a "permanent plateau of prosperity," total productions increased from just under 150 after World War I to a peak of 264 in the late twenties. They fell rapidly, as can be seen in Chart I-1, during the thirties. Buoyed by a populace in search of release during World War II and the Korean War, the number of shows opening rose slightly. The trend in new plays and musicals parallels the record of total productions. If the trend since World War II continues, the average number of openings on Broadway by 1970 will be 43; by 1980, it will be under 34.[7]

To the casual theatergoer, the number of openings must be an irrele-

3. We are assuming, falsely, that all theatrical activity in other cities is supported by local people. Undoubtedly part of the audience must be tourists as well. Thus other cities would have an even smaller number of establishments supported by residents than the figures in Table I-1 suggest. New Yorkers, then, must visit the theater considerably more frequently than do people in other areas.
4. New York *Times*, May 26, 1963, Sec. 2, p. 1.
5. *Variety*, June 26, 1966, p. 64.
6. *Ibid.*
7. Based on an extrapolation of the regression of time on openings, in logarithms, from 1945/46 to 1962/63.

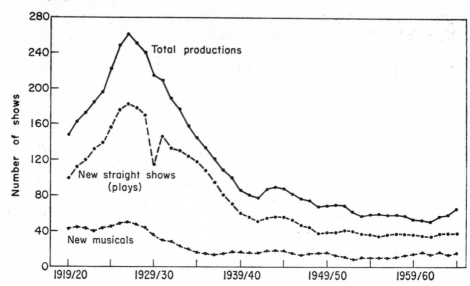

Chart I-1 Three-year moving average of total production and new shows, 1919/20 to 1962/63

Source: See Appendix A, Table A-1.

vant statistic trotted out by the Broadway pundits each June. John Q. Public is far more impressed with the range of his selection. If, as during a typical week in February, 1927, twenty-seven plays and seventeen musicals are gracing the boards, the playgoer is more likely to find agreeable fare than if, as in February, 1963, there were only fifteen straight shows and nine musicals.[8] While productions per season have contracted 80 per cent, during an average week in February the number of shows playing has declined only 50 per cent (see Chart I-2).

From the roaring twenties to the pit of the Depression, the playgoer's selection of shows shrank by considerably more than half. The musical theater was especially hard hit; in February, 1934, only two shows were bringing song and dance to New York, compared to seventeen just seven years earlier. Theatergoers responded to Broadway's offerings as might be expected. Tickets sold at musicals dropped precipitously;[9] but since Americans love pretty girls, music, and dancing, the musical stage recovered strongly from those bleak days, although it never reached the pre-Depression, pre-sound motion picture level of the twenties.

Serious theater was more in keeping with bread lines. The non-musical stage, even though it contracted from 1930 to 1934, fell less than the

8. All data referring to a typical or average week in February are an average of the four weeks of the month.

9. See Appendix A, Table A-3, for data and sources.

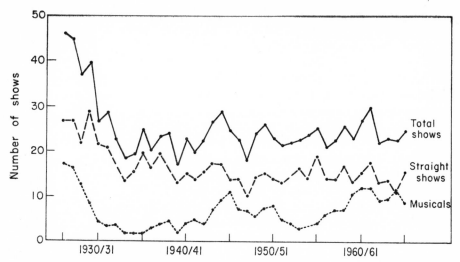

Chart I-2 Number of shows playing during an average week in February, 1926/27 to 1962/63

Source: See Appendix A, Table A-2.

musical theater, but unfortunately for those in search of serious nourishment, it has remained static since the time of the New Deal. Because of rise in attendance at musicals, however, more theatergoers are visiting the Times Square area than at any time since the twenties with the exception of the booming war years.

The disparate trends in openings and shows playing point up an important phenomenon—shows have been running longer. Around the time of the Civil War a play that ran for two or three weeks was a smash hit; today a moderate success will last for over a year. In the late twenties the average play ran for 70 performances, but today the mean number of performances is about 150—more than twice as long. The number of performances for musicals has grown from around 115 to over 300: the average run has more than doubled.[10]

What is the best criterion for evaluating the health of the theater? Those concerned with the variety of shows available within a season will consider that Chart I-1—the number of openings each season on Broadway—most accurately reflects the situation. Note, in support of this position, that Broadway is the final test for new plays. It is the source of most properties used in summer, community, amateur, and university theaters; it is also an inspiration for motion pictures and sometimes television; it feeds scores and librettos to the record industry. Hence, from the point of

10. See Appendix A, Table A-6, for average runs.

view of the theater outside New York and of other entertainment media, the more new productions per season the better. For them the contraction in Broadway has naturally been unfortunate. As a source of new scripts, Broadway has diminished. At its peak, over two hundred new plays and musicals a season (many were of course unsuitable for use outside Manhattan) were being made available to summer, community, college, and local theaters. In the fifties, only forty to fifty new productions became available each season; the situation is only slightly better today.

Yet if we evaluate Broadway as a source of entertainment, the picture is brighter. Today, those who attend the theater irregularly and out-of-towners who visit New York infrequently are offered a wide selection. A potential patron of the theater in every year since 1933 has been able to choose among fifteen to eighteen straight shows; and while during the Depression he had a choice of only two musicals, he could select from ten in 1963.[11] Clearly, casual theatergoers—those who attend less than fifteen times a year—can almost always find shows they have not seen. On the other hand, since turnover is slower nowadays, theater votaries more often find themselves in the annoying position of having seen everything available.

Performers, stagehands, musicians, and box office personnel heed most the number of workweeks available during the year. Total performances—a measure of weeks of work—fell to half the level of the late twenties by 1933/34, aggravating a chronically bad unemployment situation. Throughout the thirties and into the war, the number of performances annually remained low and employed actors were rare. Under the impetus of swarms of servicemen in search of an evening of entertainment, theatrical activity boomed during the war, pushing total annual performances to a peak that had only been exceeded during the late twenties and early thirties and which has never been topped since. In recent seasons, performances have totaled between 8,000 and 9,500 per season, about the same as during the Depression.[12] Job opportunities in terms of weeks of work have thus not declined during the last thirty years.

From the financial end, with the possible exception of profits, gross receipts chart more accurately the health of the theater than any other measure. The earnings of theater proprietors, producers, and playwrights depend on box office receipts. After 1930, the decline in receipts—they fell 60 per cent—was so sharp and abrupt that numerous theaters—the Shubert chain for example—were unable to pay their creditors. From the disastrous year 1933/34 to the present, total gross has inched upward

11. During February.
12. See Appendix A, Table A-7, for data and sources.

mostly as a result of box office gains for musicals.[13] But when changes in the value of the dollar are taken into account, average receipts per show per week have not improved.

Theaters

Towards the end of the twenties, when Broadway was still flourishing, as many as eighty legitimate houses were in operation on an average for over 200 performances.[14] With property owners generally keeping 45 per cent of the box office receipts, theatrical real estate was profitable and new theaters were being built as late as 1929. As stage activity dwindled, the mean number of performances per season declined to a low of 139 per house in 1931/32. Theater owners suffered; only a few houses could become cinemas and share in the Depression-reduced film audiences. Competition for the few productions led to a decline in rentals, and theater terms fell from 45 per cent of the gross to about 30 per cent in 1939.

Almost twenty years went by, it appears, before theaters again made profits for the owners. From the 1929/30 season until 1948/49, the number of houses on Broadway continued to shrink. During the fifties, as houses became television studios and then shifted back, the number of theaters oscillated between thirty and thirty-three. Then the reclaiming of the Little, the Biltmore, and the Ziegfeld from television and motion pictures pushed the total upward. By the middle of 1964, Broadway could boast thirty-six houses, and counting the thirty-four to thirty-six off-Broadway theaters, Manhattan had about seventy legitimate theaters.

Moreover, houses are in operation for more performances than ever. From the 1942/43 season, the average number of performances has been consistently above 220 and through much of this period has hovered over 280.[15] The restoration of theaters to Broadway and the strong demand for their services as reflected in performances per house, suggests that real estate operations have become more profitable.

Profits and risks

But are there profits for the investor in a Broadway show? Those Broadway "angels" who supply the backing do not put up $100,000 solely because they love the theater. Almost to a man, they hope and expect to receive their money and more back. Until their investment is repaid, the backers receive the operating surplus—the difference between weekly operating costs and box office gross. Once their investment is returned (only about one out of five is completely recouped) they receive half the operat-

---

13. See Appendix A, Table A-4, for data and sources.
14. See Appendix A, Table A-8, for data and sources.
15. *Ibid.*

ing surplus as their share of the profit. The longer a show runs, normally, the greater the profits.

The payoff to investors depends on production costs and operating surplus as well as length of run. As noted above, runs have approximately doubled since the twenties; however, the average cost of mounting a production has tripled.[16] There has been some gain in operating surplus over the last thirty-five years, and the net result is probably that average profits have remained constant. Yet averages can conceal more than they reveal. Not all shows last for twice as many performances as the average production could boast during the twenties. In fact, although a few productions now run for years, many close immediately. In 1927/28, 12.8 per cent of the straight shows played fewer than ten performances; but in the three seasons following 1957, 23 per cent remained open for fewer than ten nights, many shuttering after one or two evenings. A comparison of Charts I-3 and I-4, which show the distribution of length of runs of shows open-

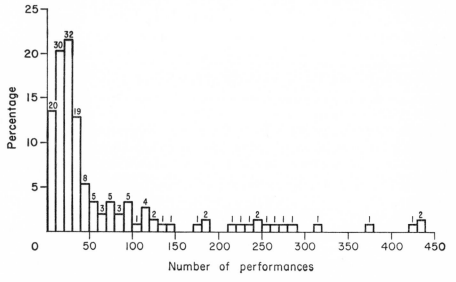

Chart I-3 Distribution of performances for 156 plays opening 1927/28 season

Note: Numbers above bars show the number of plays running that long.
Sources: The Best Plays of 1927-1928 and *The Best Plays of 1928-1929,* ed. Burns Mantle (New York: Dodd, Mead, 1928 and 1929).

ing in the two periods, is startling. In 1927/28 no play ran for more than 440 performances; but in the more recent period, twelve plays—10 per cent of the total—lasted for more than 450 performances.

The contrast between the two charts also reveals an interesting change

16. See Chapter III.

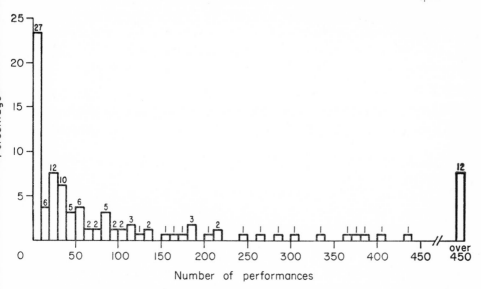

Chart I-4 Distribution of performances for 116 plays opening 1957/58 to
1959/60 seasons

Note: Numbers above bars show the number of plays running that long.
Sources: Best Plays volumes for each season and *Variety,* June issues.

in the Broadway climate. During the twenties, many shows persisted for
two, three, or four weeks. By the late fifties, however, plays either shut
promptly or made a substantial go of it. Note how few straight shows ran
between eleven and twenty performances. After a few nights, it became obvious whether or not a production could cover its operating expenses. If
not, it quickly closed. No longer do producers hope that word of mouth
will build an audience. In earlier years, it was possible to run a production
until an audience developed. Whether this is now out of the question because costs are too high to risk running at a loss, or because audiences have
changed and will attend nothing less than a hit, is uncertain. Certainly the
difference between the two charts indicates there has been a real polariza-
tion in length of run: a play becomes either a great success or a quick failure; a moderate success is becoming less and less frequent.

The proportion of plays that recoup their investment has remained constant over this period. For the three seasons in the late fifties, *Variety* listed
twenty-six straight shows—22.4 per cent—as having made some profit.[17]
Most plays that returned a profit had run over 250 performances; the few
that made it with a short run either had successful road tours before opening or an extraordinarily low initial investment. A typical play during the

17. *Variety,* May 29, 1957, p. 68; May 28, 1958, p. 72; May 27, 1959, p. 71.

twenties, on the other hand, took only 64 performances on the average to become financially successful.[18] Thirty-three plays or 21 per cent of the total produced during the 1927/28 season ran more than 64 performances. The proportion of hits in that season is apparently no different from the proportion in the late fifties.

With the investment per play being considerably higher and with failures folding faster, the theater appears to have become a riskier venture. While on the average it may be as profitable as ever, taking into account changes in the value of money, investors lose more with an unsuccessful production and gain more with a profitable one than they did before the Depression.

Backing plays can be lucrative: Mr. and Mrs. Howard S. Cullman earned about $2,000,000 on three hundred productions from 1938 to 1961; Mr. Arthur Cantor, who invested in forty-one shows between 1957 and 1961, had twenty-five successes which produced roughly a 50 per cent profit on his investment of $103,000.[19] According to one study, an investor who supported all the shows between 1948 and 1958 would have earned 19.5 per cent annually on his money.[20] Unfortunately, it is impossible to become an investor in all shows. Whereas some producers finance their own shows, others have a coterie of backers and seek new sources of money only when a property looks particularly dubious. New producers will also accept financing from all sources. Neither situation is normally profitable. Nevertheless, compared with profit rates in other sectors of the economy, 20 per cent appears high.[21] The theater is more perilous than most other enterprises, however, and investors may require a higher rate of return as compensation for the added risk.[22]

Critics and success

Playwrights and producers frequently complain about the power of critics to make or break a show.[23] Profits often hinge, they claim, on six or seven men, writing hurriedly, usually late at night, a few words on an unsettled performance—the opening. Universally poor notices have normally resulted in the quick shuttering of productions and good notices

18. Alfred L. Bernheim, *The Business of the Theatre: An Economic History of the American Theatre* (New York: Actors' Equity Association, 1932; reissued, New York: Benjamin Blom, 1964), p. 206.

19. New York *Times,* June 5, 1961, p. 40.

20. John Gaydon Watts, "Economics of the New York Legitimate Theater, 1948–1958" (Unfinished Ph.D. dissertation, Columbia University, n.d.), chap. v.

21. See George J. Stigler, *Capital and Rates of Return in Manufacturing Industries* (Princeton: Princeton University Press, 1963).

22. See W. B. Hickman, *Corporate Bond Quality and Investor Experience* (Princeton: Princeton University Press, 1958), for evidence that investors do require a premium to bear risk.

23. See Chapter II, p. 38, for some complaints about critics.

have often been followed by substantial runs. Yet exceptions stand out: *Tobacco Road* and *Abie's Irish Rose* were received with critical scorn but had record runs. If a correlation exists between reviews and profits, it may only mean that critics reflect public tastes. To prove they control the destiny of a play it would be necessary to show that profits would have been different had the reviewers written more or less favorably. Such a proof is impossible to establish; however, as Chapter V notes, the longer a play runs, the less and less theatergoers depend on the notices and the more they rely on word-of-mouth for choosing shows.

To measure the relationship between reviews and profits, the views of the New York daily newspaper critics were tabulated and the percentage of favorable reviews were correlated with the profits of the productions. Only 34 per cent of the variance in profits could be "explained" by the notices (holding musical or non-musical constant).[24] The results are unimpressive. Reviewers can hardly be said to have a major effect on profits; it does not even appear that they are a very accurate reflection of public preferences.

Reasons for the decline

What do these figures and charts reveal about Broadway? In the late twenties and early thirties, three developments decimated the theater: the Great Depression, the introduction of sound motion pictures, and the growth of radio. The sharp fall in income and employment from 1929 to 1933 cut attendance drastically. While the 1932/33 season was bad, probably the worst one in the stage's modern history was 1933/34. Most industries were depressed at that time, but by the end of the thirties, the rest of the economy had regained its pre-Depression level. The theater never recovered. Some other factor or factors were at work.

When dialogue, music, and songs came to the screen, a whole new dimension of entertainment opened. While Mary Pickford, Rudolph Valentino, and Charlie Chaplin had brought tears and laughter to millions, it was not until October, 1927, when *The Jazz Singer,* starring Al Jolson, opened that the musical stage had competition. An instant hit, it was the harbinger of a wave of sound films. According to the *Census of Manufactures,* 1,347 motion pictures were produced in 1927, almost all of which were silent; two years later, 1,204 films were produced, of which only 270—22 per cent—were silent.[25]

The effect of sound on motion pictures and on the theater can be seen

24. A multiple regression with a dummy variable for musical-straight show was used. The F statistic was 37.39, which, for the 149 observations, is significant at considerably better than the 1 per cent level.

25. Bureau of the Census, *Census of Manufactures, 1927* (Washington, D. C.: Government Printing Office, 1929), pp. 1203–1205, and *Census of Manufactures, 1932* (Washington, D. C.: Government Printing Office, 1930), pp. 1323–1325.

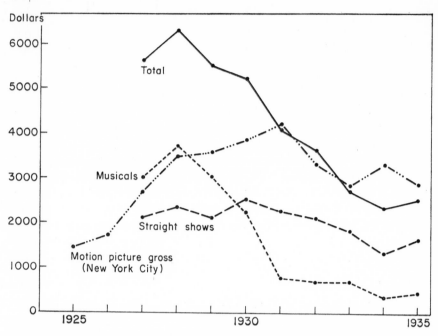

Chart I-5 Total box office receipts, 1925 to 1935 (1963 dollars)
Source: See Appendix A, Table A-4, for data and sources.

in Chart I-5. With the invention of the synchronous sound track, motion picture grosses at downtown New York theaters doubled.[26] Note that in February, 1929, before the onslaught of the Depression, box office receipts at Broadway musicals had begun to wither. By 1931, when the film houses were at their pre-Depression peak, sales for musicals had fallen to 20 per cent of their previous crest. As might be expected, talking motion pictures had less effect on straight shows. Box office earnings of dramas and comedies reached a maximum two years after the musical theater had started to slide. Although gross receipts of plays have never returned to their pre-1930 level, the reduction in earnings was considerably less sharp than it was for musicals.

Besides changing the entertainment habits of millions, sound revolutionized Hollywood. Some stars found themselves laughed at when their voices were heard. One by one, these unfortunates fell into limbo. Directors, masters with the camera, had to learn the most elementary principles of integrating dialogue with motion. Plot and situation writers became inadequate. Picture companies turned swiftly to the great reservoir of trained

26. Computed from 1926 to 1929. The basic data and sources are given in Appendix A, Table A-4.

artists—the New York theater. Talented writers, inspired thespians, and famed directors were lured with large offers to forsake the legitimate stage. Since Hollywood could offer much more than Broadway, they went.

The Jazz Singer had two effects on the New York theater: the audience deserted the stage for the cheaper substitutes, and personnel (stars, writers, and directors) were diverted to films. If the former effect were dominant, we should expect a decline in Broadway ticket prices, since those resources which were unable to shift easily out of the theater—such as the Broadway houses themselves[27]—would be forced to accept lower prices for their services. Costs, therefore, would come down and ticket prices would fall. But the cost of a seat rose! Between 1926/27 and 1934/35—in the face of a 60 per cent contraction in the number of tickets sold[28]—ticket prices to plays climbed 21 per cent and to musicals, 5 per cent.[29] Simultaneously, theater rentals were being reduced. Production and operating expenses, therefore, must have shot up: from the late twenties to 1940, production costs almost doubled and operating outlays advanced by 43 per cent (see Chart III-1). Although responsible for only part of this rise, Hollywood must certainly have been a major factor.

Also contributing to the difficulties of the stage was the growth of radio. Even though it seems an unsatisfactory substitute for live drama, and even though it appealed to a mass audience which rarely attended the theater, radio did attract creative theatrical personnel. The networks as well as Hollywood and Broadway now bid for Helen Hayes. Undoubtedly, both radio and motion pictures forced production costs higher during the thirties.

In the long run, though, it was the combined effects on supply and demand that cut weekly attendance in half. By 1940, an individual in search of entertainment could listen at almost no cost to "Amos and Andy," "Stella Dallas," or "The Firestone Hour." He could see *Gone With the Wind* for $0.75 and most other films for less. To lure him to Broadway at $2.00 or $3.30, producers had to offer finer entertainment—the best actors, the best scripts, and the best effects. Yet talented individuals are always in short supply and with the advent of sound films and radio were much in demand elsewhere. Faced with a crippling shortage of gifted practitioners, producers offered fewer shows.

The reader may believe that since motion pictures and radio had such an effect on the stage, television also must have hurt Broadway. The data,

27. Theaters can easily become movie houses; however, while the number of motion picture theaters in midtown New York increased 50 per cent from twelve to eighteen between 1926 and 1930, the rise was too small to compensate for a 50 per cent reduction in performances in the more than sixty legitimate houses. To remain profitable, thirty theaters would have had to shift to motion pictures, and the market was inadequate to support that many new film houses.
28. See Appendix A, Table A-3, for basic data.
29. See Appendix A, Table A-5, for data and sources.

however, do not support such a supposition. From a few experimental programs in 1945, television grew rapidly. By 1950, antennas were spouting from almost every New York rooftop. Five years later almost every city in the country was within reach of a station. Yet during that period no particular trend downward in attendance or box office receipts can be detected (see Chart I-2), nor is there a divergence from trends in effect before the war or after the middle of the fifties. Television appears to have taken the audience from the cinema and put it in an armchair at home but left theatergoers completely unmoved.

While the stagnation of Broadway has often been blamed on a rise in ticket prices since the war, most of the upward trend can be attributed to inflation. Since the end of World War II the price of the best seat at a straight show has risen, in real terms, only 15 per cent and at a musical, only 8 per cent.[30] Compared with the thirties, today's seats cost, in real terms, less: in 1934/35 the average price for the best seat at a play was $7.76, in 1966/67 it was $7.23. If inflation is taken into account, ticket prices have not changed up through the 1966/67 season. Surprisingly, musical prices have dropped: in 1929/30 the charge was $10.15, but in 1966/67 it was down to $9.18.[31]

In summary, then, it is the shortage of qualified performers, accomplished writers, and masterful directors, rather than of excessively high seat tariffs, that has prevented Broadway from expanding. As we shall see in Chapters II and III, mounting costs have forced producers to rely more on those shows which are almost sure to have a long run. The result has been a slow growth in total attendance (musicals and straight shows), in total box office receipts, and in total performances. The improvement in these statistics, however, has been due solely to a growth in the musical stage. The stagnation in non-musical productions and the unceasing slide in new offerings contribute to pessimistic predictions for Broadway's future.

Off-Broadway

During the last decade and a half the New York theater has been supplemented by off-Broadway, which has grown from insignificance into an active and thriving business. While small off-Broadway houses were known in the twenties or even before, their activity was peripheral to Broadway.

No large movement occurred until the fifties. As men and women with fresh ideas flocked to New York after the war and found their way blocked on Broadway by fierce competition, they established their own theaters.

---

30. Up to 1962/63.
31. In 1966 dollars for the most expensive seat for a regular weekly performance. See Appendix A, Table A-5.

Although very few of these early companies survived, the Circle in the Square dates from that time. The small theaters first came to public notice when, in 1953, Brooks Atkinson penned a glowing notice of Geraldine Page and the production of *Summer and Smoke* at the Circle in the Square. From that time to the 1961/62 season, the ferment downtown spread until it included productions as far north as 103rd Street and as far south as the New Village South Theatre on Vandam Street.

Total activity in the small theaters now exceeds that uptown: 1963/ 64 saw 7,975 performances on Broadway compared to 9,000 off-Broadway; while 53 shows originated uptown, 90 were put together elsewhere in Manhattan. In spite of the frenetic ferment in the little houses, the life expectancy of a production (musical or straight show) is only 100 performances; yet uptown straight shows average over 150 and musicals normally run 300.

During the 1953/54 season, 17 shows, 10 of which were new productions, opened in the little houses. By 1961/62 the number of straight shows, musicals, and revues had climbed to a record 115, of which 49 were new plays and 20 were new musicals. In the two seasons following, production was below its previous peak (see Table I-2); however, off-Broadway shows continue to run longer and total performances are still rising. What this augurs for the future, if anything, is uncertain.

Fragmentary data and statements by downtown producers suggest that the small theaters are generally unprofitable. They are often financed by relatives and close friends, and the intent is not always to make money. A would-be director, fresh from college, may believe that a production of *Man and Superman* will attract critical acclaim and result in Broadway work. Inveigling $15,000 to $20,000 from unwilling parents and friends, he may produce and direct the show. A relatively simple play should not cost him more than $15,000 to mount, though some off-Broadway musicals have cost as much as $40,000. If his gross receipts exceed $2,500 per week or about 55 per cent of capacity gross, he should be in the black. (The break-even point for straight shows uptown also averages about 55 per cent of capacity.) A survey of eight off-Broadway straight shows and three musicals revealed that four of the eight plays were earning less than their weekly operating expenses, and the eight plays as a whole barely cleared their average break-even point.[32]

Information on total box office receipts and attendance for the little houses is non-existent. On the basis of this survey, however, estimates of these figures can be made. The three musicals surveyed in 1962 reported

32. A survey of off-Broadway productions was conducted by the author in January and February, 1962, by mail. The data were supplemented by interviews with several off-Broadway managers.

an average gross of about $3,500, while the eight plays each took in roughly $3,000. During a fairly typical week, February 3–9, 1963, twenty plays and two musicals were running. If we assume no change in prices and a representative sample, total gross receipts off-Broadway for that week must have been about $67,000—approximately the same as a sellout musical on Broadway.

Table I–2   Off-Broadway, 1953/54 to 1964/65

Season	Total productions	Total performances	Productions still running at end of season	Average number of performances during season
1953/54	17	875	1	51.5
1954/55	33	1,682	2	51.0
1955/56	38	1,913	7	50.3
1956/57	43	2,913	9	67.7
1957/58	73	4,382	10	60.0
1958/59	84	5,768	13	68.7
1959/60	101	6,758	21	66.9
1960/61	117	7,713	18	65.9
1961/62	134	7,957	19	59.4
1962/63	89	7,767	24	87.3
1963/64	90	9,000	20	100.0
1964/65	65	n.a.	n.a.	n.a.

n.a. Not available.
Source: New York *Herald Tribune*, first Sunday in June, 1953–65.

With this estimate of gross receipts, it would be relatively simple to estimate attendance if we knew average prices *paid* for seats downtown. Whereas posted box office prices are known, actual prices paid tend to be lower and are unknown. Customarily, downtown managers issue "twofers" authorizing the bearer to purchase two tickets at a reduced rate (usually for the price of one) for certain performances and in certain sections of the house. They are distributed before opening and abandoned only with a great hit. As would be expected, the poorer the show, the more the prices are cut. The survey shows that the public paid the list prices for shows operating near capacity and about 65 per cent of list for a moderate success. Presumably, actual tariffs are even less for outright failures.

Assuming that all tickets were sold at list and the sample is representative, approximately 15,000 people attended off-Broadway during the selected typical week. On the other hand, if actual prices average 65 per cent of list, attendance could have been as high as 24,000. On Broadway, assuming no cut-rate tickets (and there are usually one or two theaters providing such tickets), about 155,000 seats were sold.

What then is the nature of the off-Broadway movement? It is obviously not primarily an entertainment medium designed to make a profit. The productions generally lose money, the audience is small, and the spark for the operations does not appear to originate in demand. Why has it flourished? For one thing it employs about half as many actors as do the big houses, thus giving an additional number of performers a chance to exhibit their skills. Casts downtown average 12.8; uptown, 14.1—an insignificant difference statistically.[33] On the other hand, because the chorus is usually omitted downtown, the cast for musicals averages 17.8, whereas on Broadway it averages 45.6 including the chorus.[34] Assuming these averages generally hold, we can estimate that during the week of February 3–9, 1963, employment ran as follows: on Broadway 196 actors were working in the fourteen straight shows and 410 performers were in the nine musicals; off-Broadway, 256 actors, some non-Equity, were drawing pay in twenty plays, and 35 performers were in two musicals. In all, over 600 members of Equity were receiving salaries on Broadway while less than half that number were gainfully employed downtown at less than half the average weekly wage.

The more rapid turnover of off-Broadway productions increases the opportunities for fledgling performers to practice. Since almost twice as many shows are mounted on the little stages as see the footlights on Broadway, and since the size of the average cast for non-musical productions is approximately the same for both, more acting jobs appear off-Broadway during a season. Excluding the chorus, the same conclusion would probably hold for performers in the musical theaters.

Opportunities to act, to exhibit one's skill for critics and producers, and to practice a variety of roles, help explain the willingness of off-Broadway performers to accept low salaries. In 1963, they were often paid as little as forty-five dollars per week.[35] In a similar manner, playwrights, directors, and producers achieve experience and renown on the little stages. The opportunity to have their work professionally performed has provided valuable practice for new authors. With *The Zoo Story* and *The American Dream,* Edward Albee established his ability as a dramatist; recently with *Who's Afraid of Virginia Woolf?,* his first full-length play, he moved to Broadway. In the 1963/64 season, Frank D. Gilroy successfully made the jump to Broadway with *The Subject Was Roses.* Directors also need training before they can be trusted with an uptown production. Many an off-Broadway show is launched by a would-be director who has been frus-

33. Based on a sample of fifty off-Broadway plays and all the Broadway plays for the 1960/61 season as reported in *Theatre World,* various issues.
34. Based on all musicals opening off and on Broadway during the 1960/61 season.
35. Richard Barr, "Off-Broadway Theatre," a report for the Special Studies Project, Rockefeller Brothers Fund, mimeographed, May 17, 1963, p. 7.

trated by his inability to secure a Broadway assignment. Among directors who started downtown, José Quintero is perhaps the best known.

Besides serving as a school for the midtown theater, off-Broadway has other functions as well. There is a market, albeit a small one, for revivals and classics. Broadway, which in the last decade has concentrated almost exclusively on new productions, witnessed not a single revival during the 1959/60 and the 1960/61 seasons. During the 1963/64 season, while Broadway mounted only two revivals, managers downtown launched thirteen. The small market for the more esoteric types of theater, such as the "theater of the absurd" is catered to off-Broadway. Practically the only hearing such movements have received in the United States is in the small theaters of New York and elsewhere. The plays of Genet, Kopit, and Adamov, to cite a few, have been performed much more frequently off than on Broadway.

Thus there are really two off-Broadway theaters: the first is a training ground for actors, directors, playwrights, and producers; the second is the off-Broadway that serves a small audience who want either the classics or avant-garde theater. Since these functions are probably necessary to a thriving theater, we can expect the off-Broadway movement to continue even though it is generally unprofitable.

Quality and quantity

From this analysis of the New York theater, three points emerge. There exists no reason to believe that rates of profit have declined for investment in Broadway productions. There has been some but not much growth in weekly theatergoing since the middle thirties. Considering off-Broadway, there has been a substantial increase in dramatic activity in New York since the war. What is yet to be discussed is the quality of the theater.

Considering statistics alone can be misleading. For example, more plays may not mean better plays. In the 1927/28 season, 264 plays were produced, an all-time high. Burns Mantle, in *The Best Plays of 1927–1928;* wrote caustically about that season, "You can count its outstanding successes on the fingers of two hands. It would require the seeds of a watermelon to tally its failures."[36] Others familiar with that year have called most of its productions valueless.[37] More recently, the 1963/64 season saw only 7,975 performances, the fewest since 1953/54. Yet theater critics believed it was a definite improvement over the preceding seasons. Howard Taubman, in the annual New York *Times* survey of the legitimate stage, wrote that "it has marked, in my judgment, a turning point for the New

36. (New York: Dodd, Mead, 1928), p. 3.
37. See Stuart W. Little, "The Broadway Producer," a report for the Rockefeller Brothers Fund, May 20, 1963.

York theater. . . . The tone was unmistakably better than in recent years—on and off-Broadway."[38] Walter Kerr in the New York *Sunday Herald Tribune Magazine* concurred.[39] And at the end of the season, Louis Calta wrote, "Broadway has rebounded from one of its worst years with a season dominated by an unusually large number of new hits—ten."[40] The rise in the number of shows playing on Broadway, the 55 per cent increase in serious dramas, and the improved economic climate may all have helped the quality of the season.

While we have chronicled the fall in productions, there is no reason to believe that simultaneously there has been a reduction in the quality of the stage. It seems more likely that the quality of Broadway shows is higher today than thirty-five years ago.[41] Certainly the taste of theatergoers has become more sophisticated, as witnessed by the number of revivals that fail. Only a few playwrights, such as O'Neill, Shaw, and O'Casey, have withstood the test of time. Whether our contemporary dramatists will become dated is impossible to say. A few, such as Williams and Miller, may survive, but it seems unlikely that anyone of this generation will challenge O'Neill as America's greatest playwright.

The next few years may well see a further decline in total number of Broadway productions and an increase in the average length of run. Off-Broadway appears to be waning. While the New York theater will certainly not die, fewer scripts will meet the approval of a New York audience. Summer stock, repertory companies, and community theaters may have to depend more heavily on new and untried works.

38. June 28, 1964, Sec. 2, p. 1.
39. May 31, 1964, p. 17.
40. New York *Times,* June 29, 1964, pp. 1, 33.
41. Herman Shumlin and Samuel Taylor in separate interviews claimed it has improved.

II | Producers and playwrights

In the theater of mid-twentieth-century America, the producer is innovator, entrepreneur, and guiding force. His decisions make a season memorable or better forgotten; his decisions may make a show a smash hit or a costly failure; his decisions determine which thirty or forty scripts among the thousands offered will be seen by the public. Impresarios can only present, however, what playwrights, composers, lyric writers, and librettists offer. If writers produce little that is good, then Broadway fare will be skimpy; if authors pen great works, the New York theater can bloom. Out of the acumen and creativity of these people is woven the tapestry of the theater.

The producer

A handful of men determine the size and quality of a Broadway season. For example, in 1961/62, sixty producers launched forty-nine shows. Of these entrepreneurs, twenty—one-third—were novices to the business. In recent seasons about 40 per cent of all producers were inexperienced; they usually sponsored about 30 per cent of all openings.[1]

Very few men launching their first show are actually new to Broadway, however. Most have worked in some capacity, often as company and business managers for veteran entrepreneurs. In some cases directors who wish to govern the purse strings become producers, as do playwrights who want *their* conception of their work to reach the stage. Several of the most active entrepreneurs have entered the theater through real estate: Roger Stevens, Joel Schenker, Lester Osterman, Robert W. Dowling, Gerard Oestreicher, and David J. Cogan. Usually a theater acquired in a real-estate deal introduced them to Broadway. As theater owners must, they took an interest in the productions that filled their houses. Becoming enamored with the stage, they themselves have tried producing.

Many producers do one show, few go on to produce a second, and still

1. A list of producers was collected from the *Best Plays* volumes for the 1959/60, 1960/61, and 1961/62 seasons. If a man was not listed in *Best Plays* in the previous ten years as a producer, he was considered new.

fewer become well established. Of the sixty-two who sponsored their first effort during the 1927/28 season, for example, three-quarters produced nothing in the next ten years. Only one became an active impresario putting on more than five productions during the next ten years.[2] Considering that only 5 per cent of the unseasoned producers launched financially successful shows, it is not surprising that so few went on to produce again. While entry to the field is easy, becoming well established is difficult.

Most established producers appear to be stage-struck. Since the financial rewards from presenting shows are, on the average, modest, producers would work elsewhere if they did not love the stage. Only about half a dozen individuals earn their living entirely by mounting new shows: Kermit Bloomgarden, David Merrick, Alexander H. Cohen, Harold Prince, Cheryl Crawford, and Feuer and Martin.[3] While the producer nominally keeps half of the profits of a show, he often must give away a portion of his share to stars, directors, large backers, and playwrights. David Merrick, it has been rumored, has been willing to keep as little as 12.5 per cent of the profits.[4] Until a show repays its backers, a producer will normally receive only office expenses—and sometimes 1 per cent of the gross—from the production. If he has a great hit the rewards can be substantial. Herman Levin, for example, sold 23.5 per cent of his 30 per cent producer's interest in *My Fair Lady* for $450,000. After paying $112,500 in capital gains tax he kept $337,500.[5]

Understandably, backing an experienced impresario is much more likely to be profitable. As Table II-1 indicates, the probability of a hit with a veteran is five times as great as the probability with someone green. Veteran producers are likely to put on more shows and do less collaborating than the untried. Since the twenties, however, the number of joint operations has grown. Producers do fewer shows per season and work more often with colleagues.[6] Undoubtedly, the higher cost of launching a show on Broadway and the increased chores involved with the production have made Broadway impresarios more willing to band together.

2. Computed by searching through the *Best Plays* volumes for the seasons from 1928/29 to 1938/39 for other shows produced by the new producers of 1927/28.

3. Little, "The Broadway Producer," p. 6.

4. New York *Times*, June 5, 1961, p. 40.

5. *Ibid.*

6. Since the number of productions new producers were connected with per producer remained constant—that is, each novice entrepreneur produced roughly one show—and since the number of productions per inexperienced producer declined from the late twenties to the sixties, we can conclude that collaboration must have increased. The same conclusion holds for established producers; the decline in the average number of productions that producers are involved with indicates that impresarios are, on the average, launching fewer shows; the fact that the number of openings per producer fell even further than productions per producer demonstrates that collaboration must have become more common.

The production process

A producer's expenses, like those of any other businessman continue throughout the year whether he has a show on the boards or not. There is a permanent office staff: secretary, playreader (a critical employee, particularly needed when searching for new properties), and a production assistant who may also act as casting director and general manager. Once contracts are signed with the playwright, the general manager takes control and handles all the routine business elements.

Research and development expenses loom large for the producer. He and his playreader must scrutinize dozens of scripts. Every possible source of material is investigated: novels, short stories, magazine fiction, even plays produced abroad. As a general rule, almost all good scripts are submitted by writers' agents. Of the innumerable unsought plays sent by embryonic writers, few are even worth the effort of reading. Roger Stevens, producer of such hits as *Mary, Mary* and *A Far Country,* reported that in ten years of constant reading not one unsolicited script was found satisfactory.[7] One author-director reported that "they are mostly bad. . . . My only suggestion for expediting production of a script is to tell the playwright to write better."[8]

Travel, adaptations, and option money are also high cost items. The more active producers often fly to London, Rome, Paris, and Berlin to inspect a foreign show or to negotiate with an author and his agents. On occasion they keep people on salary to preview foreign productions. Kermit Bloomgarden estimates that optioning plays or commissioning adapters costs him over $25,000 yearly—a non-recoverable item since the play may never see Broadway.[9]

Would-be impresarios have even greater difficulty in finding adequate material. Established dramatists have favorite producers and are understandably unwilling to trust their works to inexperienced hands. As a result, the novice producer must often turn to the novice author.

After selecting a script, an entrepreneur must sign the Dramatists Guild contract.[10] The standard agreement establishes minimum royalties and the author's rights. On signing the contract, the entrepreneur advances the author a non-refundable deposit (to be repaid from future royalties, if any) for the sole right to produce the show within a specified period which

7. Interview, March, 1962.
8. A comment written on one of the questionnaires from the survey of playwrights described below, pp. 34–39.
9. Little, "The Broadway Producer," p. 10.
10. All producers and all playwrights who have had productions on Broadway have agreed to sign no other contract. If both parties are novices, theoretically they would be free to make their own agreement. In practice, all sign the Dramatists Guild contract.

Table II–1 Broadway producers, new and established, 1959–62 and 1927/28 seasons

Seasons	Number of producers	Percentage new producers	Number of productions	Percentage presented by new producers	Percentage hits[a]		Percentage musicals		Openings per producer[b]		Productions involved in per producer[b]	
					Established	New	Established	New	Established	New	Established	New
1959/60	66	38	65	29	27	0	20	14	1.12	.76	1.56	1.03
1960/61	68	46	59	40	28	12	20	20	.95	.77	1.65	1.00
1961/62	60	33	49	35	26	0	22	7	1.07	.85	1.70	1.03
Total												
1959–62	194	40	173	35[c]	27[d]	5[d]	21[e]	15[e]	1.05	.79	1.63	1.01
1927/28	161	40	245	26[c]	n.a.	n.a.	n.a.	n.a.	1.88	.99	2.09	1.03

a. Percentage classified by *Variety* as hits on basis of whether profits were earned. *Source: Variety*, third week in June.
b. Productions per season is total production divided by number of producers. Productions involved in per producer is found by counting for each producer the number of shows he was involved with ignoring double counting and then dividing by number of producers.
c. No significant difference between 1959–62 and 1927/28.
d. Significantly different at better than .005 level.
e. No significant difference between established and new producers.
Source: Best Plays volumes. Lists of producers were prepared; any producer who had not produced a show during the previous ten years was considered new.
n.a. Not available

cannot exceed one year. If the producer fails to stage the play within the period, the deposit is forfeited.

While many proven playwrights receive a flat 10 per cent of the weekly take, the minimum contract specifies that for a straight play the dramatist will receive 5 per cent of the first $5,000 of the box office gross, then 7.5 per cent of the next $2,000 and 10 per cent of everything above that. The minimum royalty for a musical is 6 per cent of the gross, to be divided among the lyric writer, the librettist, the book writer, and the composer. The compact specifies that the show must run for twenty-one performances in New York or for sixty-four performances within any eighty-day period on the road for the production to receive any part of the subsidiary income. If these conditions are met, the producer and the backers will earn 40 per cent of the net subsidiary income—after deducting commissions—for the first ten years after the Broadway closing.[11] The writer keeps the remaining 60 per cent. (Subsidiary income includes the earnings from the sale of the rights to produce the play abroad, earnings from stock companies and amateur groups, and earnings from the sale to the motion picture industry. Also any income from television or from recordings would be included.) When the run is shorter, all earnings from sources other than the box office revert to the author; in such a case, however, they are likely to be small.

The contract limits the latitude of the producer and in turn gives the playwright right-of-approval. Not only is the producer prohibited from changing one word of the author's dialogue without his permission, but he must also obtain the writer's approval on cast, director, musical conductor, and dance director. Some playwrights take an active hand in choosing the personnel and participate actively in producing. Others ignore their power and leave the decisions to the producer. Still others delegate their authority to their agents.

After the script comes the financing. Yet rarely can backers be found without first selecting the director and one or more stars. The director and stars generally insist on reading the play before agreeing to participate. The featured actor is vitally interested in the director; the director is concerned with who will star; and, finally, the backers want to know who will direct and who will star. The circle completes itself.

Capital is customarily raised through a limited partnership agreement which guarantees the backers half of any profits in the show. The backers in turn must provide all the financing. While their liability is limited, they are usually subject to some overcall[12] (20 per cent is common) above their

11. For the two years following it receives 35 per cent; for the thirteenth and fourteenth, 30 per cent; for the fifteenth and sixteenth, 25 per cent; and for the seventeenth and eighteenth years, 20 per cent.
12. "Overcall" is the extra amount over his original investment that a backer of a show must furnish the producer at the producer's option.

original investment. For example, a new play may be capitalized at $150,-000 with a 20 per cent overcall. An investor who ventures $15,000 (10 per cent of the capital) will be entitled to receive 5 per cent of the profits. At the same time, he is liable, if additional money is needed, for 20 per cent of $15,000.

In order to raise capital, the producer may take in a full partner. Sometimes a person who can furnish funds will become an associate producer. In most cases, an associate producer has no responsibilities for the production aside from financing, but he shares the billing on the program and in advertisements.

For a successful producer—one whose last show made a profit or whose shows have, in recent years, generally made money—the chore of securing backing may amount simply to placing a few phone calls to previous investors. For a new producer or one who has been unsuccessful, raising capital may necessitate advertising, holding auditions for potential backers, and pleading with friends and acquaintances.

At the same time a producer is raising capital, a director and stars must be secured. The director customarily receives a flat fee plus a percentage of the box office receipts. The average for a straight show during the 1960/61 season was roughly $4,000 plus a percentage of the gross, which may range from 1.5 to 3.5 per cent. In addition, he may get as much as 5 per cent of the profits. Stars are well paid, often as much as one-tenth of the gross with a guaranteed minimum, ranging from $1,500 to $5,050. If there are two leading actors or actresses, both may secure a share of the box office: the total can go as high as 20 per cent of the weekly take; more often it is limited to 15 per cent. In recent years a "name" actor has frequently obtained a percentage of the profits, ranging from 1 to 15 per cent. The usual arrangement is for the featured performer to make an investment in the show under a "one for one" deal. Normally, backers share in half the profits; a contributor who furnishes 10 per cent of the capital receives 5 per cent of the profits, but under a "one for one" understanding, a 10 per cent participation draws 10 per cent of the profits. The additional 5 per cent comes from the producer's portion. Not only stars, but authors, directors, and other individuals in a position to furnish much of the backing of the show have negotiated "one for one" arrangements. "One for one" pacts are often very profitable for the actor or director, since, if the show is a success, the share in the profits can easily be sold. The gain on the sale is subject only to the capital gains tax.

The director or a casting director hires the remaining cast subject to the approval of the author and producer. Often much of the company is obtained through one of the big agencies, such as the William Morris Agency, General Artists Corporation, and Allied Artists Casting Agency. These firms act as agents for actors, actresses, and other performers. Almost all players are procured through an agent or agency; rarely does an actor secure a job by walking in off the street and auditioning. Each performer or his agent individually negotiates his salary. Actors' Equity specifies that the minimum an actor or a chorus member can receive for a Broadway show is $125.00 a week;[13] in straight shows most players receive more than the minimum.

The director having been hired, the producer chooses a scenery designer (usually with the director's approval); sometimes a costume designer and a lighting designer are retained as well. All designers receive a flat fee for their work; in 1960/61 the mean payment for planning the sets was slightly more than $4,000. Frequently, the individual who designs the scenery will receive in addition a small weekly royalty; in recent years, it has ranged from fifty dollars to two hundred dollars a week or roughly 0.5 per cent of the gross.

Most of the routine business matters are handled by the general manager. He often negotiates with scenery builders to construct the sets in exact conformity with the approved design, makes arrangements with the costumer or a large department store, and arranges with a lighting house for the electrical equipment. In addition, he rents a rehearsal hall (sometimes he can use an empty theater at cost), completes the arrangements for the tryout tour, and negotiates for a theater.

A theater is usually rented on a sharing basis. From a straight play the house operator will collect between 25 and 30 per cent of the box office. Quite frequently, a house holding a straight show will receive 30 per cent of the gross on the first $20,000 and 25 per cent of everything beyond that. A few big profitable musicals have obtained a stage for a straight 20 per cent. Out of total box office receipts, the production normally receives from 70 to 80 per cent; this sum must cover all operating expenses and leave something to repay the backers or for profits. The theater typically supplies utilities, box office personnel, ushers, and maintenance men. In addition, the playhouse often pays the wages of several stagehands and, for a musical, of several musicians; the number varies from show to show and depends on bargaining. The house owner also shares the cost of advertising up to a specified limit in the same proportion as he shares in the gross. If the limit is $2,000 and he is receiving 30 per cent of the gross, the owner of the house will pay up to 30 per cent of $2,000, or $600 per week.

In the fall, when Broadway is booked tight, an unknown producer with an unknown property can find it incredibly difficult to get a house, and even known impresarios must take poor terms. In the spring, with fewer shows opening, the owners of empty theaters are more amenable to concession. But this situation too has its drawbacks. Producers are reluctant to launch

13. Through May, 1966. In the 1966/67 season the minimum will be $127.50 and in the 1967/68, $130.00.

a new work in the spring because box office receipts slide drastically during the summer months. By May, patronage is already noticeably lower than it was during the winter. If a show opens in the fall, there are six to eight good theater months to come, but if the premiere is in March, April, or May, the summer doldrums are just around the corner.

In choosing a house, a number of factors are kept in mind. The location of the theater is important. The magic streets—Forty-fifth and Forty-sixth—where many houses are concentrated, are the most valuable. It can be profitable to be located next to or across the street from a sellout. People often wander through the area to determine what is playing and what tickets are available. Those who are unable to purchase seats for a sellout may settle for another show nearby.

The producer who is negotiating for a theater must also consider the type of show he is mounting. Several houses, generally the larger ones, have signed musical contracts with Local 802 of the American Federation of Musicians. Under this compact, the theater must employ a minimum of four musicians whenever it is in operation, no matter what the show. Each musician's salary in the contract houses is only $170.00 per week for a musical and $119.50 for a drama; in other theaters it is $213.20 and $159.90. Naturally, shows planning an orchestra desire contract houses while those without song prefer the others.[14]

Now the actors are rehearsed, the scenery constructed, and the costumes purchased. It is time for the tryout. Producers often open in a city near New York, although many now prefer to hold a series of previews in Manhattan itself. Testing is vitally necessary; no one can tell just how good a show is and what parts need work until it plays before a paying audience. If the reaction is good and the out-of-town reviews are favorable, the producer heaves a sigh of relief and heads for New York, where only polishing remains before the premiere. More often, changes are needed in the script, scenery, and acting. If the play shows ailments that the writer is unable to cure (comedy lines or situation changes), the producer, with the author's permission, calls in a "play doctor" who is usually a playwright himself to give the show the mental tranfusion it needs. If his help is substantial, he may gain joint billing on the program. Usually he is compensated by a percentage of the gross.

During the tribulations of the out-of-town tryout, the publicity wheels have been set in motion. Over a period of approximately six months before the premiere, the producer, or his press agent, steadily feeds items about the director and the star to newspapers. Several weeks before the curtain rises[15] the agent begins his real campaign. He places advertisements through one of two agencies announcing the forthcoming opening; a poster

14. Some straight shows need music for special effects.
15. By this time, all shows have press representatives.

is designed, billboard space is rented, and feature articles are prepared to run in the drama sections of the major newspapers the Sunday before the commencement of the New York run.

At this point the curtain goes up; the play has opened. The best of the notices are publicized and blown up for various uses. If the show is a smash hit, the producer often reduces his expenditures on advertising until demand begins to slacken. If the play is a failure, there is little advertising can do: it dies an ignominious death. But when the show is on the border-line, expenditures are large.[16]

Before seats can be advertised, ticket prices must be arranged in collaboration with the theater operator. Normally, the house owner lists several alternative scales of prices and the capacity gross for each. The producer often chooses the scale in effect most recently. If he believes, though, that he has a great success, or if he calculates that at that scale income will be insufficient to assure a reasonable prospect of profit, he may decide on higher prices. At other times, if he estimates that demand for tickets will be light or that his costs will be moderate, he may charge less.

Customarily, the nominal cost of attending a show remains constant throughout its run. In fact, though, prices fluctuate. They often decline when demand slackens. A common way to reduce the tariff is through "two-fers," a small stub entitling the bearer to buy two tickets for the cost of one. They are generally good only for weekdays and only in certain sections of the house. Producers, intending "two-fers" for individuals whose demand for theatergoing is relatively elastic, distribute them through schools, clubs, and large corporations. Occasionally, ticket prices are simply cut.

Producers claim that if they raised prices for a smash hit those theater-goers who bought their tickets before the prices rose would have paid less than those who were more tardy. The people who had to pay higher prices would be antagonized, according to the argument. This point of view, however, has failed to deter them from reducing ticket prices for part of their audience through "two-fers." Union pressure apparently accounts for a large part of the reluctance to raise the published scale. Most of the theatrical associations, Actors' Equity in particular, would oppose boosting the cost. Equity realizes that raising the scale, *ceteris paribus,* shortens the run. Consequently, performers will be haunting the casting offices that much sooner. In 1939 it defended its position for resisting higher ticket prices for hits by asserting, "Equity can only say that from long and careful consideration it has reached the conclusion that the average theatre patron lives on a budget which allows just so much money for tickets to the theatre. Now if that patron has to pay high prices for his tickets when he

16. See Chapter V for a discussion of advertising.

does go, he is going to be able to go much less often. . . ."[17] Moreover, before the 1965 change in the law, theaters could not charge different prices for seats in the same section, with the result that if seats had been sold for six months in advance, the producer would have to wait that long before raising prices. (The law was repealed on December 31, 1965.) Notwithstanding this reluctance, prices do rise, and people pay more than the box office list. Those who want tickets immediately can buy them from "scalpers"; those willing to wait can purchase them at the list price. (Chapters V and IX discuss ticket scalping in more detail.)

After the opening, operating earnings depend not only on ticket prices but also on costs. During the run of the play, operating expenses consist of actors' salaries; salaries of the crew (backstage personnel, such as grips, flymen, electricians, and carpenters); royalties due the author, director, and scenery designer; office expenses; taxes; rental of electrical and sound equipment; maintenance of costumes and scenery; insurance; and miscellaneous costs. The house takes a significant portion of the gross. As mentioned above, a number of people also take a percentage of the box office; in fact, over 60 per cent of the gross can be committed among the theater, the author, the director, the stars, and the producer before the payment of a cent to the crew, managers, and the remainder of the cast. With the surplus, if any, over operating expenses, the producer must repay the backers. Once the investment has been returned, the show can begin to make a profit. Half the profit usually goes to those who provided the capital; the rest is distributed to the producer and to those with whom he has agreed to share.

Other sources of income for the Broadway production

The Broadway stage is both an end in itself and a test market for new plays. If a production is successful, one or more companies can be organized to tour the country. The script can be sold to a motion picture studio. A musical often profits, as well, from the original cast recording (the producing company and the author usually split 10 per cent of the net proceeds from the record sales). In addition, royalties come from summer stock, amateur performances, and foreign adaptations.

Some shows that lose money in New York are profitable in the end because of subsidiary income. For box office successes, subsidiary earnings add significantly to profits. Through the middle of 1962, for example, *My Fair Lady* had yet to receive a cent for amateur or stock rights, but it had collected $5,500,000 from Warner Brothers for the motion picture rights (plus 47.5 per cent of the picture's gross above $20,000,000).[18] In addition, the original cast recording had netted the company about $1,350,000

17. *Equity*, January, 1939, p. 9.
18. New York *Times*, May 24, 1962, p. 29.

by September, 1961, and sales have continued.[19] Total profits, excluding the film's proceeds, were probably already greater than $10,000,000.[20] Even now, after the show has closed, the backer, Columbia Broadcasting System, can expect to go on reaping profits.

A successful show, therefore, can be extremely lucrative not only for the backers but for the producer. He shares in the Broadway profits, the earnings from touring companies, the income from subsidiary rights, and any movie sale. On the other hand, an entrepreneur whose show closes quickly may find that he toiled for a year with no recompense for a financial fiasco. As a result, producers tend to be cautious and are deeply concerned about costs and revenues.

Types of shows produced

Unfairly charged with being animated only by money, most, if not all, established producers have a passion for the stage and a longing to achieve artistic recognition. Limited by what the public will accept and the necessity to repay their backers, impresarios tend to emphasize their own preferences. While some concentrate on musicals and others specialize in straight shows, many offer varied programs.

A Broadway stage presenting nothing but musicals and comedies has recently been predicted.[21] Fortunately, the data do not support such a prophecy. The proportion of light-entertainment productions has remained unchanged over the last thirty-five years. For example, during the 1927/28 season, 35 per cent of the openings were comedies and 20 per cent were musicals. In the 1963/64 season, 30 per cent of the openings were comedies and 23 per cent were musicals.[22] A mixed menu continues to be offered. Relative attention to dramas, as Table II-2 indicates, has, if anything, grown since the late twenties. The belief that in the future the theater would present only musicals appears to have arisen from the small upsurge in song and dance shows during the late fifties. Even the apprehension that comedies were multiplying has no foundation in fact; the data suggest the contrary. A smaller proportion of comedies are being mounted now than before World War II.

Critics have implied that an increasing proportion of Broadway shows have been imported from England and the Continent.[23] They claim, moreover, that mounting production costs have led to an increase in the im-

---

19. *Ibid.*, September 25, 1961, p. 39.
20. *Ibid.*, May 24, 1962, p. 29.
21. See, for example, New York *Times,* June 5, 1961, p. 40.
22. The number of comedies and musicals opening during the 1927/28 season was computed from *The Best Plays of 1927–1928,* and the number for the 1963/64 season was taken from *Variety,* July 8, 1964, p. 54.
23. See, for example, Marston Balch, "Theatre's Creative Core—Where Is It?" *Prologue,* XIX, No. 2 (December, 1963), 1.

Table II–2 Types of productions on Broadway by five-season intervals, 1927/28 to 1965–66

	Number of:			Percentage		
	All shows	Musicals	Comedies	Dramas	Musicals	Comedies	Dramas
1927/28 to 1931/32	949	148	365	318	15.6	38.5	33.5
1932/33 to 1936/37	609	53	258	244	8.3	42.3	40.0
1937/38 to 1941/42	409	49	168	155	12.0	41.1	37.9
1942/43 to 1946/47	375	72	144	127	19.4	38.4	33.9
1947/48 to 1951/52	319	50	100	131	15.7	31.4	41.0
1952/53 to 1957/58	251	39	80	89	15.5	31.8	35.4
1958/59 to 1961/62	269	55	66	106	20.5	24.6	39.5
1962/63 to 1965/66	220	37	65	75	16.8	29.5	34.1

Note: "All shows" includes all productions opening on Broadway, including reviews, solo performances, and dance groups; it does not include touring limited-run productions, City Center revivals, or Lincoln Center shows. If *Variety* classified a show as a comedy-drama it was not included in either comedy or drama but was included in the total.
Source: Best Plays volumes and *Variety*, third week in June.

portation of already prepared and tested shows. The day may come when London is a tryout town for New York, but there are as yet no signs of it. Over the last few decades, imports have not appreciably increased. Over 14 per cent of all openings in 1927/28 were British or were translations; in the 1959/60, 1960/61, and 1961/62 seasons, 19.5 per cent were foreign.[24] The difference in percentages could easily occur by chance.[25] Moreover, the tabulation of imports for the 1927/28 season underestimates the real number, while the percentage for the more recent seasons is probably correct. Hence, the notion that producers are drawing increasingly on non-American dramatists appears to be false.

The playwrights

Broadway producers claim that more plays would be produced if more suitable scripts were available.[26] The shrinkage in Broadway activity is blamed on a dearth of good scripts. If the number of satisfactory manuscripts has declined, many explanations might be offered. The three following seem most plausible: authors could be devoting less time to the theater; incentives for writing for the stage have declined; or types of scripts that were satisfactory years ago are no longer adequate. This last factor has clearly been at work—only shows that appeal to a large audience are economically feasible. For those seeking entertainment, the screen

24. Based on *The Best Plays of 1927–1928*, a list of thirty-five imports was compiled. Undoubtedly some shows were missed; consequently, the 14 per cent is an underestimate. The percentage of imports for the more recent seasons was taken from *Variety*'s season summary.
25. The difference is insignificant at the 5 per cent level.
26. Herman Shumlin and Roger Stevens in separate interviews.

and broadcasting are less expensive than the legitimate stage. The theater can compete only by offering better diversion than is offered in other fields, and producers have responded by concentrating on the finest productions. Many scripts that once might have been successful are now rejected either by producers or by the public.[27] Furthermore, rising production costs have led producers to weed out the short runs. On the average, a play must attract over 64,000 patrons to break even today;[28] thirty years ago, less than a third of that number would have made the production profitable.[29] The result is that the marginal production of the twenties has been dropped.

Also contributing to a diminution in playwriting has been the growth in competition for the author's energy. Dramatists can no longer devote all their time to the theater. Even for a successful playwright, theatrical earnings must usually be supplemented. According to a survey of active dramatists, only about one-fourth earned 90 per cent or more of their income from the stage, while another fourth received less than 50 per cent. (The survey, conducted by the author, covered the forty-seven playwrights who had had two or more shows on Broadway from 1959 through 1963; thirty-three responded.) In 1963, over half the respondents had written for motion pictures. Only one-fourth, however, had earned money from television. Hollywood was the most aggressive competitor for the playwrights' time, and roughly 60 per cent of the dramatists reported that, outside the theater, they had earned the most money from films.

On the average, authors probably fare better in motion pictures than in the theater. According to one study,[30] half of those who wrote for Broadway in 1957 earned less than $1,548, while more than half of those writing for television made over three times as much, with a median income of $5,250. Films are even more lucrative. The median income for those employed by the cinema was $10,000. The low median income of playwrights is undoubtedly a result in part of the extensive fluctuations in earnings. One year a dramatist may earn over $50,000; for the next two, nothing.

Motion pictures and television clearly compete for dramatists' talents and have undoubtedly reduced the time devoted to the writing of plays. Have incentives for dramatists also declined? If the scarcity of good scripts is the factor that has been limiting the production of plays on Broadway, it

27. Shumlin and the playwright, Samuel Taylor, both claimed in separate interviews that the average quality of plays has risen.
28. Estimated by dividing the average production cost for a straight show in 1961/62 by the average total earnings over operating costs for a play running at capacity in order to compute the number of weeks a play must run at capacity to break even. The latter figure was then multiplied by the total capacity gross and then divided by the average ticket price to measure the number who would have to attend to cover all costs (operating and production). The basic data come from the Broadway financial summary published each week in *Variety* during the 1961/62 season and from Chapter III.
29. Estimated by the procedure outlined in n. 28, above.
30. Data taken from William J. Lord, Jr., *How Authors Make a Living* (New York: Scarecrow Press, 1962), pp. 82, 84, 162.

is likely that the average earnings of playwrights have climbed substantially. And in fact financial rewards from playwriting have multiplied tremendously over the last century. In the nineteenth century, when copyrights were weak or non-existent, dramatists were often little more than hired help. While authors were usually paid a flat fee for each performance, they were sometimes merely employed by the house on a weekly salary to write dialogue. In 1889, for example, Richard Mansfield paid Clyde Fitch $30.00 a week to write *Beau Brummel* and $7.50 a performance until the total reached $1,500, after which Mansfield used the play free of royalty.[31]

By 1926, when the Dramatists Guild signed its first minimum basic agreement, an experienced playwright, by the usual arrangement, received 5 per cent of the first $5,000 gross, 7.5 per cent of the next $2,000, and 10 per cent of all additional box office receipts. Normally all income from subsidiary rights was split evenly with the producer. The Guild in its first contract prescribed these rates as the minimum for any playwright, even for novices.

The lot of the scriptwriter has continued to improve. During the thirties, dramatists raised their share of subsidiary rights to 60 per cent. Coupled with the fact, as Table II-3 manifests, that the premium from film rights has shot up, proceeds from subsidiary rights must have multiplied. Inflation, moreover, has pushed a much larger proportion of box office income above $7,000, thus augmenting the average share of receipts captured by the author. In 1929, for example, inasmuch as most straight shows earned between $10,000 and $15,000, the minimum compensation for the author would be about $900 (at $12,000 gross) or 7.5 per cent of the gross. By 1964, most shows took in over $25,000 per week, giving the author a minimum of $2,200 or 8.8 per cent of the gross.

Furthermore, because productions play about twice as long now as they did in the twenties, royalties continue to pour in considerably longer. The combination of inflation, increase in real box office receipts, and longer runs has pushed box office earnings for playwrights up 250 per cent.[32] Altogether, we could conclude that since an average play runs for about nineteen weeks with box office receipts averaging about $30,000 a week (producing weekly earnings of $2,700 for the dramatists), a writer could receive from an "average" Broadway production—if there were such a thing—a total of over $51,000. In addition, expected receipts from subsidiary income are probably greater than $15,000, and there would be additional income from any touring production.[33]

Unfortunately, life is neither that simple nor that lucrative for a play-

31. George Middleton, *The Dramatists Guild* (New York: Dramatists Guild, 1959), p. 7.
32. See Chapter IV.
33. Table II-3 shows higher expected receipts from motion pictures; however, such income includes musicals, which probably tend to sell for more than straight shows.

Table II–3   Sales of motion picture rights, 1926 to 1955 (Musicals and straight shows)

	Number of sales	Percentage of productions sold	Average price paid (1947–49 dollars)	Average cash receipts for playwrights from an opening[a] (1947–49 dollars)
1926–30	134	12.1	$45,990	$2,500
1931–35	144	18.8	50,431	4,250
1936–40	73	14.9	94,980	8,200
1941–45	100	27.7	142,729	21,300
1946–50	56	19.4	185,258	19,400
1951–55	69	27.0	112,434	16,500

a. For 1936–55, 60 per cent of average price paid for shows that opened minus a 10 per cent commission; 1926–35, 50 per cent of the net.
Source: George Middleton, *The Dramatists Guild*, p. 16.

wright. According to the survey of active dramatists, the playwright spends approximately a year (eleven months on the average) from the time he starts writing until the script is completed. Even among such successful dramatists as were sent the questionnaires, scripts go unproduced. In the last decade those who had been writing for the entire period had authored, on the average, just under five scripts each (co-authors were counted one-half). Yet only 3.6 shows per author had been performed on Broadway. Thus, only three-fourths of the playbooks written by these twenty-three dramatists, all of whom have been in the trade for ten or more years, had been seen on Broadway. On the average then, these active playwrights had had one show every two and one-half years.

Consequently, our "average" playwright with his average play might be earning over $23,000 per year, not $65,000.[34] Such an "average" dramatist would be far from average; he would be one of the most active and successful dramatists in America. As might be expected, playwrights vary considerably in their activity. While one author had written ten scripts in ten years, all of which had been produced, others (counting half for shows co-authored) had seen two or fewer of their plays reach Broadway.

The variation in income for playwrights is tremendous. For example, one playwright in 1955, one in 1956, and one in 1957 earned over $200,000 from writing for the theater alone,[35] but a considerable number of professional dramatists—those who have earned money from writing for the stage and who belong to the Authors League of America—received less than $1,000 a year from the theater. William Jackson Lord, Jr., who prepared these figures, reported that "less than a third of all playwrights (31.5

34. One play every two and a half years at $65,000 per play is equivalent to $26,000 per year.
35. Lord, *How Authors Make a Living,* p. 174, Table LXVIII.

per cent) derived personal income from playwriting every year between 1953 and 1957."[36]

When we consider those who are attempting to break into the field, the writer's situation is even darker. While no figures exist, thousands who will never succeed must be attempting to become dramatists. In the twenties, a study conducted for Actors' Equity Association reported that one producing firm "examined more than 5,000 plays over a period of five or six years. Its list included the works of authors whose plays had previously been produced on Broadway as well as those of hitherto unknown dramatists. Of all these plays only thirty were produced, and of these thirty only five were outstanding financial successes, none, however, falling within the hit class."[37] Paul N. Turner, counsel for Actors' Equity Association (who related the above), also estimated that the royalties accruing to the authors of the plays that were produced was far less than the cost of typing all the plays. He believed that the time consumed in writing and in attempting to sell the 5,000 plays and in rehearsing the thirty produced plays probably exceeded a half million days and that if the royalties had been divided among the authors they would have provided an average compensation of between twenty-five and fifty cents per day.[38]

A similar statement would probably accurately reflect the situation today. If total earnings of writers were divided by the total hours spent in writing and typing scripts, the resulting hourly wage would most likely be far below the United States legal minimum. The appeal of writing for the theater can hardly be the expected average earnings, so it must stem from the possibility of large receipts, from the satisfaction of seeing one's work on the stage, and from the love of drama. Only four of the respondents to the questionnaire sent by the author mentioned income problems, however, as reducing their incentive to write. Most of those who discussed the matter referred to the wide fluctuations in earnings which made sustaining a family difficult. One felt that writing for the stage could never be more than a part-time occupation; it would always be necessary to earn a salary in another field. Another dramatist, in contrast, complained that theatrical incomes were too large; they attracted individuals to the theater who had neither interest nor talent. Consequently, Broadway was flooded with too many poor pieces.

In summary, the development of television and sound motion pictures has benefited the dramatist enormously. Since both media use vast amounts of material, the demand for writers has waxed greatly. The relatively low median earnings, however, suggest that while the number of would-be play-

36. *Ibid.,* p. 175.
37. Bernheim, *The Business of the Theatre,* p. 113.
38. *Ibid.*

wrights has multiplied, there is still a large group with little ability. Those with exceptional gifts do well; they are needed for the best films, for the best television series, and for the legitimate stage. As was suggested above, the theater, to compete with these other fields, must offer a better product by employing the most talented writers. In order to be attracted, they must be compensated well. The climb in playwright earnings since the twenties is thus fully comprehensible in light of the competition from other media.

Preparation of playwrights

Since incomes have risen so sharply for dramatists, it might be expected that the supply of theatrical authors would have burgeoned. Certainly there is no shortage of individuals with sufficient training to be dramatists. Only one-fourth of the dramatists queried by the author had either taken a course in playwriting or attended a special school; only six of the nine thought that their training had been helpful. The remainder had had no specific education for the stage. Some of the group had not finished high school; 21 per cent had never attended college; only nine out of thirty-three had spent time in graduate school. We might, therefore, conclude that it is not a lack of formal training which prevents the rise of more dramatists or the creation of more scripts. It is possible that the supply of authors is restricted by other factors. People choose occupations only partially on the basis of the income they can earn. Personal satisfaction, an urge to write, and the agreeableness of the work are also important.

Factors affecting the incentive to write for the stage

The questionnaire requested that dramatists jot down all complaints they had concerning writing for the theater. Almost half were disheartened with the Broadway productions of their work; directors were incompetent, actors unskilled, and producers "stupid." Typical is the remark of one playwright: "The stress and strain of having to find a producer, and *then* a director, and *then* actors—and the frustration of having to 'filter' the work through all of them. The direct writer-to-reader relationship of the novel is more satisfying, infinitely so, but the theatre, damn it, is more alluring."

While unhappy with the interpretation of their scripts, many authors denounced, as one writer put it, "the most irresponsible, most ignorant and most dangerous (to the health and future of the theatre) element of all: the critics." Not only was the dramatist's conception inadequately conveyed, but it was misunderstood by the reviewers. These complaints may come from those whose work quickly closed after it was justifiably panned. The grumbles about the interpretation may be only self-justification for a failure. Yet the large proportion of writers voicing them indicate that an undercurrent of discontent with Broadway performances might be affecting playwriting. Dissatisfaction with the interpretation of their works can, however, only have been decreasing over the last few decades. Actors are better trained; scores of schools teaching the histrionic arts have sprung up in the last thirty years. The playwright has greater control over the production. He has the right to agree on the director and on the actors, and no word of the script can be altered without his permission. The only way he could have more absolute control would be to produce and direct the play himself. Some playwrights have taken this option; but in this day of specialization, it is difficult, time-consuming, and exhausting. More importantly, most dramatists do not have the experience necessary to direct and produce.

Restrictions on the type of play that is acceptable to Broadway also aroused strong feelings among these writers; this difficulty was cited by over 20 per cent. As one author put it, "The impediments to getting scripts bought by producers are few for me now. Just follow simple rules like: one set—few characters—and never never criticize the Soviet Union will do it." Another voiced his disillusion by writing, "I have no desire (or talent possibly) to turn out slick sex comedies or I.B. Machine-made musicals or portentous historical biographies. The plays I write are apt to be unshowy and aim to reveal some truth about human character—which makes them attractive to an audience quite different from the people who subscribe to theatre parties, etc."

What an author could produce has always depended on public taste. Sophocles wrote to please the judges and the Athenian citizens; Shakespeare dramatized those characters and plots that would please his audience; the playwright of today must also create for the viewers. If the public is too small to sustain a particular type of show, then the play will have to be done off-Broadway—where the financial rewards are meager—or be relegated to the scrap heap.

As a consequence of the increase in production costs—to repeat an earlier conclusion—plays of limited appeal have been squeezed out. This is the eternal problem of the artist: he may wish to create certain works, but if too few of the public care for his efforts he may starve. Since the Broadway market has narrowed and off-Broadway inadequately compensates the playwright, some authors may have turned to other fields with fewer restrictions. To the extent that this may have happened, the theater has been made poorer.

In short, the unhappiness of a few playwrights with the restrictions that the commercial theater places on their works may have reduced their incentive to write for Broadway. Moreover, the frustration of filtering work through others may have discouraged them. On the other hand, since earnings of dramatists have increased considerably, it is difficult to believe that writers have turned away from the theater for these reasons. It seems more plausible that they have been lured away by money to motion pictures and television. Coupled with an increased concentration by producers on shows deemed likely to have substantial runs, these factors have led to a steady shrinkage in openings season after season.

III | Production and operating costs

The precipitous drop in straight shows opening on Broadway from the late twenties to the recent season—a deep 80 per cent—can be explained on several grounds.[1] First, demand for seats may have decreased because of good substitutes, such as motion pictures and television. Normally in such cases, prices and costs decline. If there are substantial economies of large-scale operation, however, prices might be forced higher when demand contracts. Alternatively, costs may have gone up for the reasons suggested in previous chapters. Let us consider then how costs have changed and what the forces are that have caused the changes.

If there are distinct external economies for the industry, that is, if the cost of essential elements such as scenery, costuming, and lighting declines as the industry becomes larger because of economies of scale, then costs will rise with a decline in demand. Marshall[2] and Stigler[3] suggest that when there are such economies, an industry tends to become localized and to delegate decreasing and increasing cost factors to independent producers in subsidiary industries. The concentration of the theater suggests that there may be external economies. Moreover, the Broadway stage does farm out certain subsidiary functions such as scenery construction, costuming, lighting, printing programs, and advertising. If expenses have risen primarily because demand has declined and there are external economies, we should find that the outlays that have grown most have to do with scenery and costumes. (The theater is such a small part of the printing and advertising industries that those costs would be unaffected by a decline in the stage.) If other outlays such as actors' salaries have been the primary factor in pushing up expenses, it would appear that either forces outside the industry or labor unions have been primarily responsible. But if costs have decreased or remained constant, we can conclude that the prime factor behind the decline has been a shift in demand.

1. See Chapter I.
2. Alfred Marshall, *Principles of Economics* (7th ed.; New York: Macmillan, 1948), p. 137.
3. George J. Stigler, *The Theory of Price* (revised ed.; New York: Macmillan, 1952), p. 148.

The data

Before we examine theatrical expenses, it is necessary to have an appreciation of the sources of the data and its limitations. The analysis is based on data gathered from a variety of sources, but mainly from the records of the major producers. All data refer to plays.

Information on the 1927/28 and 1928/29 seasons is drawn from the records of the Theater Guild at the Yale University Library and *The Business of the Theatre,* by Alfred Bernheim, a study of the economics of the theater done for Actors' Equity in the late twenties. The figures presented by Bernheim are based on a survey he made of one hundred producers; he obtained responses on twelve productions from ten individuals. In addition, he secured data on production and operating costs for two shows from other sources. In all, *The Business of the Theatre* gives usable information on nine Broadway straight shows (and four musicals). The Theatre Guild papers contain data on six straight plays, giving a total sample of fifteen.

Seven plays constitute the sample for the 1939/40, 1940/41, and 1941/42 seasons. Six are drawn from the University of Wisconsin's collection of financial records of the Playwrights' Company and of Kermit Bloomgarden, the producer. The other is from the personal records of Max Gordon, a major producer of the period. The 1949/50 and 1950/51 figures also come from the University of Wisconsin's statements and from the records of the Theatre Guild at Yale University. From this period eleven dramas and comedies are represented. Facts on the 1954/55 season are based on some limited partnership statements in the theater collection at the New York Public Library (presented by Hobe Morrison, drama editor of *Variety*) and on the financial statements now in the library of the University of Wisconsin. There are a total of fourteen plays for these years. The data for the 1960/61 season were compiled from the files of the League of New York Theatres. In order to make a study of costs,[4] the League asked Broadway producers for a copy of their financial statements. Some of the twenty-five reports were subsequently, by request, returned to the producers, so that data presented here derive from fifteen Broadway productions whose financial reports remained on file with the League.

Bias in the data

None of these may be considered a truly representative sample; problems existed with each set of seasons. (Appendix B discusses the data in detail.) It is sufficient at this point to recognize that the productions included in the samples tend to be the more successful ones and that the shows from which figures were collected for the period around 1940 prob-

---

4. The study was conducted by Robert A. Baron, a Broadway business manager who had earlier done similar work for Actors' Equity.

ably had higher than average operating costs. Some adjustment for the bias in the figures for the 1960/61 season was possible. The League files included the average production cost and the average operating cost for the original twenty-five plays. Inasmuch as the League's production figures were 11 per cent lower than the average for the shows remaining in the files upon which our detailed figures are based, all items were adjusted downward by that percentage.[5]

It must be noted that some vital facts were generally unavailable—receipts from the sales of motion picture rights, record rights, amateur and stock rights, television rights, foreign rights, and so forth. This exclusion is especially serious since the importance of these rights has changed with time.

Table II-3 shows that the average sale price to the movies (excluding percentage arrangements) has about tripled since the twenties. The same table presents the playwrights' expected cash receipts from the film rights. The productions' expected incomes from motion picture rights have followed a similar pattern, except that from 1926 on they received only 40 per cent of the net. Clearly, motion picture rights since the war bring more to the production than they did during the twenties.

There have been changes as well in the distribution of the proceeds from the sale of other rights. In the twenties, the producer and author often split the revenue evenly. By 1936 the playwright was keeping 60 per cent of the film money, but income from the rest of the rights was still divided in half. During the forties, the contract was amended to require that the dramatist keep 60 per cent of all income from the droits. At the same time, the producer's claim to a share of the income from rights was extended from a seven-year period to eighteen years.

While average subsidiary receipts may be small compared to box office earnings, they can be extremely high for shows in demand. It is unfortunate that data on subsidiary income are scarce and poor; information is likely to be incomplete since revenue from droits may dribble in over a decade or more. (For illustrative purposes, Table III-1 lists figures on ten shows.) Since receipts from subsidiary rights have, in all likelihood, climbed, the gain in average box office receipts over the last thirty-five years will understate the gain in the earnings of Broadway plays. This bias must be kept in mind in evaluating the relative profitability of Broadway productions.

Costs on Broadway

The expenses of a Broadway play fall into categories representing the stages from birth to death. First are the pre-production costs—discussed in Chapter II—which usually involve outlays for advertising, the limited

5. For a few small items, the average for the twenty-five shows was available, and these figures were used when possible. See Appendix B, Table B-1.

Table III–1   Profits and Sources (Current dollars)

Play	Season opened	Capitalized at	Profit or loss	Operating surplus[a]	Motion picture sale[b]	Other royalties
Heavenly Express	1939/40	$ 30,177	−$ 36,290	−$ 5,248	−$ 0	−$ 0
The Male Animal	1939/40	25,000	250,000	100,000	60,000	20,000
The Corn is Green	1940/41	25,000	450,000	250,000	54,000	25,000
Montserrat	1949/50	60,000	n.a.	7,421	n.a.	15,773
The Man	1949/50	60,000	− 38,000[c]	− 3,617	7,200[d]	6,500[d]
Legend of Sarah	1950/51	60,000	− 51,854	− 5,530	0	1,174
Cat on a Hot Tin Roof	1954/55	102,000	490,813[e]	330,979	135,000	19,457[e]
The Bad Seed	1954/55	78,000	316,552[e]	92,587	158,689	6,175[e]
The Ponder Heart	1955/56	104,040	− 96,085	14,814	0	2,819
The Lovers	1955/56	102,000	− 141,933	− 5,466	0	0

a. Operating surplus in New York.
b. Net to company (usually 40 per cent of total).
c. Approximately.
d. Through the end of 1954.
e. As of June 28, 1958.
n.a. Not available.

partnership agreement, and negotiations with the author, star or stars, and director. Actual production costs consist of all other disbursements required to raise the curtain in New York. After the premier, weekly outlays for actors, advertising, and other requirements determine operating expenses, which in turn limit the operating surplus.

When the drama has completed its New York run, it can either close or go on the road, in which case operating expenses must still be met from the weekly receipts. Sooner or later the curtain must come down for the last time, but that in itself entails expenses. If the production has run for more than a few weeks, the theater often shares the charges for scenery removal. Partially offsetting closing expenses are receipts from the sale of scenery and props. A quick shuttering may result in substantial closing expenses, since the house must generally be paid for two weeks and the cast and other personnel are guaranteed a minimum of two weeks' salary.

We will concentrate primarily on the costs for the theater and on production and operating breakdowns. Except for the tryout's profit or loss, the other outlays are normally minor. As might be expected, there is a large variance in the out-of-town profit or loss, which is a residual depending on the same factors which affect operating surplus, that is, income and costs. It will be implicitly covered in this and following chapters.

Total costs and income

Chart III-1 presents the major factors affecting Broadway during the last few decades. It indexes changes—in terms of constant purchasing power dollars—in total production costs, weekly company income, weekly box office receipts, weekly operating costs, and the theater's weekly income.

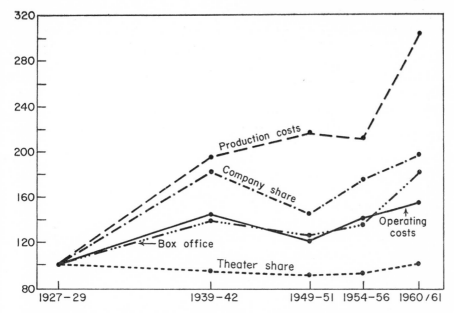

Chart III-1 Change in real weekly income and real cost to the theater and the production, 1927-29 to 1960/61 (1927/28 and 1928/29 = 100)

Source: See Appendix A, Table A-9.

Since the gross receipts are split between the company and the house, it can be seen how each has fared.

The house. From the diagram it is evident that the house's income in constant dollars declined from a high during the twenties to a low around 1950. The major factor in this fall was the reduced percentage of the box office received by the house. Since 1950, with climbing box office receipts, the theaters' earnings have gone up.

The late Jack Small, general manager of the Shubert chain, remarked shortly before his death that the theater's percentage of the gross had declined from between 40 and 50 per cent in the early thirties to between 25 and 30 per cent today.[6] He also maintained that the number of stagehands being furnished by the house was as great as or greater than the number furnished during the Depression. He emphasized, however, that since shows run longer and theaters are in operation more of the time, theater owners are better off today. While profits of Broadway houses have undoubtedly improved since the Depression, they are still considerably below the level of the twenties, when new houses were being built. Today no one is building.

6. Interview, December 15, 1961.

The reversal of the downward trend in the number of Broadway theaters—which fell from over sixty to thirty in the early fifties but has risen in recent years to thirty-six—indicates that profits have improved.

The company. Profits for the production depend on its share of gross receipts, operating costs, length of run, and production outlays. As the house's percentage fell, the share kept by the company rose. Chart III-1 shows that it more than covered the rise in operation costs. Production outlays, however, have risen considerably faster than either company income or operating expenses.

The larger the production expenses, other factors being equal, the longer a show must run before it breaks even. Conversely, as a play runs longer, the expenditure needed to raise the curtain declines in proportion to total disbursements.

In Chapter I we found that a Broadway production's average length of run had roughly doubled since the twenties. This change is to be expected. The weekly surplus—the difference between operating expenses and operating income—must pay for the investment in the play. Since production charges have climbed twice as fast as the weekly operating surplus dramas must run twice as long today to repay the backers.

Production costs

Actors' salaries. Why have production costs risen so rapidly? What elements have increased most? Over the thirty-year period, the salaries paid to actors for rehearsals have been one of the fastest-rising elements. Since Actors' Equity has laid great emphasis on actors being paid for rehearsing, this rapid increase would be expected. Before Equity was organized, actors often rehearsed for nothing and were paid only after the show opened. If one performance was given, the actor was paid for one performance. Bernheim reported that in the days before Equity, John Goldsworthy played twenty-two weeks with salary in a two-year span and rehearsed fifty-seven weeks without salary. Another actor in one season rehearsed twenty-two weeks with no compensation and received a total of four days' wages.[7]

One of Equity's first demands was that actors be paid for a minimum period of work no matter how long the show ran. During the twenties, performers normally rehearsed for nothing but were guaranteed two weeks' acting salary.[8] By 1962, an actor received a minimum of $87.50 per week during rehearsal.

In spite of this increase, only a small part of the inflation in costs of production can be attributed to actors. Rehearsal salaries for perform-

7. Bernheim, *The Business of the Theatre,* p. 132.
8. *Ibid.,* p. 129.

ers in 1927/28 and 1928/29 were generally negligible—only the Theatre Guild reported paying them; during the 1960/61 season they accounted, on the average, for 6 per cent of the total.

Costumes. Outlays for costuming actors have also grown. Chart III-2 indicates a 179 per cent rise in company expenditures on this item. This sharp rise, however, is misleading, since there apparently has also been an increase in the proportion of period plays. In a random sample of 120 plays from the 1928/29 season,[9] seven were historical, compared to eleven out of twenty-nine in the 1960/61 season. The samples from which the data were drawn reflect this change. Of the fifteen plays included in the sample for 1960/61, only one is a historical drama, but five others are, at least in part, set in the first two decades of this century and need costuming; one other deals with Roman Catholic officialdom and involves special apparel. None of the sample from the twenties is a period piece or needs unusual clothing. In the twenties, the average outlay for dress was $3,030 (in 1960/61 dollars); in 1960/61 it was $6,574 for the eight plays in modern civilian attire. Therefore, the cost of garbing actors for plays in modern civilian dress has risen approximately 117 per cent, not 179 per cent as Chart III-2 shows.

It should also be noted that expenditures on clothing have risen faster than the price of clothing generally.[10] But why? Contributing to the upsurge has been the rise in the proportion of the expense of actors' garments paid for by the limited partnership. Before the formation of Actors' Equity, players often had to supply all their dress, including that needed for historical pageants. Equity has been working to enlarge the proportion of attire furnished by the producer. In the twenties the production normally provided all garb for actresses but only historical costumes for the men. By 1962, only actors paid more than $250 a week were expected to furnish their own modern civilian dress.

Undoubtedly, part of the higher clothing cost stems from a desire by producers to furnish better costumes. Herman Shumlin, a noted producer, asserted that costumes had improved greatly during the last thirty years.[11] As Chapter I indicated, the growth in outlays on costuming performers is probably a response to the increased competition of motion pictures.

Advertising. More important than costumes in the total rise in costs has been the multiplication of expenditures on pre-opening publicity. In the early period, publicity accounted for 7.2 per cent of the outlay before opening night; by 1960/61 it averaged 12 per cent. We can see from Table

9. All new plays that opened between June 1, 1928, and December 31, 1928. The sample was gathered from *The Best Plays of 1928–1929,* ed. Burns Mantle (New York: Dodd, Mead, 1929).
10. See Bureau of Labor Statistics, Consumer Price Index of retail clothing prices.
11. Interview, 1963.

Table III–2   Average production costs, selected seasons (1966 dollars)

	1927/28 1928/29	1939/40 1940/41 1941/42	1949/50 1950/51	1954/55 1955/56	1960/61	1960/61 (Baron's figures)
Total	$33,134	$62,192	$71,455	$69,413	$111,422	$100,609
Scenery	10,414	n.a.	19,850	16,506	25,243	22,445
Props	4,945	n.a.	2,836	2,499	5,213	4,707[b]
Costumes	3,312	n.a.	7,980	5,557	10,247	9,253[b]
Electrical and sound	3,397	n.a.	3,406	4,620	5,661	5,111[b]
Scenery designers	2,089	4,415	3,656	3,108	4,432	3,532
Directors	3,047[a]	n.a.	4,939	4,220	5,172	4,449
Cast	1,510	n.a.	4,189	4,397	6,661	6,015[b]
Crew and stagehands	2,934	n.a.	3,165	4,479	5,865	5,296[b]
Advertising	2,376	n.a.	6,447	4,963	13,318	12,026[b]
Legal and audit	n.a.	n.a.	1,771	1,876	3,481	3,143[b]
Managers	n.a.	n.a.	2,931	3,345	4,587	4,142[b]
Theater	n.a.	n.a.	1,220	1,377	2,205	1,991[b]
Press agents	n.a.	n.a.	1,310	1,535	1,588	1,434[b]
Office	n.a.	n.a.	1,545	1,535	1,844	1,665[b]
Hauling	493	n.a.	693	1,060	n.a.	n.a.
Total itemized costs	34,138	n.a.	63,238	60,998	94,946	85,000
Mean of remainder	3,656	n.a.	6,789	9,074	15,825	14,290[b]

a. Producing directors only.

b. Reduced by the same proportion Robert A. Baron's total is to our total.

Note: While the data for all plays include total production costs, the data for some plays are incomplete. Therefore, the sum of the cost items may not equal total production costs since each item is an average of the available data.

n.a. Not available.

Source: See pp. 42–43. Baron's figures are taken from his unpublished, untitled study in the League of New York Theatre's files.

III-2 that advertising rose from about $2,376 in the earliest period to $12,026 in the latest season for which we have data. Chart III-2 reveals that the increase in advertising expenditures was more rapid than the growth of any other factor.

The steepest climb in paid publicity during this period took place in the last half of the fifties, but this cannot be attributed to higher newspaper rates. For example, advertising charges per agate line advanced only 12 per cent in the New York *Times,* while total expenditures on publicity were doubling. Since total expenditures for linage in the New York *Times* grew only 26 per cent, increased outlays to inform the public must be attributable to an attempt to reach a wider audience. Unless spending in other New York newspapers expanded more rapidly, which seems unlikely since the *Times* carries the bulk of the amusement advertising, producers must have expanded their outlays for billboards, television, radio, magazines,

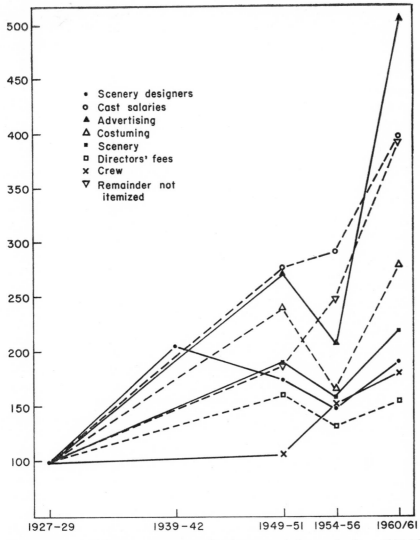

Chart III-2 Change in real cost to the theater and the production, 1927-29
to 1960/61 (1927/28 and 1928/29 = 100)
Source: See Table III-2.

and out-of-town newspapers—an obvious attempt to attract the non-New
York public.

Another explanation may lie in a changing pattern of theatergoing.
Before the Depression, when playgoing was casual, the public was willing
to patronize a wide variety of plays. With the development of films and

television, people became more selective; they were unwilling to attend mediocre plays. Accordingly, a show now tends to be either a hit with a substantial run or a failure that closes promptly.[12] To counteract this tendency, producers lean heavily on advertising. If enough tickets can be sold prior to the opening, much of the investment might be recouped, even in the face of pallid reviews.

Miscellaneous expenses. Another factor which has pushed production costs up is the growth in legal and auditing fees. Since Bernheim fails to mention such expenditures, they were probably negligible in the twenties. And in spite of their insignificance in 1960—accounting for only 3 per cent of the total—legal and audit fees increased more rapidly (77 per cent) in the decade of the fifties than any other item.

Other incidental expenses which have proliferated include telephone bills; insurance; secretarial services; penalties from the cancellation of contracts; various small bills for the stage and general manager, for the carpenter, for the wardrobe and properties, and for the press agent; expenses incurred in the acquisition of stage rights; out-of-town expenses for staff and producer; mail order expenses; Blue Cross and hospitalization; and miscellaneous items. None of these expenses is consistently large enough to be listed separately. But when taken as a group these unclassified outlays have grown from roughly $4,000 during the twenties to an average of about $14,000, or 15 per cent of total costs—a sizable increase.

The sprouting of incidentals reflects a greater division of labor and a generally higher cost of doing business. There are more insurance premiums to be met (Blue Cross, for example, was unknown in the twenties); there are more and higher taxes to be paid; there are bigger and better forms to fill out.[13] The requirements by Equity, Dramatists Guild, and others that bonds be posted and records kept, the requirement by the Securities and Exchange Commission that information on the limited partnership be filed, and the required financial statements to backers have all added to paper work. The growth of telephone bills and transportation expenses undoubtedly reflects the employment of more stars, directors, and authors who normally live in Hollywood, Rome, Paris, or London.

Also contributing to the multiplication of little outlays may be the changing role of the producer. During the twenties the entrepeneur usually took an active role in the day-to-day work on the play. Often he directed, but even when he did not, he kept a close eye on all items and handled many minor tasks himself. Today, by necessity, he is more absorbed with the business portion of the production. As Broadway has become less

12. See Chapter I, pp. 10–12.
13. The new statute passed in 1964 to safeguard the rights of backers has added to paper work.

profitable,[14] the producer has had to devote an increasing proportion of his time to raising capital for the production. As a consequence, he has had to delegate to hired help many of the small tasks he once perfomed himself.

Scenery. While the expenses of advertising, costuming, actors' salaries, and incidental items have been rising markedly, some items which are traditionally accused of inflating costs have been going up more slowly. The largest single outlay in preparing for opening night—accounting normally for over 20 per cent of the total—is the building and painting of scenery. In recent years it has not risen at all, but from the late twenties until roughly 1950 it almost doubled.

The climb in expenditures for scenery is probably the result of improved quality.[15] Moreover, sets are now mechanized more frequently, and revolving scenery is quite common. Since the bulk of the growth took place in the first twenty years of the period under study, it might be partially explained as a response to sound motion pictures. Producers may have attempted to create more realistic effects to compete with that more naturalistic medium. In addition, sets are still constructed almost entirely by hand, since there is as yet little room for automation, and the price has kept step with carpenters' wage rates. The decline in cost of scenery during the fifties could have been caused by changing fashion in scenery (starker, sparser sets), or by change in costs of materials (lumber, furniture, etc.), or by some automation in building. However, the price changes during the fifties were modest compared to the rise between 1928 and 1950.

Properties (items on the stage that the actors can or do move themselves) are usually listed separately in theatrical accounts. Nevertheless, they contribute to the general scenic effect on stage and cannot be completely separated from scenery. The costs of scenery and props together, which amounted to about 27 per cent of the total production costs in 1960/61, have soared about 77 per cent since the twenties, mostly before 1950.

The crew. In many discussions of Broadway's ills, the stagehands' union has been castigated for contributing to higher costs. Yet total payments to the crew amount to only 5 per cent of production costs. Moreover, during

14. From the decline in the number of productions, we can assume that total profits in the industry have diminished. It may be that expected profits for any one show have remained unchanged. To assume this, however, would be to assume that the supply curve for capital is infinitely elastic with respect to average profits; while this may be so in most fields, it seems unlikely for the theater. Part of the recompense for "angeling" a show is non-monetary and involves a psychic income from being connected with the theater. For a fuller discussion of the motivation of play backers, see "Angels Without Wings: An Exploratory Study of Investors in the Living Theatre," a research study by Weiss and Geller Research (Chicago: mimeographed, March, 1956).

15. In the 1963 interview, Herman Shumlin testified that better scenery was being used now.

the last thirty years—even though, according to Herman Shumlin, more stagehands are being used than earlier—total wages of the backstage personnel have less than doubled, while earnings in manufacturing have increased more.

With the sharp reduction in theater activity during the thirties, there was no increase in real payments to the crew. Only since the fifties with the advent of television, in which many of the stagehands' union find employment, has there been an improvement in the wages of the crew. In 1960/61, backstage personnel received about 67 per cent more than they had a decade earlier.

Other items. Most of the other items for which we have data make up only a small portion of the total. Directors' fees have crept upward barely 53 per cent, considerably less than the growth in income for almost all important sectors of the economy. The payment for scenery designers has grown 92 per cent; during the same period average weekly wages in manufacturing have risen 111.5 per cent, according to Department of Commerce figures.

The Theatre Guild records for the twenties reveal no payments for the services of company managers, stage managers, general managers, legal and audit fees, rent for rehearsal space, press agents' salaries, or office expenses; part of these must have been absorbed into the general overhead of the Theatre Guild. Unfortunately, only scattered figures for these items—insufficient to compute meaningful averages—are available from the Bernheim data. Bernheim reports that all shows use press agents and stage managers and that most plays employ company managers and general managers, must pay for rehearsal space, and must have office expenses. The wages of managers—general, company, and stage—went up almost 50 per cent in the last decade; however, they still accounted for less than 2 per cent of the total in 1960/61. Press agents' salaries and producers' office allowances each rose less than 20 per cent, and each accounted for less than 2 per cent of the entire production cost.

Chart III-3 shows the growth of the more important items during the decade of the fifties. It can be seen from the chart that the most rapidly rising costs were for advertising and the wages of the crew and stage hands. Directors' fees actually fell during the period. Cast salaries improved approximately 40 per cent, while costuming bills went up only 16 per cent.

We can conclude that production costs have advanced significantly in the course of the last thirty years, that they shot up most rapidly in the last half of the fifties, and that they have been pushed up by the factors discussed above. Especially important in the upswing has been the growth in the number and importance of many small incidental items. Of the other factors involved in launching a play, advertising, cast salaries, and costum-

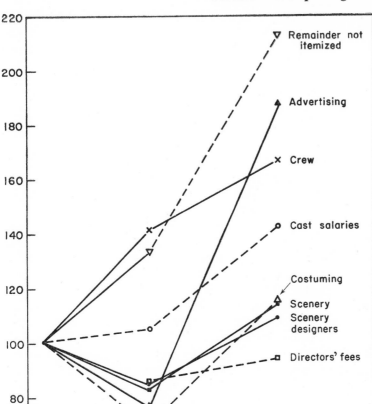

Chart III-3 Change in real cost of selected production items, 1949-51 to 1960/61 (1949/50 and 1950/51 = 100)
Source: See Appendix A, Table A-10.

ing expenses have contributed most to high production costs. Yet production costs are only one part of a play's expense. Their complement is operating expenditures; again they can be regarded as income for someone or as costs to be met out of the box office gross.

Operating costs

Operating outlays in general have increased much less rapidly throughout the whole period than those connected with the production process. Chart III-1 shows that they have nearly kept pace with changes in the company share of the box office.

In Chart III-4 are exhibited the most important factors affecting the weekly operating surplus. What should be noted from this graph is that the box office gross since the 1939/40, 1940/41, and 1941/42 seasons has fluctuated within rather small limits. During the thirties the theater's share of the box office declined, leaving a greater proportion of the gross available to the production. Chart III-1 shows that the amount left to the company has moved parallel to changes in operating costs.

Actors' salaries. The most important single item to be met out of current operating income is actors' salaries, which account, on the average, for 37 per cent of the weekly outflow. Chart III-4 indicates that this item advanced rapidly from 1920 to 1940 and then declined to roughly the same level it had held in the twenties. In the last five-year period, wages of performers recovered somewhat, although it is apparent that the weekly take-home pay of actors in a play on Broadway is only slightly larger today in real terms than it was in 1928. The graph also indicates the changes in the weekly earnings in manufacturing. The difference between the increase in manufacturing wages and actors' salaries is striking; in terms of increase in weekly take-home pay, stage performers have fallen considerably behind the average for manufacturing.

It should be remembered, however, that plays run longer today than previously. Once a performer finds a part, he can expect it to last longer. In the next chapter we will consider the joint effects of the increase in production pay and the small increase in operating pay.

Advertising. The second highest item in weekly operating costs in 1960/61 (an average of 15 per cent of the total) was advertising. Chart III-4 shows that advertising expenditures actually decreased a little from the twenties through the 1955 period. After that they exploded; in the last five years of the study, as the figures show, they doubled. Such a result demands explanation.[16]

Why have advertising expenditures increased so fast? As suggested above, theatergoing has changed. When patrons of the theater could be counted on to attend any show of reasonably good quality, advertising was necessary only to inform the public that the play was being performed and to keep the name of the show in the mind of the theatergoer. Now that people are seemingly willing to attend only the biggest hits, it is necessary

16. The standard error of the mean of advertising expenditures in 1960/61 is $605. Therefore, there is a 2.5 per cent chance that the true population mean is as low as $1,819 (in 1949/50 and 1950/51 dollars). If it were that low, it would be 20 per cent higher than it was in 1927/28 and 1928/29. However, that is still an increase of approximately 44 per cent over the expenditures in 1949/50 and 1950/51. Consequently, we can conclude that there has been some significant rise in advertising expenditures in the last few years. In fact, there is less than a 5 per cent probability that advertising expenditures have remained unchanged in the period between 1955 and 1960/61.

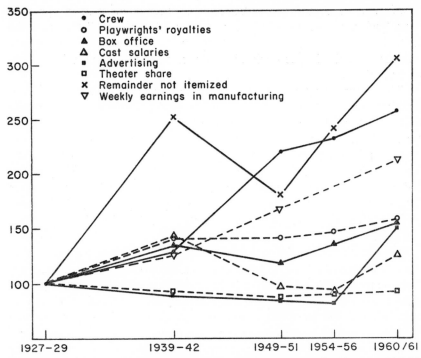

Chart III-4   Change in real weekly cost of selected operating items, 1927-29 to 1960/61 (1927/28 and 1928/29 = 100)

Sources: Table III-3. Weekly earnings in manufacturing are the Department of Labor's averages of gross weekly earnings in manufacturing and are taken from the *Economic Report of the President* (Washington, D.C.: Government Printing Office, 1962), p. 242, Table B29, and from Department of Commerce, *Statistical Abstract of the United States* (Washington, D.C.: Government Printing Office), for the earlier years.

to persuade them that each production is a special treat, which naturally involves more publicity.

Several other hypotheses seem plausible. Theatergoing appears to be less spontaneous and more planned than in the past. In the twenties, few tickets were bought by mail, judging from advertisements which did not list specific price information. It seems likely that most were bought at the box office or through brokers, probably shortly before the performance. Today, advertising must furnish more information and inducement. The probable rise since the war in the proportion of tickets sold to out-of-towners has contributed to the increased outlays for publicity.[17] In addition, the marked rise in advertising expenditure since 1955 suggests that television, either as competition or as a medium through which an audience may be attracted, has affected the theater.

17. Due to improved transportation facilities. See Chapter I.

Playwrights. Authors' royalties form another major item of operating costs. Such payments usually amount to about 8 per cent of the gross and 12 to 15 per cent of operating costs. Chart III-4 shows that playwrights' incomes have also lagged behind in comparison to wages and salaries elsewhere in the economy.

The picture painted in Chart III-4 of playwrights' incomes, however, is unduly somber. To an author the important factor is not the receipts per week but the total proceeds from writing a play. In this respect two factors must be kept in mind. First, plays run longer today than formerly; therefore, even if the playwright's weekly returns have remained substantially the same, his expected earnings from writing a play have increased. Second, a major component of the revenue received comes from the sale of subsidiary rights. It appears that the amount paid by motion picture companies for the rights to a play has climbed considerably during the last thirty years.[18]

Stagehands. The belief that stagehands are responsible for higher theater costs is based on the 157 per cent advance in their wages and salaries since the twenties. Most of the upsurge in this item took place in the forties, undoubtedly in response to the new demand for backstage personnel to work in television. In recent years, crews' wages have increased less than the box office gross or the company's share of the box office. Notwithstanding the tremendous growth in payments to the crew, they remain a minor item for the producer, accounting for only about 7 per cent of the total weekly costs.

Miscellaneous expenses. Chart III-5 demonstrates that in the decade between the 1950 and 1960 seasons the small incidentals not separately listed have zoomed upward; the increase was almost 70 per cent. From the twenties to the present, they tripled. (It should be remembered that the same unitemized production expenses have also shot up.) The incidentals consist of legal and audit expenses, office charges, payroll taxes, insurance, dues, mail order expenses, transportation charges, departmental bills, stationery and printing bills, New York City business tax, telephone expenses and postage, the cost of printing tickets, and miscellaneous outflows. In all they amount to about 23 per cent of the total operating expenses, up from roughly 13.5 per cent in the twenties.

The same factors that led to a growth in the number of incidentals before opening night—more paper work, increase in overhead business expenses, and some upgrading of the product—have probably been mainly responsible for pushing this item higher as an operating cost.

Directors and designers. A small item, but one that mounts up, is the weekly royalties of directors. As can be seen from Table III-3, the list of

18. See Table II-3, p. 36.

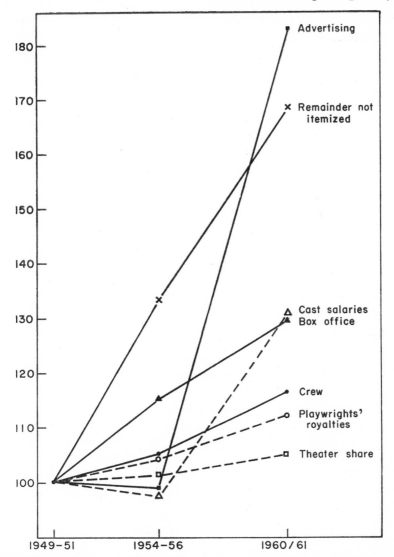

Chart III-5 Change in real weekly cost in constant dollars of selected operating items, 1949-51 to 1960/61 (1949/50 and 1950/51 = 100)

Source: Table III-3.

operating expenses for the 1927/28 and 1928/29 seasons includes no directors' royalties. Many of the plays produced by the Theatre Guild at this time were directed by staff members; consequently, it is not surprising to find they received no weekly royalty. Bernheim reports for the same period that directors occasionally earned 1 per cent of the gross as royalties.

Table III–3 Average weekly operating income and expenses, selected seasons (1966 dollars)

	1927/28 1928/29	1940/41 1941/42	1949/50 1950/51	1954/55 1955/56	1960/61
Box office gross	$18,747	$25,711	$22,453	$25,858	$29,170
Theater share	8,160	7,423	7,254	7,372	7,639
Company share	10,587	18,288	15,199	18,486	21,531
Actors' salaries	5,744	8,106	5,569	5,426	7,297
Crew and stagehands	492	630	1,086	1,148	1,268
Authors' royalties	1,472	2,084	2,079	2,168	2,334
Publicity and advertising	2,019	1,773	1,659	1,640	3,050
Directors	n.a.	467	401	378	573
Designers	n.a.	n.a.	57	99	111
Stage and company managers	189	264	734	818	974
Total listed expenses	9,413	10,923	10,801	11,082	15,120
Total operating expensives	10,900	14,678	13,493	14,686	19,670
Unlisted expenses	1,487	3,756	2,692	3,603	4,549
Maximum size of sample	15	8	11	15	15

Note: While the data for all the plays include total operating expenses, the data for some plays are incomplete. Therefore, the sum of the cost items may not equal total costs since each item is an average of the available data.
n.a. Not available.

However, of the nine shows for which figures are given, only one reports a payment, $100 weekly, to a director. Since the 1940/41 and 1941/42 seasons, directors have averaged between 1.7 and 2.1 per cent of the gross, with some directors collecting as much as 3.5 per cent of the box office.

Designers' royalties as well as directors' have risen sharply since 1950, though neither bulks larger than 3 per cent of total operating cost. Since neither directors nor designers drew royalties in the twenties, no percentage increase from the earliest period can be computed. During the fifties, designers' weekly remunerations almost doubled, rising from an average of $57 per week to $111 (in 1966 dollars), and directors' weekly incomes increased from $401 per week to $573, a rise of 42 per cent.

We can conclude then that the single most significant change in operating expenses over the entire period is the decline in the house's share of the gross. This reduction was concentrated mostly in the thirties when there were too many theaters for too few plays. The decrease has had the effect of increasing the potential revenue to the production, enabling producers to meet higher costs and repay backers more quickly. But offsetting the fall in the house's percentage have been increased outlays for miscellaneous items. More than any other factor or factors, their proliferation has decreased the profitability of Broadway productions.

IV | Income, costs, and unions

Almost all Broadway expenses have gone up, some more than others, and even though these expenditures are costs to the producer, they are income to the recipients. Many theater people receive income both before and after the play opens. Others receive their entire compensation before the premiere, while still others are paid strictly from operating income. To judge properly which people have gained most and which costs have climbed most and why, we must combine operating expenses with production outlays. The producer is concerned primarily with total outlay during the run of the show; those employed by the producer are probably concerned mainly with annual income. Let us look at both.

Income in the theater

Payment is made to most theater professionals both during the production process and during operation. For some, such as scenery designers, the major part (and often all) of their income comes before the show opens; for others, such as playwrights, almost all remuneration (except for the non-refundable advance) accrues after the premiere. To the extent that a professional is paid only out of operating receipts, he assumes part of the risk of the production. For example, theater owners receive revenue from houses only when they are in operation, and the amount they derive is dependent, within limits, on the success of the show.

Before the formation of Actors' Equity, players had to gamble on the success of a new production. Today, with their guarantees, they have shifted much of their share of the risk to producers and backers. Directors and scenery designers, on the other hand, have increasingly been sharing in a percentage of the gross or in the profits and have consequently increased the chance they take with a production.

To measure changes in annual income of various production factors, it is necessary to know how long each person is employed. For example, a playwright will presumably be most interested in the total receipts from a script. Even if weekly compensation is lower, he may be in a better position if—as a result of longer runs—his total income from playwriting rises. However, if fewer of his shows are staged during a year, either because it takes longer to write them or because producers reject a higher proportion of works, his financial position may have deteriorated.

Those professionals who perform all or almost all of their services prior to the opening—such as the playwright, director, and scenery designer—are concerned primarily with their total receipts from a show, which depend at least in part on the length of the run. Actors, on the other hand, while benefiting from longer-running productions, profit less than proportionately. If they can find new employment immediately, they should be indifferent or almost indifferent to the length of run of plays. And, in fact, there is some disadvantage to being in a hit and being required to play the same role over and over again for months. Offsetting these disadvantages is the cost of shifting to a new part: rehearsal pay is lower than performance pay, a new part must be learned, and the critics must again be faced. Moreover, actors cannot usually find new parts immediately. How much a performer benefits from a long run depends on how much it increases the average number of weeks he works in a year. The most that can be said is that once he has a part, he can expect it to last over twice as long as it would have thirty years ago. Whether he stays with the show as long as it runs is a different matter.

Reputedly there is little unemployment today among stagehands; indeed, they do much "moonlighting." Hence, they are probably indifferent to the length of run of plays. If a show closes, they can find new employment immediately. Their position may have been different in the twenties. If the number of weeks they work per year has risen, their income has undoubtedly improved more than the rise in the weekly pay of crew members would indicate.

Measuring changes in the welfare of theater owners is also difficult. The average number of weeks theaters are in operation increased from 33.6 weeks in the 1927/28 season to 38.5 weeks during the 1955/56 season. During the 1960/61 season the average was 35.8 weeks; in 1964/65 it was 34.7. At the same time, the number of shows playing per operating house has fallen from 3.2 to 2.4 per season. From these statistics we can conclude that theater owners are better off for two reasons: theaters are in operation more of the time, and there is less turnover. Turnover creates costs for theaters, which often share in the expense of bringing in a production and in advance advertising. Theater owners therefore prefer a smaller turnover to a larger one, *ceteris paribus*.

It appears likely, however, that the theaters' outlay to launch a new show has climbed per production. Unless expenses have gone up less than 38 per cent per show since the twenties, total expenditures per year for bringing in new productions have increased. (A 38 per cent rise in costs per show would just offset the fall in the number of productions per house per season from 3.24 to 2.36.) Total revenue has improved little; the product of the house's weekly share of the gross and the average number of weeks in operation per season has advanced 8.7 per cent, and costs to bring in a play have grown more than 38 per cent. Therefore, profits for theater owners appear to have declined. (It should be noted, however, that the fall in number of theaters has been reversed. In 1964, the number of Broadway theaters expanded to thirty-six from a low of thirty in the 1955/56 season.)[1]

Authors now average 250 per cent greater financial return per play than in 1927/28, but yearly incomes may have increased considerably less.[2] If playwrights must spend more time creating a script or if more manuscripts are rejected currently than before, income will have grown less than 250 per cent. Nevertheless, it appears very likely that active playwrights are better off in the sixties, relative to other occupations, than thirty years earlier.

Directors and scenery designers also appear to have improved their positions. Their income per play has risen 430 and 215 per cent, respectively.[3] It may be, however, that they do fewer plays a year now than formerly, so that their annual income may have risen considerably less.

In contrast to our knowledge concerning income per play, we know little about how annual income has changed, since for most occupations we can only speculate about change in weeks worked. Nevertheless, it seems likely that income of theater owners has declined and incomes of authors, directors, and scenery designers have increased both absolutely and relative to incomes in general.

Total costs

Charts IV-1 and IV-2 show a combined index of the average costs (in dollars of constant purchasing power) of the New York City operations of a play. The index was computed by adding the outlays during the production process to the product of the weekly expenditures from operations and the average length of run.[4] Unfortunately, the estimates for those items which depend on the box office are proably biased. The average gross of the sample is undoubtedly lower than the average weekly box office for all shows. The mean gross, in general, is derived from averaging box office receipts for the third, fourth, and fifth weeks[5] for each play, regardless of how long it ran. But if the show ran less than five weeks, the mean gross

1. See Appendix A, Table A-8.
2. Computed by multiplying average length of run by weekly compensation.
3. Computed by multiplying average length of run by weekly compensation and adding the fees paid before opening.
4. See Table A-6 for average runs.
5. See Appendix B.

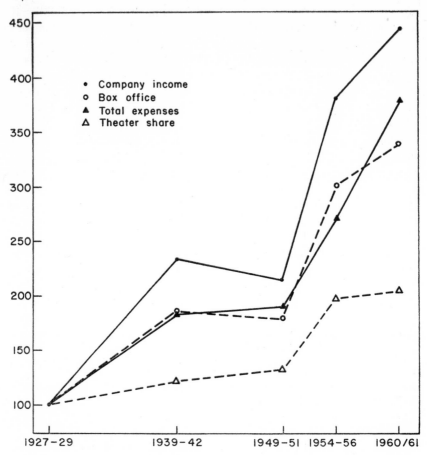

Chart IV-1 Change in total average income and cost for the theater and the production, 1927–29 to 1960/61 (1927/28 and 1928/29 = 100)

Source: Table A-9.

is the average of the last three weeks if the play lasted three weeks. Hence, failures are given as much weight as successes that last several years. While for many items there is no correlation between cost and the success or failure of the production, the correlation is high for some expenditures, primarily those based on a percentage of the box office gross. Thus, the income from all factors receiving a percentage of the box office, such as authors and directors, is probably underestimated. In comparing the companies' share of the box office and of total expenses, there is, as well, a presumption that the former is biased downward more than the latter, since total costs are only in part a function of the box office.

Inasmuch as our interest lies in changes over a period of time, the

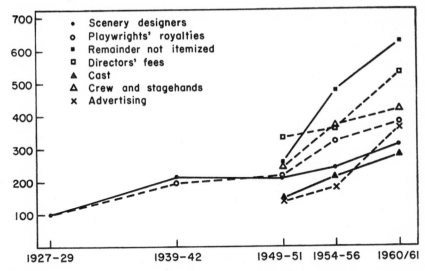

Chart IV-2 Change in total average cost of major items, 1927–29 to 1960/61
(1927/28 and 1928/29 = 100)

Source: Table A-9.

above bias would be unimportant if it led to no bias in the index. But because of the increase in average length of run, the importance of the underestimated figures in the total has grown.[6] Chart IV-1 understates the growth in income for the production as a whole. For the same reasons, the advance in playwrights' earnings, as shown in Chart IV-2, is biased downward. Yet, it seems plausible that the amount of bias is small and that while the increase has been larger than indicated, the pattern of costs over the period of time has been unaffected.

Chart IV-1 also reveals that box office income and the theater's share of the gross grew only slightly before the fifties. This chart presents a rather optimistic picture of the company's financial state. The company's share of the box office has climbed faster than total expense. Most of the increase in the production's income relative to costs occurred in the period before World War II. Because of the bias from the growing variance in length of run, however, income has climbed even faster than indicated relative to the increase in costs.

The figures suggest that investments in straight shows have become more profitable. But to draw this conclusion would be unwise; the variance in box office receipts and expenses as a whole is high, and only part of the

6. See Chapter I, p. 7. The total is computed by adding production costs (unbiased) to length of run times operating costs (biased). Since average length of run has increased, the effect of the bias on the total has gone up.

Table IV–1 Operating and production costs, selected seasons (percentages)

Cost item	1927/28 1928/29	1939/40 1940/41 1941/42	1949/50 1950/51	1954/55 1955/56	1960/61
Playwrights	10.0	10.4	10.9	11.8	9.1
Crew	5.6	n.a.	7.0	7.5	6.2
Directors	2.4	n.a.	4.1	3.3	3.3
Scenery designers	1.6	1.9	1.8	1.4	1.3
Cast	40.4	n.a.	31.0	30.8	30.0
Managers	1.3^a	1.3^a	5.1	5.4	4.8
Advertising	15.6	n.a.	11.3	10.4	14.7
Scenery and props	12.0	n.a.	9.2	5.5	6.3
Costumes	2.6	n.a.	3.2	1.6	2.1
Electrical and sound	2.7	n.a.	1.4	1.3	1.2
Total itemized costs	90.7	n.a.	82.5	77.9	78.8
Remainder	13.0	n.a.	16.9	22.2	21.1
Production costs	26.0	26.5	28.9	19.9	23.0

^{a} Only stage and company managers; other years include general managers as well.
Note: Items calculated by summing production outlays and the product of operating outlays times number of weeks of operation.
n.a. Not available.

total income is reflected in the data. If investors tend to avoid risks, however, we should expect profits to have increased as risks have gone up.

Chart IV-2 and Table IV-1 give a more detailed picture of the changes in costs over a period of time. The most spectacular increase has been among the items labeled "remainder not itemized," which, as the table shows, have risen from a small proportion of total costs (13 per cent) to about one-fifth of the entire outlay. In terms of index numbers they rose to over 250 by 1950, almost to 470 by 1955, and to about 620 in the 1960/ 61 season. The rate of growth of these miscellaneous expenses has been consistently higher than the rate for any other factor.

Note that scenery, props, and costuming, which are often blamed for higher costs in the theater, are responsible for a smaller proportion of total outlays in 1960 than they were around 1928. Wages and salaries of backstage personnel made up just under 6 per cent of the total in the twenties and just over that figure in 1960. In other words, most of the factors commonly blamed for high costs contribute no more or contribute less to the total than they did in the twenties.

Unions

Are unions primarily responsible for ballooning costs? Chart IV-2 shows that the answer is no. The items which have grown the fastest are the "miscellaneous" ones and directors' fees and royalties. Since directors belong to one of the few occupations (the only one shown in Chart IV-2) that were non-union during this period,[7] neither of these factors has been directly affected by union activities. (Scenery designers have been unionized since the early twenties, actors have been organized from the time of World War I, playwrights formed an association in the late twenties, and stagehands have had a closed shop for the entire period under consideration.) And, in fact, three out of four of the fastest-climbing factors—directors' fees and royalties, advertising, and miscellaneous items—are unrelated to union activity.

Furthermore, the increase in the payments to unionized occupations can be explained by other factors. In spite of the fact that there has been no increase in cast size, salaries of performers (including stars), on a weekly basis, have gone up 28 per cent in real terms since the late twenties.[8] Meanwhile, weekly wages in manufacturing have risen 112 per cent. Unless the supply of actors were completely unaffected by what the actors could earn in other fields, some increase in the salaries of performers would be expected. And, if performers were very sensitive to earning opportunities elsewhere, actors' annual incomes should have gone up close to 110 per cent. By the very nature of the industry, a performer's productivity cannot increase. Hence any change in weekly pay should be reflected entirely in weekly expenses. Average annual pay is, of course, the product of weekly income and number of weeks worked. If the amount of time actors work in a year has remained unchanged, annual pay will have risen only 28 per cent. If actors are now employed a greater proportion of the time, their income will have grown more. The number of weeks they work would have had to go up 64 per cent for their annual income to keep pace with income in manufacturing. Unfortunately, the change in weekly income gives no conclusive evidence that the union is effective. Thus, the 28 per cent increase in weekly pay is consistent with the assumption that Actors' Equity has had no effect on wages and that the supply is fairly insensitive to relative wages. On the other hand, the possibility cannot be ruled out that Equity did in fact raise performers' salaries.

We should note, however, that the mere setting of minimum wages can lead to the exclusion of low-cost substitutes. If a producer could hire a novice performer for $40 per week or a seasoned actor for $125 he might easily take the novice for a walk-on part. But if he must pay the inexperienced man $125 (the minimum wage in 1964–66), the entrepreneur would naturally prefer the knowledgeable performer. Certainly minimum wages make it more difficult for those who have little experience to find a

7. Directors organized in the summer of 1962.
8. A sample of 58 plays during the 1927/28 season had an average of 14.4 performers; 28 of the plays that opened during the 1960/61 season have an average of 15.0. These figures were computed from *Best Plays* volumes for 1927/28 and 1960/61.

Broadway part. In part, Broadway minimum wages may explain the off-Broadway movement; young performers seeking a chance to work and unable to secure Broadway employment settle for off-Broadway wages and conditions.

To the charge that Equity is partially responsible for higher theater costs we must give the verdict of not proven. While it is possible that they did contribute to the upsurge in expenses, it seems unlikely that their effect was considerable. If the number of weeks worked has increased more than 64 per cent, or if more people desire to be actors at any relative wage, Actors' Equity may be partially responsible. Since job opportunities have grown with the development of motion pictures and television, it seems reasonable to assume that actors are employed a greater proportion of the time now than during the twenties, independent of union activities. How great the increase has been is impossible to say with the data available.

There is room for more automation backstage than behind the footlights. Nevertheless, because each show is different, the possibilities are limited. Crew costs have risen 90 per cent on a weekly basis, which still is below the rise in weekly wages in manufacturing. It might be reasonable to attribute part of the growth in salaries of backstage personnel to the unions. From the producer's point of view, though, this is a small item which affects his costs only marginally; the outlay for the crew and extra stagehands was 6.2 per cent of total expenditures during the 1960/61 season, up from 5.6 per cent in the twenties. If, in the absence of unions, there had been no rise in the payments for grips, carpenters, electricians, and others, total outlays during the 1960/61 season would have been only 4 per cent lower.

The other unionized occupations, such as managers and scenery designers, account for an even smaller proportion of total costs than does the crew. On a weekly basis, the outlay for designing sets has grown 43 per cent. The figures on managers' salaries are not comparable over the whole period, since for the twenties they fail to include general managers' salaries, while later they are included. Consequently, while it is possible that the unions may have been very effective in raising the wages of their own members, we can attribute very little of the increase in total costs to union activity.

Slightly over 9 per cent of the increase in real total outlays can be accounted for by the advance in earnings of playwrights. It is impossible to determine from our data whether this rise was due to union activity or to competitive forces. To an author the relevant price is his receipts per play or more exactly, his receipts per hour devoted to playwriting. To the producer the relevant expense is the royalty per performance, which has risen about 59 per cent—considerably less than wages and salaries in general have increased—while the playwright's returns per play shot up about 250 per cent.

Three factors may have led to such a large growth in compensation for playwriting: costs of writing a successful script may have increased, the competition of television and motion pictures for scarce writing talent may have increased, or union activity may be responsible. Chapter II indicated that much of the advance in playwrights' earnings can be explained by the competition of television and motion pictures for their services. Moreover, on a weekly basis, the greatest advance in payments to scriptwriters took place during the thirties, suggesting that sound motion pictures were responsible. Producers, we saw in Chapter II, tend to have become selective. This indicates that the time spent in writing a marketable script has probably increased.

Let us assume, however, that it takes just as long today, on the average, to fashion a script as it did thirty years ago; i.e., direct costs of writing have remained constant.[9] Then we should expect, if authors were very sensitive to wage scales in other fields, that income for playwrights would follow the national trend. Thus, if there had been no changes in relative wages and if the time necessary to write a play had remained the same, authors would receive about 110 per cent more in real terms today for a script than in 1929. But we find that they are receiving 250 per cent more. If we make the further assumption that this difference is the result of the Dramatists Guild's activities, we find that of the rise in the cost of putting on a show, 5 per cent can be attributed to the organization of the playwrights.

Of the unionized occupations, only playwrights appear to be receiving more than would be expected if relative wages had remained constant over a period of time. In fact, assuming that the average number of weeks worked per year is unchanged, the other theatrical vocations—stagehands, scenery designers, and actors—would appear to have experienced a fall in relative wages. It seems likely, though, that unemployment has decreased in these callings; if so, income for organized personnel may have kept pace or even exceeded the growth in wages and salaries in general.

At a minimum, we can deny that any part of the advance in costs is attributable to union activity. A reasonable estimate of the portion of the rise for which unions are responsible is 5 per cent, the gain accounted for by authors' increased royalties. Sensitivity to wages elsewhere in the economy explains away the betterment of weekly pay for all other organized occupations. At most, if we assume that the entire improvement in payment to unionized crafts is the result of union activity, about 50 per cent of the total addition to expenses can be imputed directly to unionism. The

9. Opportunity costs, however, would have risen.

other half is primarily ascribable to such factors as advertising and increased incidental disbursements.

Conclusion

It would appear, then, from these statistics, that total expenses on a weekly basis in the theater have risen roughly 70 per cent in real terms during this period.[10] Income to the production has kept pace with or has even risen slightly faster than costs. Ticket price and box office gross, however, have gone up more slowly, while the house has received a smaller share of total receipts. Except for the period of the thirties, expenses have tended to mount modestly. Chart IV-1 shows that costs grew most rapidly in the period from the late twenties to around 1940. Most of the inflation in Broadway expenses appears, therefore, to be a result of the competition of motion pictures and is consequently not easily remedied.

At most, 50 per cent of the advance in costs is attributable to unions. It seems more likely, however, that the organization of these occupations has affected expenses only marginally, probably by about 5 per cent. If such is the case, the growth in outlays can be ascribed primarily to three factors: first, to the industry's being mainly of a handicraft type not subject to important gains in productivity; second, to mounting overhead expenses and sprouting incidentals which have accounted for about one-fourth of the upsurge in outlays; third, to advertising, which is responsible for 14 per cent of the growth.

Market forces outside the control of the producer can explain almost all of the rise in costs. Apparently the only way entrepreneurs could reduce expenses would be to reduce advertising outlays; however, to compete successfully in today's market probably requires publicity for all but the biggest hits. Since multiplying paper work has forced outlays up, efforts should be made to reduce or eliminate the requirements which have contributed to these costs. Only by reducing such incidentals and trimming advertising can the theater expect to reduce costs and prices.

10. The total rise in outlays (operating costs multiplied by average weeks operating plus production costs) divided by average weeks operating.

V | The audience

It is the audience that finally determines what will be seen on the stage: if playgoers desire trash, it will be supplied; if they want excellence, the theater will respond. Without viewers the stage would die. Since spectators are so vital to Broadway, they should have been studied. Manufacturers long ago discovered the importance of knowing their customers, advertising agencies spend millions annually to measure the likes and dislikes of potential buyers, but the managements of Broadway enterprises have never sponsored a full investigation of their patrons. Certain information, partially as a result of this work, is now available. By syncretizing three studies—the *Playbill* audience survey,[1] a sociological investigation of theater audiences by Weiss and Geller Research,[2] and an audience inquiry conducted by the author—a composite portrait of the theatergoer—who he is, why he goes, and what affects his attendance—can be drawn.

The data

Depending on their sources, figures can mean much or little. A small unbiased sample of a population can accurately predict its likes and dislikes, while a large unrepresentative sample may mislead. The importance of understanding the limitations of the data and their sources must, therefore, be stressed.

The PLAYBILL study

Professional interviewers, employed by *Playbill,* annually distribute printed questionnaires in Broadway theaters. In 1960, for example, forty-eight shows were sampled (some more than once) for a total of 384 performances. Each interviewer chose thirty playgoers, one from every other row, starting at 8:00 P.M. and continuing until curtain time. Those who came late received forms during the intermission. John W. Enders, who conducted the survey, reported that there was no apparent difference be-

1. This study is published annually in *Who's Who* (New York, Playbill). It is based on a fifty-two-week study conducted for *Playbill,* the weekly magazine distributed in Broadway theaters, by John W. Enders, Head, Marketing Department, Manhattan College. Professor Enders had additional information prepared especially for this author.
2. Weiss and Geller Research, "An Exploratory Study of Theatre Audiences, Present and Future" (Chicago: mimeographed, March, 1956).

tween individuals who arrived late at the theater and those who arrived early.[3] Every attempt was made to keep the sample random, he averred; the researchers were instructed to ignore appearance and to choose according to location.

The Weiss and Geller study

Unfortunately the report on this work fails to disclose how the study was conducted and whether there was any attempt to insure that the group chosen to be interviewed was representative. All we know is that twenty-nine men and thirty-seven women were questioned. Of the total, twenty-seven were from the Midwest and the rest lived in eastern cities or suburbs. Sixteen of those interviewed had an elementary school background, twenty-two had attended high school, and twenty-six had some college education.

The Broadway audience survey

In April of 1962, the author conducted a survey of theatergoers in seven Broadway houses for a total of eighteen performances. Questionnaires were inserted in all *Playbills*, but it was requested that only one member of a family fill out the form. The audience was asked to drop the completed form in one of several large boxes placed in the lobby or near the exits.[4] If the responses came from a random sample of the audience, they can be treated as representative of everyone in the theater. However, there is no assurance that the responses were a random sample of those in the audience. Did the 24 per cent of the audience who were represented in these responses differ significantly in any important way from those who ignored the questionnaire? Unfortunately, we cannot know. Since those sitting in low-priced seats responded more frequently than those in higher-priced sections, minor adjustments in the data have been made for the differing rates of response. We have assumed that the responses from each price range represent a random sample of those sitting in seats in that range.

A comparison of the author's survey and the *Playbill* results is encouraging (see Appendix C): the studies are, with minor exceptions, consonant.[5] Therefore, while we must recognize the possibility of biases, we can have some confidence that our figures are close to the true facts. Still, one difference in the data for the *Playbill* study and the author's audience survey should be noted: all data from the *Playbill* study refer to respondents,

3. An interview with the author in January, 1962.
4. Appendix C discusses the method of conducting the survey, its problems, and the possible major biases in the data.
5. Comparing age, percentage of audience from out of town, and with adjustments in income. See Appendix C.

Table V-1   Patronage by seasons in 1960

Period	Percentage of out-of-town respondents
Jan.-Feb.-March	29.6
Apr.-May-June	20.1
July-Aug.-Sept.	25.0
Oct.-Nov.-Dec.	33.1

Source: Enders, *Who's Who in the Audience, 1960*, p. 6.

while the figures from the audience survey are often for the audience as a whole; that is, respondents were weighted by the number of people in the party. In the remainder of the chapter, all unidentified figures are from the author's audience survey.

The composition of the audience

Contrary to popular opinion, the New York theater is sustained by New Yorkers: only about 30 per cent of the audience are from outside the metropolitan area. Patronage by out-of-towners, as Table V-1 shows, varies with the season. It also differs by type of show: musicals attract more visitors than do plays, comedies more than drama, and long runs more than the recently opened show. Matinees also are favored by those who are in Manhattan temporarily.

Of playgoers from the metropolitan area, 60 per cent came from within the city limits, 12 per cent from Westchester and Connecticut, 8 per cent from Long Island, and 20 per cent from New Jersey.[6] Notwithstanding the substantial proportion of local respondents who came from New York City, the audience did not live close to Broadway: the average time noted to return home that night was 51.6 minutes—almost an hour. Those attending the theater in the afternoon spent more time commuting: 66.6 minutes. Weekend playgoers had longer trips than did weekday ones.

Those visiting Manhattan are inclined to be older and earn higher incomes than local theatergoers. The median age for visitors was forty-four, while for local individuals it was just under thirty-six. The median family income for out-of-towners was $16,300 (see Tables V-2 and V-3), and for those from the area, under $12,000. Ticket prices are higher in the evening than for matinees, and higher for the weekend than during the week, so it is unsurprising that matinee and weekday audiences had lower annual earnings on the average than did evening and weekend audiences.

Inasmuch as high incomes are often associated with above-average education, the fact that 68 per cent had been to college is understandable.[7]

6. Enders, *Who's Who in the Audience, 1960*, p. 7.
7. *Ibid.*, p. 10.

Table V–2 Weighted characteristics of the evening audience for all shows and the audience at two matinees

	Straight shows	Musicals	Matinees[a]	Total
Percentage responding to questionnaires	35.4	19.8	15.7	25.8
Percentage of respondents from New York or within commuting distance	70.2	59.4	75.1	64.3
Percentage of local respondents on expense accounts	4.9	3.0	3.7	4.2
Percentage of out-of-town respondents on expense accounts	11.0	13.1	6.9	12.1
Percentage of local audience who went to a restaurant	72.0	70.3	72.8	71.1
Percentage of out-of-town audience who came to New York for pleasure	42.3	54.1	72.1	49.4
Median income				
Local	$12,200	$11,800	$ 9,900	$12,000
Out-of-town	15,000	17,900	11,800	16,300
All	13,000	13,400	10,300	13,200

[a] Weighted by number attending matinees of *A Man for All Seasons* and *How to Succeed in Business Without Really Trying*; since these were the only shows sampled at a matinee performance, no attempt was made to represent the entire matinee audience.

Note: In order to generalize the results, each of the twenty-four shows running on Broadway during the survey week was matched with one of the seven productions surveyed on the basis of type of show, length of run, and success of the production at the box offices. The last characteristic was measured by taking the actual box office receipts as a percentage of capacity receipts. Assuming that the sixteen evening performances of seven shows—matinees were omitted—represented a random sample of the characteristics of the other seventeen productions, the sample preformances were given weights corresponding to the proportion of the total audience that the sample performance represented.

Median incomes are estimated by assuming that the proportion of individuals making $11,001–$12,000, $12,001–$13,000 and so on declines linearly throughout the median category $10,000–$20,000.

With the large incomes went high-income occupations: 47 per cent were in professional, semiprofessional, and managerial fields; clerical and sales jobs employed 22 per cent; 13 per cent classified themselves as craftsmen, foremen, and operators; 11 per cent were employed in service industries or were manual laborers; students, retired, and others not working made up 4 per cent; about 2 per cent were housewives.[8]

Tourists contribute substantially to the coffers of Broadway houses. About half of the out-of-towners reported that they came to town for pleasure. In addition some of those who reported that their trip was for business also mentioned recreation as a factor in their visit. Because tourists are more likely to be free in the afternoon, it is not astonishing that 79 per cent of the New York visitors at a matinee performance of *How to Suc-*

8. *Ibid.,* p. 12.

Table V–3 Characteristics of people in the audience

	Straight shows	Musicals	Weekday straight shows	Weekend straight shows	Weekday musicals	Weekend musicals	Matinee straight show	Matinee musicals	Weekday totals	Weekend totals	Grand total
Percentage responding	31.0	16.7	34.2	31.2	19.7	15.6	19.2	12.6	27.2	22.8	23.6
Percentage local	70.4	59.9	69.1	71.7	51.3	61.8	78.9	65.7	61.9	66.1	65.8
Percentage single	29.0	22.2	31.0	23.1	22.4	15.8	45.2	47.5	28.3	20.2	26.6
Median age	39.3	38.1	39.0	39.7	36.6	39.9	38.2	28.1	38.3	39.8	38.9
Percentage of local respondents on expense accounts	4.8	3.5	4.9	4.9	2.3	4.7	4.5	2.4	4.2	4.8	4.4
Percentage of local audience who went to a restaurant	65.8	67.6	71.8	62.2	74.9	65.1	58.6	64.3	73.6	63.8	66.5
Percentage of out-of-town respondents on expense accounts	9.3	10.6	11.7	6.8	12.6	9.7	8.6	5.3	12.0	8.1	9.8
Percentage of out-of-town respondents who came to New York for pleasure	49.6	55.5	42.4	53.9	56.0	49.0	66.6	79.0	47.9	52.0	52.0
Travel time one way (minutes)	53.55	50.70	47.01	50.00	49.84	53.90	71.09	62.00	47.8	51.5	51.6
Median income											
Local	$13,992	$13,052	$13,176	$15,516	$12,750	$13,979	$ 9,461	$11,509	$13,139	$14,938	$13,553
Out-of-town	14,979	15,777	16,548	14,127	16,617	17,246	10,416	14,232	16,234	15,764	15,805
All	14,288	14,058	14,234	15,120	14,684	14,908	9,602	12,553	14,329	15,167	14,981

Note: The totals are not weighted by the other shows running during the survey week (see note for Table V-2). Medians estimated by assuming individuals are evenly distributed throughout the entire median category.

ceed in Business Without Really Trying and 67 per cent at a matinee of
A Man for All Seasons asserted that they were in town seeking diversion.

The expense-account trade, on the other hand, turns out to be exaggerated. It is almost negligible: only 12 per cent of the visitors were enjoying an expense account, while New Yorkers whose expenses were being paid by their firms made up only 4.2 per cent of the local respondents. Answers, however, to the question, "Are you on an expense account?" may not be accurate. A man who is entertaining may be unwilling to admit in front of his client that his company is paying for the evening, and for this reason, these percentages may be low. As a control, at one performance of *A Shot in the Dark,* questionnaires were distributed with business reply envelopes, and the audience was requested to return them by mail. At that performance, only 3.9 per cent of the local theatergoers claimed to be on expense accounts. Thus, while we must admit the possibility of bias, it seems remote.[9]

Individuals on expense accounts, as is widely believed, do favor light shows. New Yorkers whose companies were paying for their tickets showed that musicals tended to be slighted by expense-account executives. Visitors on expense accounts, on the other hand, favored comedies and musicals over more serious fare. Table V-4 illustrates the emphasis on lighter entertainment by those on expense accounts.

Do the people in the audience differ from those who do not attend? In age and in the proportion who are married, the local audience—those who came from around the city—resembled the average for the adult population of the New York area. Almost 73 per cent of the respondents were married—not significantly different from the proportion of married adults in the area. But the average individual at a performance was better educated, much more affluent, and more likely to be in a managerial or professional job than are the people of the New York metropolitan area generally. Except for matinees the audience varied little from performance to performance. Compared to evening spectators, the proportion of an afternoon audience that was unmarried was higher, incomes were lower, and patrons commuted longer to and from the theater.

9. An unusually high proportion of the audience—over 50 per cent—at the control performance were from out of town; in fact, a two-by-two chi-square test of the hypothesis that the proportion of the audience that was from out of town was the same as the proportion for the sample as a whole produced a value of 8.2, leading to the rejection of the hypothesis. In this unusually large group of visitors, there was an extraordinarily high percentage of people on expense accounts—23 per cent. Since it seems less likely that the method of collecting the responses would affect the answers to questions concerning expense accounts by out-of-towners who are unlikely to be entertaining clients than by local people who probably are, we need not reject our original figures. It seems quite possible that a convention was in town and that a large number of people who were on expense accounts decided to view *A Shot in the Dark.* We must admit, though, that at any one performance a substantial minority could be on expense accounts.

Table V–4 Percentage of local audience and out-of-town audience on expense accounts at different types of productions

	Comedies	Musicals	Dramas
Percentage of local audience on expense accounts	5.9	3.7	4.2
Percentage of out-of-town audience on expense accounts	13.3	11.2	6.0

Theatergoers

We are concerned here with three groups: the adult population, men and women, in the New York City area as a whole; theatergoers—people who go to the theater, whether frequently or rarely—from the New York area; and the people in the audience—for a particular show or group of shows—from the area. All people in the audience are theatergoers by definition, but they are not a random sample of playgoers. In the audience, there are a great many theatergoers who visit Broadway frequently. They undoubtedly have high incomes and differ from the average inhabitant of the metropolitan area. Thus, active playgoers will be overrepresented in the audience and the average income of the audience will be higher than that of all theatergoers. But do theatergoers (regardless of how frequently they attend the theater) in turn differ from the population generally?

Since those who often attend may be unusual—they may have higher incomes, they may be older, or they may live closer to Times Square—the typical audience is unlikely to be representative of people who have gone to the theater one or more times, that is, of theatergoers generally. To answer the question, "Are playgoers unique?" the overrepresentation of active playgoers must be removed from the data. To do this, our responses have been weighted in inverse proportion to the frequency with which the respondent visited Broadway. Thus a questionnaire which indicated that the person who filled it out went twice as often as another was given half the weight of the first person's questionnaire.[10]

The most striking difference between all theatergoers and the individuals in an audience is in their income. While median income for the entire audience was almost $15,000, the median for theatergoers was only $7,400 for local people and $8,800 for out-of-towners. According to the 1960 census, the median family income in 1959 for all families in the New York

10. One item on the questionnaire requested the respondent to indicate when he last saw a Broadway show. This can be considered a measure of how frequently this particular individual attended the theater. It was believed that this indirect method of measuring frequency would be more accurate than would be the answers to a direct question concerning the frequency of attendance. See Appendix C for more details on the questionnaire.

metropolitan area was $6,696.[11] Undoubtedly, three years later, in 1962, incomes were higher. Earnings of New York theatergoers, therefore, do not seem substantially different from earnings of the population generally. On the other hand, visitors to New York were more prosperous than people throughout the United States.

On the basis of income, therefore, theatergoers appear to resemble the local population. The playgoer, however, is considerably younger than the average for the local inhabitants: while the median age of New York area patrons is only 28.1, the median for all individuals above fourteen is 42.7, considerably higher.[12] Since incomes normally rise with age, such a young group as are the frequenters of Broadway should, if they were similar to the public, have a low income compared to the average for everyone. But earnings are about the same, so we can conclude that theatergoers are above average in income as well as younger than average.

The desire to see a play

Enthusiastic playgoers are better educated, older, less encumbered with young children, and have more time available for recreation, according to the Weiss and Geller study, than those who attend less frequently. Men tend to be less interested than women in the theater, an attitude which the study attributed to a "prevailing tradition that makes much show of emotion unmanly. The 'gang' may label the theater 'long-hair' and 'sissy stuff.' "[13] Some playgoers gained pleasure from the anticipation of a big evening at the theater: almost half of those interviewed by Weiss and Geller spoke of the expectancy as the lights dimmed or the thrill as the curtain went up as factors in their appreciation of a play. Women commented on this aspect of theatergoing more frequently than men. Half of those responding in the Weiss and Geller interviews stressed the skills of the flesh-and-blood actors before them, comparing their technique favorably with the more impersonal acting of the movies. Some talked about the theater as an interpreter of life, feeling that it gave them new insights into their own lives. About 20 per cent commented on the pleasure of discussing the play with friends. A few mentioned the status of going to the theater and especially the prestige of attending first nights. In this group, naturally, were those who visited Broadway because it was the thing to do culturally or socially. Through almost all the responses ran the themes of identification and anticipation of a "big night out." These two factors were evidently the

11. Bureau of the Census, *U.S. Census of Population, 1960* (Washington, D.C.: Government Printing Office, 1964), I, Part 1, 1–309. The New York metropolitan area is taken to be the New York—Northeastern New Jersey Standard Consolidated Area.
12. *Ibid.,* pp. 1–186.
13. Weiss and Geller, "An Exploratory Study of Theatre Audiences," p. 12.

primary causes of theatergoing. Prestige and cultural interaction played secondary roles.[14]

High cost, commuting distance, difficulty of purchasing tickets, and bad plays were the most frequently mentioned reasons for failing to attend the theater more often. Eighty-one per cent of the enthusiastic group of constant playgoers brought up ticket prices as a problem. Between 50 and 60 per cent of the people who attended less frequently referred to the cost of seeing a show. From the comments quoted in Weiss and Geller, the respondents apparently had in mind the cost of the whole evening. About half of those interviewed gave commuting as a reason for not attending the theater more often. Respondents living in the East were more involved with this problem than those in the Midwest. Easterners were also more concerned with the difficulty of buying tickets. Only 14 per cent of the respondents in the Midwest mentioned this problem, as against one-half of those in the East. Disagreeable to many was the necessity of buying tickets considerably in advance. Those with young children often objected on the grounds that childhood diseases were unpredictable.

An individual's taste for theatergoing appeared to be strongly related to his early experiences with drama. If he had attended the theater at an early age and if the event was pleasant, he was more likely to relish the stage. Those who reported having been taken because "it was good for them" or having grown up in an environment in which theatergoing was considered feminine were apathetic. Weiss and Geller felt, justifiably, that lack of interest in theatergoing is a vicious circle: those who stay away know nothing, those who know nothing are indifferent, and those who are indifferent stay away.

What show to see

The content of plays—that is, what the playwright had to say to the audience through the development of the plot and its characters—was the attraction for theatergoers. While a fourth of those interviewed objected to shows with a "message," roughly half preferred them. Important to these people were productions that dealt with "real-life" characters and situation adjudged valid in terms of the respondent's personal experience. On the other hand, most young people avoided "real-life" plays but enjoyed love stories. Eight of the twenty-seven, reporting on types of plays disliked, singled out fantasies.[15]

Active theatergoers liked straight plays, while those who went to the theater less frequently preferred musicals. This conclusion by Weiss and Geller is substantiated by the audience survey: an average playgoer at the

14. *Ibid.,* pp. 4, 5, 12–17.
15. *Ibid.,* pp. 26–31.

comedies *A Shot in the Dark* and *A Thousand Clowns* had seen a Broadway show 26.1 days before; at a drama, 37.8 days before; and at a musical, 48.2 days before.

Critics are important for new productions: of the audience from the New York area attending *A Thousand Clowns* (which had been running only four weeks), almost half reported that newspaper reviews had influenced them while only 27 per cent cited personal recommendations. As shows run longer, personal recommendations become more important. For *A Man for All Seasons, Gideon, How to Succeed in Business Without Really Trying,* and *Milk and Honey,* 61, 41, 55, and 70 per cent, respectively, indicated they were influenced by word of mouth. Except for *Gideon,* which was on cut-rate tickets and doing only fair box office business, over half of those answering from the metropolitan area indicated that they chose on the basis of personal recommendations. Critics' comments are much less important for these longer-running attractions. Only 37, 37, 42, and 26 per cent of the local respondents, respectively, at *A Man for All Seasons, Gideon, How to Succeed,* and *Milk and Honey* checked this reason for attending.

The only other reason specified by a substantial portion of local people was newspaper advertising (see Table V-5). While only 12 per cent of those at *Milk and Honey* and 14 per cent at *A Man for All Seasons* suggested this had affected their decisions, 20 per cent of those at *Gideon* and 23 per cent at *How to Succeed* had been influenced by newspaper spreads. Thus, paid publicity in the dailies brings a certain amount of business, and good reviews give a substantial boost to a show. In the end, however, these figures suggest that a show's success will depend on how well the public likes it. If people who see it enjoy it, they will recommend it. Without these personal favorable comments, good notices and newspaper advertising cannot long sustain a production. The survey also suggests that advertising over the radio, on billboards, or in magazines produces few local patrons. However, advertising may influence those who suggest plays to their acquaintances, or a billboard may trigger a person's memory and lead him to go to the theater. Therefore, our data on advertising undoubtedly underestimate its effectiveness.

A significant difference in reasons for choosing a particular show exists between those who went to the theater often and those who went infrequently. Over 40 per cent of those who had been to the theater within the last week mentioned word of mouth as a factor in their decisions, while only 1 per cent of those who had not seen a show in more than eight months referred to it as a factor. People who went to the theater often usually credited several sources as influencing their choice, while occasional playgoers gave few reasons. From these figures we can draw one conclusion on ad-

Table V–5 Reasons for choosing shows (percentages)

Category checked	Total		Local		Out-of-town		Local		Out-of-town	
	Local	Out-of-town	Saw show within 2 weeks	Over 8 months since saw show	Saw show within 2 weeks	Over 8 months since saw show	Musicals	Straight shows	Musicals	Straight shows
Word of mouth	52.3	51.6	43.2	1.4	46.0	0.9	60.6	47.0	55.7	37.3
Newspaper advertising	16.0	12.1	31.1	24.9	19.2	29.4	16.7	15.9	22.4	16.6
Newspaper critics	37.7	17.6	40.1	28.9	20.3	14.1	34.3	40.4	18.4	21.5
Magazine critics	5.6	17.7	5.7	7.8	20.1	16.8	5.9	5.4	16.1	22.3
Other advertising	3.5	1.4	n.c.	n.c.	n.c.	n.c.	4.8	2.4	2.6	0.5
Radio and television critics	3.9	2.9	n.c.	n.c.	n.c.	n.c.	5.3	2.8	4.9	1.1

Note: Percentages total more than one hundred since many respondents checked more than one reason.
n.c. Not computed.

vertising: paid publicity probably has little effect on habitual theatergoers, who depend strongly on personal recommendations, but may reach the casual theatergoer.

Visitors to New York chose their shows for many of the same reasons that natives did. The importance of newspaper and other advertising, however, was somewhat less. The most significant difference between local and out-of-town respondents concerned the role of magazine critics: New Yorkers virtually ignored magazine notices, but tourists credited them with as much influence as newspaper reviews.

Substitutes. Motion pictures, television, and off-Broadway compete for the time of the Broadway frequenter. The Weiss and Geller study reports that 63 per cent of those who discussed competition cited motion pictures. Television vied for the leisure time of the young and infrequent theatergoers, but it was dismissed by those who went to the theater often. The audience survey, however, revealed that those who watched a good deal of television saw few Broadway shows. But it also demonstrated that those who went to the theater often also went to motion pictures and to off-Broadway shows more regularly than did those who rarely visited Broadway (see Table V-6). This result intimates that motion pictures, off-Broadway, and Broadway are not substitutes but complements, which is hardly likely. An alternative explanation of the results is that Broadway habitués are people who have strong tastes for entertainment outside the home. They may be unmarried, widowed, or married with no young children; they may be wealthy and bored; or they may just enjoy night life in Manhattan.

Curtain time

Among factors which attract or repel theatergoers is the time the show starts. Most theatergoers are content with the usual curtain time, but among those from the New York area—the bulk of the audience—there was a substantial feeling that a slightly earlier beginning would be preferable. Of the local people at a week-night performance, 32 per cent wanted the curtain up at eight o'clock or earlier; only 12 per cent, however, wanted it as early as seven-thirty. Weekend audiences were more partial to a late beginning: almost 10 per cent expressed an interest in a nine o'clock curtain. A greater proportion of visitors preferred later starts. In contrast, the preponderantly female audiences at matinees—whether from out-of-town or from the metropolitan area—who responded to the question about evening performances were overwhelming supporters of dimming the footlights early; 64 per cent checked seven-thirty or eight.

These results indicate that it might be profitable for Broadway theaters to experiment with an earlier curtain on one or two week-nights. While

Table V–6 Relationship between television viewing and Broadway, off-Broadway, and motion picture attendance (local residents only)

| | Median days since saw last: | | Median minutes spent viewing television the previous night |
Playgoers who had seen last Broadway show:	Off-Broadway show	Motion picture	
within last 2 weeks	144.5	11.6	4.2
over 8 months ago	over 183.0	22.3	49.2

seven-thirty was tried unsuccessfully a few years ago, the results of the survey indicate that this was too early and that eight o'clock might be a good compromise. On the other hand, there seems to be almost no support for a curtain later than the current one.

Ticket sources

Once the decision has been made to see a certain show, tickets must be purchased. As indicated above, this can be an unpleasant chore for many. Seats can be secured from the box office, by mail order, from ticket agencies, from friends, or from a myriad of other sources. Almost all theatergoers procured their tickets from the first three outlets. The percentage of purchasers by major outlets and the percentage of tickets bought by these outlets are presented in Table V-8. The percentage of purchasers by outlets is computed by counting each person who buys a ticket as one, no matter how frequently he goes or how many tickets he buys.

The figures in Table V-8 are rather interesting. While 63 per cent of local theatergoers bought their tickets through the box office, only 52 per cent of the seats dispensed to those from the metropolitan area were sold by it. Whereas only 8 per cent of local playgoers patronize ticket agencies, the agencies sold them 16 per cent of all their seats. Thus, ticket agency customers either purchased more seats per person or went to the theater more frequently than those who bought through the box office. Probably they did both. As might be expected, visitors to Manhattan traded with brokers more often. Licensed ticket agencies were utilized more frequently by those planning to see a musical than by those looking forward to a play. It is curious to note that while less than 2 per cent of the theatergoers acquired their tickets from sources other than the box office, mail orders, or ticket agents, they secured a much more substantial proportion of their seats—over 13 per cent—from these other origins. Ardent playgoers, we can conclude, procure their seats frequently through ticket agencies; conversely, those who buy by mail either are less avid devotees of the stage or attend in smaller groups or both.

Cost of the evening

Only about half the total cost of a visit to Broadway results from the purchasing of tickets. As can be seen from Table V-9, the average outlay for going to the theater per group, most often a family, is around $32.00. For those attending musicals or going on the weekend, it is higher. A night at a musical averaged $16.00 per person, compared to about $14.00 at a play, of which about $6.50 was for the seat. Since ticket prices are higher for musicals and on weekends, it is natural to find that the average ticket bought is more expensive for those performances. Individuals on expense accounts, as might be expected, were more lavish: the average cost of the evening per person was $20.00 for a straight show and $28.00 for a musical. The seats prices were $8.22 and $15.00, respectively. Note that the highest box office price for a straight show was $7.50 and for a musical, $9.90. Thus, purchasers using expense accounts paid, on the average, considerably more than the official amount for their tickets.

Of the audience who were from New York or the vicinity, 71 per cent ate at a restaurant before going to the theater. Their average check, including drinks, came to $6.50, almost as much as they spent on their seats. Frugal people reduced the total cost for an evening at the theater to $12.00 or so by eating at home. Yet since, as we have seen, much of the enjoyment of seeing a play comes from having a "big evening out," dining out must add to the evening's gratification. For much of the audience, therefore, avoiding a restaurant would diminsh the pleasure.

The dinner check points up the value of the theater to other industries in Manhattan. We can estimate that during the survey week, a fairly typical period, $390,000 was poured into the coffers of local eating establishments by commuting playgoers. Assuming that the average check for out-of-towners was about $6.50—the amount commuters spent—total restaurant receipts from theatergoers must have been approximately $690,000, a substantial sum. During the same week the legitimate gross was $1,041,-437—for each dollar spent on tickets, playgoers had laid out almost seventy cents for dinner.[16]

The total cost of an evening at the theater was affected by the marital status of the playgoer, his sex, his family income, the time it took him to

16. The total gross was computed from *Variety,* May 2, 1962, p. 177. The gross receipts of restaurants from local people was estimated by multiplying the percentage of residents of the New York area in the audience (64.3 per cent) times the total gross spent at theaters, then by the percentage of restaurant goers (71.1 per cent) among local theatergoers, and finally multiplying the ratio expenditures in restaurants to cost of tickets per person. Assuming all out-of-towners dined at a restaurant, the product of the percentage of out-of-towners (35.7 per cent) and the total gross was multiplied by the ratio of expenditures in restaurants to cost of tickets per person. This procedure overestimates the amount spent in restaurants, since some of the expenditures on tickets included brokerage fees.

Table V-7 Preferred curtain time (percentages)

| | Total | | Local | | Out-of-town | | Matinee | | | | | |
| | | | | | | | Local | | Out-of-town | | Local | |
Curtain time checked	Local	Out-of-town	Week-night	Week-end (evening)	Week-night	Week-end (evening)	A Man for All Seasons	How to Succeed in Business	A Man for All Seasons	How to Succeed in Business	Saw last Broadway show within 2 weeks	Saw last Broadway show over 8 months ago
7:30	11.8	9.1	11.8	7.0	7.4	8.1	33.8	27.4	34.3	15.8	n.c.	n.c.
8:00	19.5	15.8	20.2	15.4	15.0	13.2	30.1	36.9	42.8	28.9	n.c.	n.c.
7:30 and 8:00	31.3	24.9	32.0	22.4	22.4	21.3	63.9	64.3	77.1	44.7	32.2	37.8
8:30 or 8:40	61.2	67.4	61.7	67.9	72.2	68.0	31.6	33.3	20.0	50.0	60.5	56.0
9:00	7.5	7.7	6.3	9.7	5.4	10.7	4.5	2.4	2.9	5.3	7.3	6.2

n.c. Not computed.

reach Times Square, and the price he paid for a seat.[17] As would be expected, single people spent less on a night out than did married playgoers who had more tickets to buy. The difference, however, does not lie solely in the fact that they purchased more seats. Single individuals spent around $22.67 for the evening, while those who were married paid $31.57, a difference of $8.90. The saving for those who were not married was greater than the cost of one additional ticket. Even excluding the amount spent on seats and even on a per capita basis, a relationship existed between marital status and expenditures: a single person would have spent, on the average—holding income and place of residence constant— about $7.60 for everything but the tickets, while a married person would have paid about $9.00, a $1.40 difference.

High-income theatergoers spent slightly more on seeing a show than did those with lower incomes. A person whose earnings were 10 per cent higher than another's would spend only 4.1 per cent more than the other on a visit to Broadway. As Chapter VI notes, however, while expenditures per show did not rise proportionately with higher incomes, the frequency of attendance at the theater did go up proportionately. Therefore, on an annual basis, a person whose income exceeded another's by 10 per cent would spend about 14 per cent more on theatergoing.

Suburbanites, naturally, had greater non-ticket expenses than Manhattanites. For example, those who took from fifteen minutes to thirty minutes to travel to the theater spent about $5.11 on non-ticket expenses such as baby-sitters, taxis, and parking, while those who had to travel from one hour to one hour and fifteen minutes to reach Broadway spent $6.59. Those who lived two hours and a half away averaged $7.89.[18] A move from a place where it takes twenty-two minutes, on the average, to reach Broadway to a place where one must spend sixty-eight minutes in transit increases the dollar cost of attending the theater by $1.50. Since an evening at the theater averages $16.00 per person, the increase is relatively modest.

"Ice"

As was noted above, playgoers using expense accounts paid on the average considerably more than the box office price for their tickets. When the surcharge on tickets exceeds the legitimate ticket agency charge of $1.50 plus tax, or when a ticket is purchased at a premium from a source other than a ticket agency, the resulting excess payment is illegal and is often referred to as "ice."[19] Since there has been more wild talk

17. Linear regression analysis was used to measure the relationships.
18. Computed from the regression of costs minus tickets per person on time, income being held constant.
19. Strictly speaking, "ice" is any bribe given to the box office for supplying tick-

Table V–8   Ticket sources (percentages)

| | Percentage of ticket buyers who purchased from various sources | | | | | |
| | Musicals | | Straight shows | | Total | |
Source	Local	Out-of-town	Local	Out-of-town	Local	Out-of-town
Box offices	47.6	55.7	79.1	61.5	62.6	57.9
Mail orders	39.8	6.0	14.7	28.1	27.8	14.5
Ticket agents	10.2	37.9	1.5	10.3	7.6	27.2
Other	2.5	0.4	4.8	0.2	2.0	0.3

| | Percentage of tickets purchased from various sources | | | | | |
| | Musicals | | Straight shows | | Total | |
Source	Local	Out-of-town	Local	Out-of-town	Local	Out-of-town
Box offices	46.8	49.2	59.1	39.6	52.2	47.2
Mail orders	24.4	7.0	9.7	15.9	18.1	8.8
Ticket agents	19.2	25.0	12.5	27.3	16.3	25.5
Other	9.6	18.8	18.7	17.2	13.5	18.5

Note: Totals may not always add to one hundred because of rounding.

about "ice" than about anything else in the theater, the audience survey asked respondents to list the amount they paid for their seats and the price printed on the ticket. Asking people what they paid for their tickets presents many problems: first, they may not know, they may have forgotten, or they may lie; second, if a businessman holds complimentary tickets, he does not appear in the sample since he should list himself as a guest. The first problem is unlikely to produce a bias, but the second may lead us to underestimate the number of illegal payments. The magnitude of this bias is unknown, but the author believes it to be small. Only 3.4 per cent of the responses were from out-of-town guests, the group in which those receiving complimentary tickets are most likely to fall. Even if half of the out-of-towners who were guests were given complimentary tickets (undoubtedly a high proportion), less than 2 per cent of the audience would be involved. Since about 11 per cent of all tickets sold are scalped, according to our survey, we may be underestimating "ice" by as much as 14.9 per cent.

A few visitors to New York during the survey week were charged as much as $29.00 for a $9.60 seat at a Friday night performance of *How to Succeed* and $26.00 for a $7.50 seat at *A Thousand Clowns*. New

---

ets to be scalped. However, the term "ice" will be used here as it is often used to describe the entire illegal premium.

Yorkers tended to make smaller illegal payments. The highest, $27.00, was paid for a Wednesday evening performance of the hit musical, *How to Succeed*. While patrons from out-of-town made up only a small percentage of the audience, they accounted for over 60 per cent of the total receipts of scalpers.

Speculation on the magnitude of scalping has been widespread. A New York State investigation has charged that the amount of "ice" may reach $10 million a year,[20] which is enough to finance twenty musicals or scores of straight plays. Is this figure realistic? Our study indicates that it is not. On the basis of what patrons reported, the total of illegal premiums over box office prices would run between $1.5 million and $3.5 million, probably about $2 million per season. Illegal payments might exceed $2 million in a very good season and fall under the figure during a poor year. The source of the New York State investigation figure of $10 million is uncertain; correspondence with the office of the attorney general of New York State has failed to elicit any clues as to the source of the estimate. All that is known is that a state accountant examined 1,219 ticket transactions obtained from banks, textile companies, and other sources. On the basis of these data he estimated that "it ['ice'] could reach almost $10 million depending on the number of hits on at a particular time."[21] Since the accountant neither had a random sample of tickets sold nor knew how many tickets were scalped altogether, his estimate must be little better than a guess.

For *How to Succeed,* the biggest hit, the audience paid well over $80,000 for tickets during the survey week. The box office received about $67,000, and approximately $13,000 was paid in illegal premiums and legitimate commissions of brokers. Earlier in the run of the show, scalpers must have taken in more. The survey was conducted the week after Easter, which is a particularly good theater week. Hence, the reported "ice" is undoubtedly greater than what would have been reported two weeks earlier or later. Altogether, illegal receipts to the shows running during the survey week must have been between $30,000 and $55,000.

About half the people purchasing tickets at more than the legal rate paid less than five dollars above the price printed on the ticket. About one-fourth paid between five and ten dollars and the remainder spent ten dollars or more on "ice." Ninety per cent of those paying a premium of ten dollars or more were buying tickets to *How to Succeed*. Most of these high-priced seats were sold for evening performances rather than for matinees, for which prices and illegal payments tended to be lower.

Ticket agencies were the source of at least two-thirds of the scalped

20. New York *Times,* December 11, 1963, p. 1.
21. *Ibid.,* p. 54.

Table V–9 Average cost of evening and of tickets

Group	No expense account						Expense accounts				
	Cost of evening per group	Cost of evening per person	Cost of tickets per person	Expenditures on restaurants (for those who go) per person	Expenditures on other items	Size of theater party	Size of theater party	Percent expense account local	Cost of evening per group	Cost of evening per person	Cost of tickets per person
Straight shows	$28.28	$14.03	$6.46	$6.80	$3.07	1.94	2.08	4.9	$52.48	$20.57	$ 8.22
Musicals	35.50	18.73	8.95	6.33	5.25	2.40	3.17	3.0	99.55	28.08	15.00
Weekday	28.36	15.37	7.51	6.89	3.35	1.93	2.50	4.2	52.93	20.55	11.95
Weekend	33.01	16.13	8.18	5.36	5.13	2.04	3.00	4.8	95.80	26.68	11.96
Total	$31.98	$16.37	$7.99	$6.52	$4.19	2.20	2.66	4.2	$70.24	$24.00	$12.19

tickets and may have easily supplied an even larger proportion. According to the questionnaires, the second largest source (see Table V–10) was a miscellaneous classification called "Other"; almost a quarter of those paying illegal surcharges checked this category. We can only speculate as to the origins of these tickets: they might be bartenders, taxi drivers, or seedy-looking men loitering in Times Square. It is rumored that agencies employ such men to scalp tickets on the street; the agency spots the potential customer and notifies their man who then makes the sale. Possibly many of the seats bought from "other" sources are actually handled by licensed brokers. Hotels were the third biggest source of illegal seats. By checking the "Hotel" category, the respondents could have meant that they acquired their tickets from bellboys, doormen, or other employees, or they could have been referring to the ticket agencies located in many Manhattan lobbies. In any case, part of this category may include tickets purchased through brokers. Consequently, it seems likely that more than two-thirds of the scalped tickets passed through the hands of licensed brokers.

For most shows, the percentage of tickets sold at prices higher than the law permits is small. During the survey week, when the legitimate gross exceeded $1 million, total "ice" payments were unlikely to be more than $55,000 (or about 5 per cent of the total receipts) and were probably considerably less. In conclusion, we can say that while ticket scalping exists and will continue to exist until human nature changes or until the state and city laws inhibiting flexible pricing are repealed, the sums involved are not as large as have been rumored. Since large figures are more titillating than small figures, these estimates are unlikely to be greeted with joy by those who write periodically on the evils of "ice." It is, however, necessary to bring some perspective back to the subject.

Conclusion

The three surveys suggest that the Broadway audience is a reasonably homogeneous group of upper-middle-class Americans. New Yorkers tend to prefer more serious drama, while visitors to New York concentrate more on musicals. The fact that out-of-towners favor comedies and musicals over dramas and the fact that those on expense accounts tend to visit serious shows less frequently than light productions, may not augur well for the stage; any increase in out-of-town business or in the expense-account trade might unfavorably affect the dramatic stage.

Since approximately half of the individuals from out-of-town came to New York City for pleasure—and since the theater is one of the more important recreational facilities in the area and is not found in abundance elsewhere—Broadway is important to the economic health of the hotel

Table V–10 Ticket sources for legal and illegal transactions (percentages)

	All purchases	Illegal purchases			
		Total	Musicals	Straight shows	Matinees[a]
Box office	50.1	0.7	0.9	0	0
Mail order	14.2	0.2	0.2	0	0
Ticket agent	20.1	68.9	66.0	81.8	87.1
Hotel	2.9	6.8	5.5	12.3	0
Theater party	1.4	0	0	0	4.7
Other	11.2	23.5	27.4	5.9	8.2

a. Unweighted average of two performances (see note to Table V-1).
Note: Charging more than the box office price is legal for legitimate charities organizing theater parties.

business, the taxi industry, and Manhattan restaurants. Inasmuch as restaurant receipts from theatergoers are equal to about two-thirds of the box office gross, the Broadway audience which is pouring $45 million into the coffers of mid-town theaters is also contributing roughly $30 million to local eating establishments.

The most surprising aspect of the survey is the relatively small amount of money going to scalpers. Contrary to popular report, even for hits, over three-quarters of the audience normally pays no more for tickets than the box office price plus, on occasion, a brokerage fee.

The survey offers two practical implications: there is a market for an earlier curtain; non-newspaper advertising brings in few patrons. Radio and television critics affect almost no one's decision. Since frequent play-goers are less affected by advertising or critics than by personal recommendations, newspaper reports affect only those who go casually.

VI | Demand for and supply of Broadway shows

Broadway attendance during an average week in February, 1963, was only 20 per cent better than it was in 1933.[1] A glance at other performing arts shows that spending on admissions more than tripled during this period, ticket sales for spectator sports more than doubled, and real per capita GNP advanced 160 per cent.[2] The purpose of this chapter is to determine why the demand for seats to the most professional, most polished, and most popular theater in the United States should have grown so slowly.

In previous chapters we found that Broadway was decimated by the advent of sound motion pictures and the Depression. But this only explains the drop in attendance during the thirties. Why has not the theater expanded with the rest of the economy since then? If we can isolate the effects of rising income on theatergoing, of prices on attendance and on the incentives to produce shows, and of taxes on demand and supply, it may be possible to make policy recommendations for improving Broadway. At the least, an understanding of these forces will make it possible to predict the future of the New York theater.

To determine the relationship between prices, costs, attendance, and number of shows, the data derived from the audience survey on ticket prices, income, relative frequency of attendance, and distance from the theater (in terms of time) were analyzed. The relationship of income to frequency was investigated statistically.[3] The results showed that a change in income generally led to a proportional change in the frequency of attendance. That is, on the average, if an individual's income increases by 10 per cent, he will go to the theater 10 per cent more frequently.

1. Based on estimates of Broadway attendance made by the author. See Appendix D for the procedure.
2. Spending on the performing arts and on spectator sports is taken from Department of Commerce, *Statistical Abstract of the United States, 1965,* p. 208, Table 288, and p. 327, Table 449, and from Bureau of the Census, *Historical Statistics of the United States, Colonial Times to 1957* (Washington, D.C.: Government Printing Office, 1960), Series H507, p. 224, and Series F2, p. 139. The series are deflated by the Consumer Price Index.
3. See Appendix D for a detailed description of how the results reported in this chapter were derived.

This suggests that as incomes rise during the next decade, demand for theater tickets should rise proportionately if ticket prices do not change.

Per capita earnings influence more than just the frequency of trips to Broadway; higher incomes can be presumed to lead to greater expenditures on theatergoing. As incomes climb, individuals will buy a higher "quality" night at the theater by paying more for the tickets, dining at more expensive and presumably better restaurants, and transporting themselves to the theater in more agreeable ways. To measure these effects, income has been correlated with the price of tickets bought, with the total cost of the evening, and with the difference between the cost of tickets and the total cost of the evening. In the investigation, the effect of place of residence, in terms of the time it would take them to go home, was held constant in order to measure the pure effect of income. The results indicate that a 1 per cent rise in income would lead to a 0.2 per cent increase in the average price of tickets bought, a 0.35 per cent increase in expenditures on other items per person, and a 0.41 per cent increase in total outlays for the evening. The results are hardly encouraging for the legitimate stage: when earnings expand, expenditures on non-theater activities—such as dining out, transportation, and baby-sitters—increase 75 per cent faster than spending on better tickets.

As per capita wealth continues to rise and is reflected in increased income, we can predict a proportional growth of attendance on Broadway, a smaller jump in the amount spent on complementary goods and services, and a still smaller rise in the price of tickets bought. One result of theatergoers' desire to buy better quality seats as they become richer is that the higher-priced tickets will become relatively more popular.

The effect of prices on attendance

Without knowing how price and cost affect theatergoing, a full understanding of the forces at work is impossible. To measure this effect it is necessary to study the relationship between prices and attendance over the last few decades. However, other things have changed in that period which might easily mask or distort the simple price-quantity relationship desired. In particular it is necessary to take into account income changes, changes in costs, and random fluctuations in the number of shows playing. Since the analysis is rather technical and would become tedious to the average reader, the detailed approach has been relegated to Appendix D, and the results are only summarized here.

In brief, the analysis covers the period from 1928 to 1963, a period during which there were basic shifts in the pattern of theatergoing. In the 1927/28 season, Broadway, in terms of attendance and openings, reached an all-time high. With the advent of hard times and sound motion pictures, attendance dwindled to half its former level and the number of new productions sank even further. In correlating price and attendance, account was taken of per capita income, the number of shows playing, and the introduction of sound motion pictures. The results indicate that a 1 per cent boost in ticket prices, *ceteris paribus,* would lead to about a 0.5 per cent decline in theater attendance. The figures also suggest that, within limits, average attendance at a Broadway show is unaffected by the number of productions running. This implies that the real restraint on number of shows is not that there is a limited number of theatergoers with limited time and/or money, but that there are not enough shows of high enough quality. If more shows were performed, there would be an audience for them.

The next question to be answered is why there are not more productions launched. Some evidence has already been presented in Chapters I and II that the scarcity and high price of talent necessary for a successful run is primarily responsible. It would be useful, however, to have a quantitative estimate of the relation between net ticket prices (ticket prices minus taxes) and the number of shows presented. In other words, the supply side of the market must also be explored.

In general we would expect that the higher the ticket prices and the higher the attendance, the more shows producers will launch. In fact, it turns out that a 1 per cent rise in ticket prices (net of taxes) would lead to a little less than 0.5 per cent increase in the number of shows running on Broadway. If attendance increased by 1 per cent for some reason, say an increase in average income, producers would increase the number of shows by a little over 0.5 per cent. The industry supply appears therefore to be relatively unresponsive to price changes. This result is not surprising; the problem with the theater has been a shortage of trained, talented writers, players, and directors. Any increase in Broadway activity must mean the luring of scarce talent away from motion pictures and from television.

Conclusion

With these estimates we can make predictions about the future of Broadway. On December 31, 1965, the 10 per cent federal ticket tax was removed. On the basis of the above figures it would appear that the number of shows playing should increase by about 10 per cent, causing a similar increase in attendance. With higher attendance, still more shows will be put on, and so on, until the shortage of trained theater people ends the spiral. The data also suggest that there is unlikely to be any long-run decline in box office prices. The extra revenue derived from the lowering of the tax will go entirely to pay authors, producers, actors, directors, and others.

The slow growth in the Broadway audience appears to be a result of a modest responsiveness of attendance to income, an increase in ticket prices, and possibly the flight to the suburbs which has increased travel time and cost. The last point is substantiated by a simple correlation between travel time and relative attendance which indicates that a 1 per cent rise in travel time leads to a 1.8 per cent fall in theater attendance.

Operating expenses largely reflect wages since the theater is not subject to important productivity gains. Therefore, in the long run we can expect the climb in costs and ticket prices to parallel the movement in personal income. As incomes advance, so will the cost of attending the theater. Luckily for Broadway, attendance is more responsive to income changes than to price changes; growing levels of income should lead to a small but significant growth in the number of productions and in attendance on Broadway. But if transportation costs, baby-sitting fees, and restaurant prices also climb, the effect of advancing incomes may be almost completely offset by higher costs of attending the theater.

VII | The theater outside New York

Americans are quick to point out to visitors that New York City is not the United States. Let us add that New York theater is not the theater in the United States. In cities, in small towns, and even in hamlets, devotees of drama are staging Williams, Miller, and Jean Kerr and attracting enthusiastic local audiences. In addition, the latest Broadway successes tour from Maine to California. By dominating through sheer size the professional stage outside New York, summer stock offers millions their only opportunity to see professional actors on a stage. If it were not for summer theaters, drama enthusiasts outside a few large cities would be without sustenance. Once theater flourished across the land, but this century has witnessed the devastation of the stage outside New York. Let us trace the decline and fall of live theater throughout the United States.

Statistics on theatrical activity outside New York are scarce and conflicting, but a definite downward trend is unmistakably evident. One estimate claimed that in 1880, 250 traveling companies played 5,000 theaters in 3,500 cities.[1] Ten years later, the census of 1890 reported that out of 297 major cities, 249 contained 617 theaters and 1,746 halls.[2] Another authority put the number of legitimate houses in 1890 at 5,000.[3] According to *Billboard,* the public sustained 1,520 legitimate houses (outside the big cities) in 1910.[4] On the other hand, Arthur Hornblow, in *A History of the Theatre in America,* reported that in 1919 the United States teemed with 4,300 theaters playing legitimate attractions.[5] Many of these also housed vaudeville and the up-and-coming motion pictures.

Obviously, these sources disagree. Part of the inconsistency may turn on a variety of definitions of what constitutes a theater. Yet they all conclude that the number was large, certainly over 2,000. The disappear-

---

1. William Winter, *The Wallet of Time* (New York: Moffat, Yard, 1913), I, 23.
2. *Report on the Social Statistics of Cities in the United States* [by] John S. Billings, 11th Census Monograph (Washington, D.C.: Government Printing Office, 1895), p. 39.
3. Norris Houghton, *Advance from Broadway: 19,000 Miles of American Theatre* (New York: Harcourt, Brace, 1941), p. 14.
4. Bernheim, *The Business of the Theatre,* p. 76.
5. (Philadelphia: Lippincott, 1919), II, 332.

ance of legitimate houses between 1900 and the twenties must have been almost as rapid as the disappearance of buggy manufacturers during the same period. All the data indicate that only 400 to 800 theaters booked plays outside New York between 1920 and 1930. John F. Wharton reported 560 theaters booked outside New York City for professional productions in 1921.[6] *Billboard* reported 634 in 1925.[7] Another theater historian, Glenn Hughes, estimated that there were fewer than 500 legitimate houses in 1930.[8]

The fall has been continuing: 560 in 1921, 197 in 1953, and 193 in 1960.[9] Robert M. Lichtenberg, in *One Tenth of a Nation,* concluded that in the last three decades (1930 to 1960) the percentage drop in legitimate theaters available for road shows has been greater than the percentage drop in the number of Broadway theaters.[10] Considering the long-run trend of theater in the United States, the decline outside New York since 1900 has been precipitous. Conversely, the New York stage, including off-Broadway, has grown since 1900 and, while smaller than in the late twenties, is healthier than at any other time since. The contraction in the theater outside Manhattan originated from a fall in the number of shows touring and an almost virtual disappearance of resident stock companies. In 1900, while most theaters housed traveling shows, in the larger cities some were the exclusive province of resident stock companies. By 1950 almost all legitimate theaters outside New York were booked exclusively by road shows.

The decline of the road

Before World War I, Broadway existed largely to supply the road with shows. Productions were launched in New York and in Chicago with the intention of trying them out. After a relatively short run, they were sent on tour. In time the process was reversed: shows were tried out on the road and then brought to New York. If the play was a success, then almost as an afterthought, a touring company was organized. By 1950, during the height of the road season one-third of the touring companies would be trying out their product before the big-city opening. But in recent years this practice too has changed. Shows increasingly have substituted previews in Manhattan for pre-opening tours. If this system continues to be used, the road can only suffer. It has already dwindled so

6. *Crisis in the Free World Theatre* (New York: League of New York Theatres, 1961), pp. 19–20.
7. Bernheim, *The Business of the Theatre,* p. 76.
8. *A History of the American Theatre, 1700–1950* (New York: Samuel French, 1951), p. 381.
9. Wharton, *Crisis in the Free World Theatre,* pp. 19–20.
10. (Cambridge, Mass.: Harvard University Press, 1960), p. 234.

much that it now consists of only the most successful Broadway productions and a small number of pre-Broadway tryouts.

As mentioned above, approximately 250 traveling companies were touring in 1880. Between 1900 and 1904 an average of 308 plays were on tour each year; but between 1925 and 1927, the number fell to 68.[11] Comparable figures are unavailable for later periods, but during the week of January 5–11, 1941, *Variety* reported 19 productions on the road.[12] Table VII–1 presents data on the seasons from 1948/49 to 1965/66 for the road and for Broadway. It is apparent that while playing weeks on Broadway have remained almost constant, playing weeks on the road have been reduced. Note that the number of shows playing at the peak of the season has fallen more than the number of playing weeks. As a consequence, the number of shows playing at non-peak times must have increased. The most rapid decline in the road seems to have occurred between 1900 and the middle twenties, with the downward trend continuing more gradually during the thirties. From the beginning of World War II, however, the shrinkage became far less marked and the evidence now suggests little or no diminution of the road since the early fifties.

Why has the road declined? Part of the answer must lie in the development of motion pictures; the great fall that occurred in the first few decades of this century coincided with the growth of the newly born film industry. Undoubtedly, radio and the development of sound for films contributed to the reduced activity. Probably as significant as anything else was the development of the automobile, which made it possible for the public to travel longer distances to visit the theater. The net result: a reduction in the number of shows on tour and an increase in casual visits to New York for playgoing. This has probably been the most significant force affecting the road during the last two decades.

The low prices of road shows compared to Broadway[13] indicates that the problem in recent years has been one of demand; the public became less interested in generally second-rate touring shows when with relative ease they could visit Manhattan and see the best. It has been suggested that the problem with the road is that its costs are too high and its profits too low. While the latter is undoubtedly true, the cause must be considered. If demand were as strong as on Broadway, prices could easily be raised to earn adequate profits; and although prices are rising, they are still considerably below those prevailing in New York.

And so, the future of the road appears uncertain. It will not, however, disappear quickly. The downward trend seems to be stemmed, but the

11. Anderson, *The American Theatre*, p. 66, based on a compilation by the New York *Dramatic Mirror*.
12. *Variety*, January 15, 1941, p. 52.
13. See Chapter I, p. 3.

Table VII-1 Playing weeks, gross, and number of shows for the road and for Broadway, 1948/49 to 1965/66 (1962/63 dollars)

	Broadway		Road				
Season	Playing weeks	Total gross ($millions)	Playing weeks	Total gross ($millions)	Gross of biggest week ($thousands)	Number of shows playing biggest week	Number of shows playing during an average week in February[a]
1948/49	1,231	$37.2	1,151	$30.5	$910	35	n.a.
1949/50	1,156	36.4	1,019	26.0	830	31	n.a.
1950/51	1,139	33.9	913	24.7	794	28	19.00
1951/52	1,072	33.8	829	21.8	712	22	18.25
1952/53	1,012	29.7	1,036	26.7	805	32	20.00
1953/54	1,081	34.1	794	20.0	619	28	22.75
1954/55	1,139	36.3	879	23.9	680	28	15.25
1955/56	1,239	39.8	864	25.7	694	22	18.50
1956/57	1,182	40.7	772	21.8	758	23	15.25
1957/58	1,081	40.0	728	24.2	765	26	13.50
1958/59	1,157	42.1	687	24.4	840	24	18.50
1959/60	1,156	47.2	728	28.2	882	25	16.00
1960/61	1,210	44.8	829	34.7	1,344	21	20.25
1961/62	1,166	44.8	963	40.4	1,576	28	17.75
1962/63	1,134	43.5	822	31.6	808	21	19.00
1963/64	1,112	38.7	846	33.6	845	21	20.50
1964/65	1,250	49.4	643	25.3	805	16	17.00
1965/66	1,295	53.9	699	32.2	906	16	20.75

a. The sum of the number of shows playing each of the four weeks in February divided by 4. *Source:* February issues of *Variety.*
n.a. Not available.
Source: Variety, June 26, 1966, p. 64.

increased tendency to open plays in New York augurs an unhealthy future for the road.

The death, metamorphosis, and rebirth of resident companies

At one time, permanent stock companies were widespread throughout the United States. In the nineteenth century, all major cities and many smaller cities had their own stock companies—sometimes good, often bad. Toward the end of the century, as transportation facilities improved, shows began the trek to the hinterlands. New York road shows supplemented and then replaced permanent stock companies. The death knell of winter stock, however, was sounded with the development of motion pictures and automobiles. While there had been about 2,000 permanent stock companies in 1910/11,[14] by the 1923/24 season, only 133 remained in

14. Lichtenberg, *One Tenth of a Nation,* p. 233.

existence.[15] (See Table VII–2 for data on the decline of stock and repertory companies.) But later in the twenties prosperity touched off new development.

The number of professional theaters gradually increased, and by 1926 Actors' Equity reported 257 companies in existence. With the onslaught of the Depression and the impact of sound motion pictures, stock almost disappeared. By 1935, the total of stock, repertory, and tent theaters had dwindled to 110. One year later, according to Houghton, there were only four winter stock, repertory, and tent theaters in existence in the United States.[16] In January of 1941, the only permanent companies to raise their curtains were in Montclair, New Jersey, Portland, Maine, and Miami Beach. Two of these, in Montclair and Portland, turned out to be not so permanent; they closed that winter. (It should be noted, however, that Houghton overlooked the Barter Theater in Abingdon, Virginia, which has existed since 1932.) These figures are probably only indicative; possibly other winter stock companies were missed.

Some problems with the figures should be noted. The Equity data given above deal only with those winter stock theaters that are unionized. The figure of 2,000 that Lichtenberg lists refers to a time prior to the formation of Actors' Equity, so it is possible that some of the 2,000 were semiprofessional. The Equity figures, on the other hand, ignore theaters which could have been of professional quality, but were not organized by Actors' Equity. Notwithstanding the problems with the data, there must have been a large decline from 1910 to the twenties (the automobile), a slight rise during the next seven or eight years (the pre-crash rich days), followed by the virtual disappearance of stock theaters in the thirties (the Depression and sound films).

While 14 stock companies operated at some time during the 1948/49 season, only six maintained a regular season. In the next four seasons, the number of established companies climbed to ten,[17] but there may have been fatalities, since the *Wall Street Journal* put the number at six in 1954.[18] In 1962, the author prepared a list of seventeen Equity resident theaters from the files of the Actors' Equity Association with the aid of Theodore Hoffman, chairman of the executive committee of the Theatre Communications Group. Mr. Hoffman doubted whether all seventeen were actively operating, although they had done so in the recent past. More recently, the *Wall Street Journal,* pointing to the expansion in theatrical activity, claimed fifteen in 1964. Whatever the true number—which depends on the definition of a resident company—these figures suggest

15. Bernheim, *The Business of the Theatre,* p. 95.
16. *Advance from Broadway,* p. 48.
17. See Sources for Table VII–2.
18. *Wall Street Journal,* March 19, 1964, p. 1.

Table VII–2 Permanent stock, repertory, and tent companies, selected seasons

	Permanent stock and repertory companies			Tent theaters		
	Number	Weeks played	Actors employed	Number	Weeks played	Actors employed
1923/24	133	n.a.	n.a.	n.a.	n.a.	n.a.
1924/25	196	n.a.	n.a.	n.a.	n.a.	n.a.
1925/26	143	n.a.	n.a.	n.a.	n.a.	n.a.
1926/27	257	4,658	2,570	n.a.	n.a.	n.a.
1928/29	251	3,408	2,491	98	1,668	828
1931/32	149	1,759	1,458	107	1,070	856

	Repertory, stock, and tent companies combined	
	Number	Actors employed
1935/36	110[a]	1,100
1936/37	4	40

	Winter stock companies	
	Number	Weeks played
1948/49	14	229
1949/50	31	372
1950/51	37	390
1951/52	30	397

a. Estimated on the assumption that the usual ratio (10 : 1) of actors to companies holds.
Sources: 1923/24 to 1926/27, Bernheim, *The Business of the Theatre*, p. 95; 1928/29 to 1936, *Equity*, July, 1937, p. 10; 1948/49 to 1951/52, *Equity*, January, 1954, pp. 5–13.
n.a. Not available.

some resurgence in winter stock and repertory theaters since World War II.

A detailed questionnaire was sent to the seventeen permanent companies. Unfortunately, probably because of the complexity of the financial data requested, only three theaters responded. The sample, therefore, may be too small for generalization. All three theaters were small in size: the seating capacity ranged from 350 to 752. Ticket prices were low compared to the road or to Broadway, but were comparable to summer stock theaters. Two of the three theaters depended very heavily on recent Broadway productions for their scripts. One company largely eschewed Broadway: out of a total of eight shows per season, it averaged only two shows that had been performed recently in New York. In addition, it usually presented two or three new plays and three or four revivals. All three theaters had tried new plays at one time or another, but only a few classic revivals such as Shakespeare, Molière, and Aeschylus had been attempted.

The costs of operating winter stock theaters, on the basis of this very small sample, are similar to those of summer stock theaters.[19] All three respondents, and most likely all resident companies, depend heavily on season tickets. Actors are usually engaged for the season and paid wages above the Equity minimums. With the exception of the Tyrone Guthrie Theatre in Minneapolis, permanent resident companies forego name performers and simply hire experienced actors.

Practically all resident companies today are non-profit, in contrast to the situation before 1930, when winter stock was widespread and mostly organized to earn a profit. Since the virtual death of resident companies during the Depression, the possibility of resurgence in profit-making winter stock companies has disappeared. Unable to raise the capital to open in any other way, the Arena Stage in Washington, D.C., started as a profit-making organization, but became non-profit to attract gifts and grants a few years later. All other resident companies known to the author are non-profit.

The *Census of Business, 1958* reported 161 stock and repertory companies operating in the United States, 14 being located in Manhattan.[20] The average receipts for the country as a whole were around $87,000 for the year. By statistical analysis, attempts were made to detect the variables that affected the number of resident companies in twenty-one cities. Population, as would be expected, explained by itself over 84 per cent of the variance in number. No other variable was consistently correlated with it. Either our data are too crude or we have too few measures of the differences between cities to detect any additional reasons for the variation. Income, education, unemployment, prices of substitutes such as movies, area, distance from New York, and measures of tourism[21] are all uncorrelated with the number of stock and repertory companies. A slight positive relationship, however, was found between the percentage of the work force in white-collar jobs and the number of resident companies.[22] We might conclude that the variation in companies from city to city (after adjusting for the population) depends primarily on individual initiative: if there are dedicated people who desire to see theater in their community, it will flourish; if not, theater will be scarce.

Permanent resident companies play an important part in American

19. See below, pp. 106–107, for description of their costs.
20. Special Census Tabulation.
21. The measures of tourism used were the total and the per capita receipts of hotels, motels, and boarding houses.
22. The *t* statistic was 1.61 with 16 degrees of freedom. This is significant at the 10 per cent level.

theatrical culture. Often they offer the only opportunity for local people to be exposed to professional performances of the classics, revivals, or avant-garde theater. How well they are performing this role is a moot point. From the survey it appears they are doing few classics, although they do present a considerable number of productions that have not been done on Broadway. Their vocation appears to be to bring plays of limited appeal—those that would not be successful on Broadway but might do good off-Broadway business—to cities other than New York.

The most noteworthy aspect of resident companies is that they generally are highly dependent on one or two dedicated and talented individuals. Except for Robert Porterfield, the Barter Theatre would not exist. Without the driving force of Jules Irving, the Actor's Workshop in San Francisco folded. The Arena Stage is still another example. When Zelda Fichandler organized the Arena Stage in August of 1950, she intended to establish a non-profit organization. Unable to raise the necessary funds, she floated stock, raised $7,000 and started the company. In the ensuing years, the Arena Stage operated with a profit (the profits, while never large, were sufficient). After building an audience, the company moved to an old brewery with expanded seating capacity of five hundred; then, in the 1961/62 season, it moved to its permanent new home in southwest Washington.

In many ways, the story of the Arena is typical; it started small, in makeshift quarters, emphasized quality productions, and after attracting a substantial audience, moved into improved quarters. Most of the better-known resident companies had similar beginnings. Two recent exceptions stand out: the Tyrone Guthrie Theatre in Minneapolis and the New York Repertory Theater of Lincoln Center. In both cases, the push for the theater came essentially from the top: an excellent theater was built first, then the company was formed. It will be interesting to watch these two experiments to see if they are as successful as the Arena Stage, the Actor's Workshop, the Alley Theatre, and the Barter Theatre. The Lincoln Center company has already experienced a complete change in management and in orientation.

The summer stock explosion

According to one historian of the American theater, summer theaters were known in the nineteenth century and in England during the eighteenth century.[23] Summer stock, however, did not flourish until the Depression. As resident companies folded and acting opportunities disappeared, unemployed actors rented abandoned barns, pitched tents, and hastily constructed arenas within which to perform. (The Barter Theatre,

23. Glenn Hughes, *A History of the American Theatre, 1700–1950*, p. 442.

discussed in the previous section, started in this manner.) The first of the modern summer theaters bloomed in New England, and they have been spreading west and south ever since.[24]

While completely accurate figures on the extent of summer stock theater are impossible to find, we do know that in terms of the number of actors employed and the audience reached, it dwarfs other professional theatrical activity. Some figures are suggestive: *Summer Theaters,* published annually by *Show Business,* reported on 277 companies in the summer of 1962; for the same season, Actors' Equity listed 165 summer theaters which had posted equity bonds.

The New York *Times,* in its Sunday theater section, started reporting summer stock theaters in 1933. That year, it listed 4 productions, all new, playing in New York State; 1 in Connecticut; 2 in New Jersey; 3 in Massachusetts; and 1 in Pennsylvania. The next year, the number listed in New York had risen to 6; by 1936 it reached 21; and in 1940, 29.[25] By 1947 there were 40; in 1965, 49 entries; and in 1966, 44. As an indicator of the trend in summer stock, however, these figures may be suspect. The *Times* listing is furnished free to all summer theaters mailing in information, and some theaters, distant from New York, may have felt free listing did not justify the effort required to send in the information. But it is clear that as circulation of the paper expanded to distant places, and as transportation improved, the value of such a listing undoubtedly increased. Hence, we can reasonably expect that the percentage of distant theaters being listed has increased.

While the listings from New York State have increased, this may not mean that summer stock has gained since the war. Note that no more were reported in Connecticut in 1966 than had been reported in 1939 or 1940. Since New York State stretches hundreds of miles west of Manhattan, the additional reports from that state may be due to increased coverage as well as to more theaters. Moreover, listings from New Jersey, Massachusetts, and Rhode Island also have not increased since the war. Alternatively, the growth in listings in New York may be due to a spread of summer theaters west from their origin in the Northeast. In support of the latter hypothesis, note that the Equity list of theaters posting bonds contains mostly theaters in the East; many western states are unrepresented.

Table VII–3, which summarizes the Equity figures on the number of union summer stock theaters, indicates a slight growth in summer operations. Most summer stock theaters have signed Equity contracts and

24. Houghton, *Advance from Broadway,* p. 38.
25. These figures are a count of the listings in the New York *Times,* the last Sunday in July, various years,

Table VII-3   Summer theaters, selected years

1940	81
1941	78
1946	99
1948	130
1949	135
1950	152
1951	141
1952	146
1953	139
1961	145
1962	165

Sources: 1940, Houghton, *Advance from Broadway*, p. 38, taken from *Equity*; 1941 through 1953, *Equity*, April, 1942, September, 1946, January, 1954; 1962 figures compiled by author from list of theaters posting bond with Actors' Equity; 1961 figures taken from *Wall Street Journal*, August 7, 1963, p. 1 (the number was quoted as having originated with *Equity*).

therefore are included. The gradual growth of summer stock theaters, shown combined with the New York *Times* data, suggests that the "straw-hat trail" may lead westward.

Detailed data on summer stock

From a questionnaire sent to the 165 summer houses listed by Actors' Equity, 85 usable responses were received. It should be noted, of course, that this survey may not be a random sample of summer stock theaters: the group to which the questionnaires were sent had posted bonds with Actors' Equity and as such were reliable and well established. Most of the questionnaires were from summer theaters which had been in operation for several years. Moreover, in any mail survey, there is an element of self-selection; there is no way of knowing how those who failed to respond differed from those who responded. Since over half of those sent the questionnaire answered, however, it is safe to conclude that the data represent, at least, a large fraction of the total.

During the summer of 1963, the author visited and interviewed the managers of twelve summer stock theaters in New York, Pennsylvania, New Jersey, and Maryland. Three of these were organized as non-profit companies (two of the three did make profits, however). The remainder were all designed to make a profit. Only two were on the star system, hiring one well-known audience-drawing performer at considerably higher wages than the rest of the cast. One or two others, however, occasionally used stars in their productions. Two of the twelve had failed to answer the questionnaire dealing with the previous season. In the interviews, however, they seemed to differ little from those who had responded to the questionnaire.

Types of productions. Of the total answering questionnaires, 72 per cent were from profit-making organizations. Musical houses made up nineteen out of the eighty-five, or roughly 22 per cent; the rest did either straight shows or a mixed program. They reported having done slightly more than eight shows per season, of which approximately 8 per cent were new shows. About 4.5 per cent were revivals of classics and the rest were Broadway productions. Even though only 8 per cent of the productions were new—that is, they had not appeared on Broadway— the fact that so many theaters were operating suggests that the number of new productions done in summer stock theaters is considerable. Over fifty-five new productions were reported in the questionnaires. If our survey is typical of summer stock, approximately one hundred new scripts were tried out—many more than on Broadway or off-Broadway.[26]

Not only do summer theaters initiate more new scripts than any other branch of the theater, but they are eager to try more. Six of the inter- viewees commented on the possibility of doing new plays, and five of the six were interested in new productions that had not been presented on Broadway. A few had already experimented with untried scripts. One of the most active was Mike Ellis, at the Bucks County Playhouse, who has tested several new productions each season for Broadway.

As might be expected, producers favored comedies and musicals; only 18 per cent of the total were dramas. In the interviews, most claimed that audiences were "escape minded" and avoided heavy drama. Besides, they had neither the casts nor the rehearsal time to stage serious works prop- erly. Of twelve questioned, eight concentrated on light comedies, three offered serious fare, while only two had ever performed a classic. Some managers reported that doing a serious drama such as *Death of a Salesman* or *The Miracle Worker* would be a financial disaster; others had per- formed these plays successfully and were interested in finding scripts for serious drama. The Woodstock Playhouse, for example, reported that *Desire Under the Elms, Death of a Salesman,* and *The Miracle Worker* as well as *Come Blow Your Horn* would all make money. On the other hand, Dukes Oak Theatre in Cooperstown would not expect to cover costs on the first two. Naturally, Broadway musicals were generally thought to be profitable. Theater owners, however, were not generally sanguine about the possibility of putting on such works as *The Mikado, The Three- penny Opera,* or *Leave It to Jane.*

To choose their plays, some producers went to New York to see the shows, some read scripts, and others chose their offerings on the basis of

26. Few were of Broadway quality and would ever see Manhattan.

Table VII–4   Summer theaters, audience and type of show

	Light comedies and musicals	Mixed and serious
Tourists and summer people	2	1
Professional and business	2	4
Cross section of community	0	2

Source: Interviews with owners and managers of summer stock theaters.

reviews in periodicals such as the *Tulane Drama Review, Time,* and *Newsweek.* Often producers simply examined the list of newly released plays and made their choice from that. In choosing a show they all had to consider their audience and their ability to cast the play properly. Furthermore, they tended to avoid plays requiring large casts and those from which movies had been made.

The type of audience, which differs considerably from theater to theater, dictates the fare producers offer. Playhouses in recreation areas, such as the Poconos, cater to summer residents and tourists, while houses in the suburbs or in areas where summer residents are not common mainly serve local people. Table VII–4 summarizes the relationship between the type of show produced and the type of audience, and although no firm conclusions can be drawn from the limited data, it is interesting to note that those whose audiences are made up primarily of tourists and summer people tended to concentrate more on light comedies and musicals. Those who draw from professional and business groups and from a cross section of the community leaned toward a more mixed program.

Demand and gross receipts. On a warm summer evening, the public is often willing to go to considerable effort to sample a live production. Producers reported drawing theatergoers from as far as fifty miles away, and almost all managers competed actively with other playhouses in a fifty-mile radius. To boost revenue, to build interest in their house, and to insure a steady clientele, all the theaters but one sold season tickets. While subscriptions were of only minor importance to a few establishments, many emphasized their contribution. Theater parties, they also claimed, added substantially to their receipts—as much as 25 per cent.

Believing the market for a show to be very limited, the summer entrepreneurs changed their bills frequently. Most ran their shows for only one week; but in two cases plays were kept for one week and musicals lasted two. Three theaters found that attendance held up well for an additional week. Two of them changed their fare only every other week, while the Olney Theatre in Maryland kept its productions a full three weeks.

Earnings depend not only on the length of the season in weeks but on the number of performances per week. Summer theaters have not only short seasons (ten to sixteen weeks) but short weeks. Out of eight theaters, four gave seven performances a week, and two did only six. One-fourth found matinees so unprofitable that they eliminated them entirely.

Gross receipts, out of which the entrepreneur must cover his costs and earn his profits, depend also on the size of the theater and on ticket prices. Theaters that specialize in straight shows or in mixed programs tended to be small, with an average of 550 seats. (Musical theaters are naturally considerably larger.) Since most country playhouses are operated for profit, the large number of these smaller-capacity theaters indicates that they can and do make money, showing that large theaters are not necessary for financial success.

Summer theaters demand considerably less for a seat than does Broadway. The average top ticket price[27] for profit-making theaters doing primarily straight plays was $3.36; for non-profit theaters, $3.45. That is, non-profit theaters asked more for a ticket than those organized for profit. As is usual, musical houses charged more, averaging $4.43 for the best seat in the house; for non-profit houses, the price was $3.88. Average prices[28] for all the seats in the house for all performances ranged from $1.99 for non-profit plays to $2.98 for profit-making musicals. Most producers believed that higher prices would reduce their revenue, although a few were planning to boost charges the following season. Those who had increased their scale recently had profited by the move.

As a consequence of lower prices and smaller houses, weekly capacity gross for non-musical theaters falls considerably below the average on Broadway, with a usual maximum of $10,000, whereas musicals averaged around $63,000, a sum comparable to Broadway.

Costs and profits. The cost of producing a show for summer stock theater is considerably lower than the cost of producing on Broadway. Operating expenses of the nine summer stock theaters which responded to this question ranged between $1,000 and $7,000 per week, with the median figure approximately $3,000. Only three entrepreneurs mentioned the cost of setting up a new production; a meaningful average is, therefore, not possible. The cost per show ranged from $2,400 to $13,000.

In comparing Broadway expenses to summer stock expenses, the latter have at least three advantages. First, rents are considerably lower than in Manhattan, the normal rate being $100 to $175 per week. The rural location of summer theaters and the consequent low land values explain part of the differential; moreover, rentals on Broadway include a payment

27. The price of the most costly seat at the most costly performance.
28. Average ticket prices were arrived at by taking the capacity gross and dividing by the number of seats and then by eight performances. Since a substantial proportion of summer theaters give less than eight performances a week, this procedure underestimates the average price.

for house-supplied porters, doormen, ticket takers, stagehands, janitors, and box office personnel. In summer stock, these jobs are usually filled by apprentices, who sometimes work for nothing or for only room and board. Less frequently they are paid a small stipend. The apprentices do the detail work: they clean up, make scenery, set up advertising material. If they are very lucky, they may actually have bit parts. In return, they are registered with the Actors' Equity Association and after two seasons can join it.

Second, except for companies employing stars, the managers had set a maximum of $125.00 a week for actors' salaries. Minimums—and most players received the minimum—were controlled by Actors' Equity; they ranged from $70.00 to $92.50 a week depending upon the type of company. Many managers who were interviewed felt that Equity was squeezing them and voiced particular resentment against the old-age pension fund that had recently been instituted. Some felt that, while it was bearable at the moment, in future years it was likely to rise and become onerous.

Third, playwrights' royalties (usually between $150.00 and $350.00 per week) depended on the gross of the theater: straight shows demanded 5 per cent of the gross and musicals around 10 per cent. Thus, royalties were considerably less than on Broadway. Another major expense, advertising, amounted normally to approximately 10 per cent of the break-even budget, making the ratio of advertising to total costs about the same for summer theater and Broadway.

After the expenses are met, the residual, if any, is profit. Four of the nine profit organizations covered their expenses. Profits were reported as high as $15,000 but tended to be clustered around the $1,000 to $3,000 range. Losses loomed larger: costs exceeded ticket sales by $5,000 in one case, $17,000 in another, and as high as $35,000 in a third. One of the non-profit operations lost $42,000. If these figures are representative of summer stock theaters, earning a million dollars on the 'straw-hat trail" is difficult indeed. It is possible, however, to make a little money in the business. Table VII–5 shows the relationship between profits and the type of program produced, and even though the sample is small, it suggests that serious drama can be as profitable as lighter work.

Table VII–5 Summer theaters, profitability and type of show

	Light comedies and musicals	Mixed
Profitable	2	3
Unprofitable	4	2

Source: Interviews with owners and managers of summer stock theaters.

Large tent musical theaters have been growing rapidly in recent years, but none of the theaters visited was of this type. The *Wall Street Journal* reports that chains of theaters which exchange musicals—thereby reducing expenses for rehearsals, costumes, and scenery—have been growing.[29] These chains usually feature stars. The *Wall Street Journal* reported that when one group started using famous personalities the gross receipts of each theater jumped $150,000.[30]

The house. Five of the houses studied had been built originally as theaters, one was a tent, two were converted dance halls, two were converted barns, and one an old gristmill. One house contained an arena stage, while most of the others were conventional proscenium types.

Each producer was questioned about the adequacy of his theater. Eight of the twelve said they would build one the same size they operated; the others would expand. Three of those who wanted larger houses had made a profit the previous year; the other claimed to have broken even in the previous ten years. As might be expected, successful managers wished to expand.

The preferences of producers may tell us the direction in which the theater is evolving. Only one manager preferred an arena stage, and he operated one; six producers expressed a preference for an apron stage or a three-quarters stage; and one desired a flexible stage that could be changed from proscenium arch. That so many wished to change to three-quarters staging suggests considerable dissatisfaction with the hitherto normal proscenium form. A dislike for balconies was widespread, and only one producer said he would definitely build another.

That "an evening out" for summer theater was similar to one on Broadway was demonstrated by one interesting fact: producers almost unanimously agreed on the importance of having a good restaurant near the theater. Some already had restaurants operating in conjunction with their theaters, while others expressed a desire or a plan to establish an adjoining eating place.

Summary. From this survey of summer stock theaters, three interesting aspects stand out. (*a*) There are apparently no economies of scale in size of operation—at least for non-musical houses. Large theaters are no more profitable than those that are small. Except that profitable operations tend to expand, there is no trend toward larger theaters. On the other hand, chain operation of musical theaters may be replacing the single musical house. (*b*) Profitability seems to be unrelated to the type of material produced: light comedies and musicals make no more money —if anything, less—than do more serious plays. (*c*) Summer stock theater

29. Wednesday, August 7, 1963, p. 1.
30. *Ibid.*

appears to be at least a break-even proposition; as many shows are profitable as are unprofitable. While the management of unprofitable houses reported losses larger than the profits claimed by those operating profitably, this imbalance could be due either to chance variation or to a human tendency to exaggerate losses and to minimize profits to strangers. Since the sample is very small, little confidence can be placed in the size of the figures, but it seems likely that a large number of summer stock theaters do make profits.

Conclusion

Each branch of the theater outside New York has its own role, although some of the functions are duplicated. The road brings recent Broadway productions to the rest of the country; but while resident companies also produce recent New York shows, they tend to de-emphasize them. Summer stock, in spite of its emphasis on the latest shows from Broadway, serves also as a vehicle to train new performers, directors, designers, and playwrights. The major role of permanent resident companies is to bring to their cities non-Broadway productions—the type found off-Broadway.

What then can we say about the future of the theater outside New York City? Touring of Broadway productions seems to be on the wane; certainly no great resurgence appears to be in the offing. Assuming transportation continues to improve, the road may eventually die. Signs are more hopeful for resident companies. The number of such companies—and probably their quality too—has been increasing since World War II. With the decrease in the number of shows traveling, demand for local companies should grow slowly. Even though many cities are already actively fostering permanent local theaters, it seems unlikely that more than a few dozen such companies will be operating in the next decade or so, and resident companies will probably never rival in number either the New York theater (Broadway and off-Broadway) or summer stock. The quality of the productions put on by repertory companies, however, may in some cases equal Broadway.

Summer stock appears to be the strongest branch of the theater outside New York. Its large size and its continued growth suggest that it may continue to employ more actors than any other branch of the theater.

VIII | Subsidies and the performing arts

"In practically all of the civilized nations of the world, the United States excepted, symphony orchestras and opera companies are given government support, and this is a tradition of hundreds of years standing. If the United States has no such direct subsidy of music, it does engage in indirect subsidy. That is, through financing tours of musical organizations and individuals abroad, it helps to pay for the upkeep of such organizations and individuals."[1] This statement points up the difference between American and foreign practices in national assistance to the arts: the United States does little compared to Europe and Canada.

Subsidies are an emotional topic. Most individuals hold strong views on the desirability of subsidies. A majority of economists probably would condemn subsidies generally, but they would clearly support the proposition that in some instances subsidies are desirable. Therefore, the purpose in this chapter is to explore a few of the justifications usually advanced for subsidizing the arts. The cost of a program to stimulate the theater will be estimated and its desirability will be discussed.

Survey of aid to the performing arts outside the United States

Canada has had an arts council since 1957. The Canada Council subsidizes orchestras, opera companies, chamber groups, solo artists, music students, and composers. In past years the council has given $200,000 annually for the support of symphony orchestras. In 1959, ten Canadian orchestras each received grants ranging from $12,000 to $30,000.[2] The Canada Council also gives grants for extra rehearsal time, for children's concerts, and for commissions to composers. Opera and chamber groups have also been assisted. Scholarships have been offered to permit composers or performing artists to study and to write.

The British government has also become extensively involved in helping the arts. In 1958/59 it contributed over $7 million for the support of

1. Hope Stoddard, *Subsidy Makes Sense* (New York: American Federation of Musicians, 1961), p. 19.
2. *Ibid.*, p. 16.

museums and galleries, $2.8 million for the purchase of works of art, and a little over $1 million for colleges and institutes dealing in art, such as the Royal College of Art, academies and colleges of music, the British Film Institute, and the Royal College of Dramatic Art.[3] The last institution, the only one specifically dealing in the theater, received around £2,000, or approximately $5,600 out of the $1 million devoted to colleges and institutes. In addition, the Arts Council, a separate independent agency designed to aid the arts, had a budget of slightly over $3 million. In the 1957/58 season it allocated about $1.5 million to opera and ballet, $433,000 to music, and roughly $300,000 to the theater.[4] Local authorities contributed about £250,000, or about $700,000, to the total.[5]

By the 1964/65 season the total budget had risen to approximately $9 million for all of Great Britain and $7.5 million for England. Of the English budget, $5.3 million was for music, $1.5 million was for drama, and the rest was divided among art, poetry, and general festivals.[6]

These figures are small, compared to what is done on the Continent. In Sweden, for example, around $18 million annually is raised by lottery and allocated to the Royal Opera, to non-commercial theater, to symphony orchestras, and to art and concert societies. Sweden has seven civic theaters, four of them with two stages and three with one stage. An average on-stage theater does about nine plays annually. Its total expenditures are in the neighborhood of $240,000, and it receives about half that sum in the form of state and municipal subsidies. Private theaters do exist, but have a difficult time surviving financially.[7]

In Germany, apparently most of the subsidization is done through the city governments, with the help of state governments' contributions. For example, in the city of Bamberg, population 78,000, the city theater with seven hundred seats has an annual budget of about $125,000, of which half is guaranteed by the city and half raised through seat sales. In Nuremberg, with three houses—the Opera House, the Lessing Theatre, and the Stadt Theatre—the budget runs to nearly $2 million per year. In Coburg, a city of 47,000, there is one city theater of a thousand seats which costs approximately $450,000 a year to run; both the State of Bavaria and the city aid the theater. As a result of subsidization of the theater in Germany, ticket prices run from a low of thirty cents to a high of about two dollars.[8]

3. *Economist,* October 25, 1958, p. 300.
4. *Ibid.*
5. W. E. Williams, "The Arts and Public Patronage," *Lloyds Bank Review,* XLIX (July, 1958), 18.
6. Arts Council of Great Britain, *20th Annual Report, 1964/65* (London, n.d.), Schedule 1, p. 98.
7. *Variety,* January 10, 1962, p. 229.
8. *Ibid.*

Both the commercial and the non-commercial theater in France are helped by the French government. Funds are allocated to all new playwrights for their first production and are also contributed to theaters or producers presenting a classic. To spread French culture abroad, the government aids companies who plan to present French plays, ballet, or music outside the boundaries of France. In addition, there are the national subsidized theaters and operas: the Comédie Française, which has two playhouses in Paris; the Opéra; the Opéra Comique; and the Theatre National Populaire, which produced programs of the classics for a mass audience in two houses. (As another example of the French government's support of the arts, the late Albert Camus was in 1959 put in charge of a government experimental theater.)[9] The Opéra and the Opéra Comique receive from the federal government around $4 million annually. A special subsidy for premieres of contemporary operas goes to the opera company, La Decentralisation Lyric, which tours.[10]

Throughout the rest of Europe, the arts are also heavily subsidized. In Italy, opera is the recipient of grants from most city governments. The Greek government aids the state orchestra of Athens. In Belgium, the symphony orchestras receive aid from the municipal and state governments. Orchestras in Denmark are subsidized. The Portuguese government aids symphony orchestras in Lisbon and Oporto. The Irish government aids not only symphony orchestras but the Abbey Theatre.

Unfortunately, while it is obvious that subsidization of the arts is extensive in Europe, it is unclear how much is spent for what and by whom. Much subsidization probably takes place at the local level, and there are no good figures on this. Since many of the radio and television stations are government-owned, subsidies may be hidden in lucrative contracts given to orchestras, opera companies, and theater groups to perform on state-owned facilities.[11]

United States aid to the arts

Historically, the federal government has done relatively little, outside of some support for the maintenance of historical sites throughout the country and for institutions in Washington, D. C., such as the Smithsonian and the National Gallery of Art. To be sure, the four branches of the armed forces maintain at least one band and orchestra each, besides supporting some recreational theater activity; but this is insignificant compared to the extensive national subsidization prevalent in Europe.

Recently, however, the federal government's interest in the arts has

9. *Variety,* January 6, 1960, p. 166.
10. Stoddard, *Subsidy Makes Sense,* p. 8.
11. For a more detailed description of aid abroad, see Frederick Dorian, *Commitment to Culture* (Pittsburgh: University of Pittsburgh Press, 1964).

shown signs of growing. In 1965, Congress established a National Endowment for the Arts with a budget of $2.5 million for fiscal 1966. The 1967 appropriation was $6 million, of which $2 million was intended to aid state art agencies, and the rest to help teaching artists, composers, symphony orchestras, choreographers, creative writers, laboratory educational theater, ballet, touring exhibits, and other such groups and projects. In addition, our tax laws give an indirect subsidy to the arts. All non-profit educational and artistic institutions are tax-exempt. However, commercial operations, run for profit, must pay the usual business profit tax. Non-profit institutions, though, such as opera companies and repertory theaters, are free from all federal taxation. In addition, the government allows deductions up to 20 per cent of gross income for gifts to educational or artistic non-profit institutions. Thus the treasury may pay up to 77 per cent of a gift to an opera company.[12]

In 1960, the Legislative Reference Service of the Library of Congress, at the request of several members of Congress, surveyed the fifty states of the union to discover what aid, if any, they were providing the arts.[13] In general, the answers showed that almost all the activity had to do with historical museums and sites being maintained by the states. However, it should be remembered that most state universities probably support the arts in some manner.

The following states reported a state art council, commission, or similar agency: Alabama, Florida, Georgia, Louisiana, Maine, Massachusetts, Minnesota, Montana, New Hampshire, New Mexico, New York, North Carolina, Utah, and Wisconsin. That is, fourteen of the thirty-six replies received by the Library of Congress indicated the existence of some agency connected specifically with the arts. In many cases these agencies appear to be of very recent origin, having been established in the last ten years, which suggests that there is a growing interest in the arts and a growing involvement of the states in the arts. Since states having an arts agency are eligible to receive a matching grant of up to $50,000 per year from the National Endowment for the Arts, most states will probably soon create such agencies.

Among the states that did most for the arts, California appropriated $27,900 for the annual arts and crafts exhibit at the California State Fair and Exposition. For the fiscal year 1960/61, Kentucky appropriated $106,000 for public concerts of the Louisville Symphony. In addition,

12. For someone in the highest income tax bracket in 1964. The rate declined in 1965.
13. The report of this survey can be found in the *Congressional Record* for February 2, 1961, pp. 1625–1632, or in House of Representatives, Committee on Education and Labor, Select Subcommittee on Education, *Hearings on Aid to Fine Arts,* 87th Cong., 1st Sess., 1961, pp. 123–147.

$50,000 was appropriated to commission the painting of murals by first-class artists for the University of Kentucky Medical Center. The State of Louisiana Art Commission has an annual operating budget of approximately $20,500. The Maine Art Commission in the years 1960/61 received $6,292. Maryland gave the Baltimore Symphony Orchestra Association $25,000. Massachusetts has established an Arts Commission which has complete jurisdiction over state commissions for sculpture, design of medals, and the like. The Metropolitan District Commission, which is a Massachusetts state agency, contracted with a local drama group in the summer of 1960 for the production of plays in an open-air summer theater constructed by the commission.

Montana appropriated $66,743 for the fiscal year ending June 30, 1958, for its fine arts commission. New Mexico also appropriated $36,429 for its fine arts commission. In 1960 New York established an advisory council on the arts and appropriated $50,000 for its first year's work. Since that year it has appropriated increasing sums of money to bring concerts and art activity to smaller cities. North Carolina appropriated $137,105 for the 1960/61 season for the State Art Society, and $30,000 for the North Carolina Symphony Orchestra. Pennsylvania gave $193,600 to the Philadelphia Museum School of Art and $50,000 to the Carnegie Museum in Pittsburgh. Rhode Island appropriated various small amounts for a number of activities, including free concerts for public school students, free public concerts in general, free public operatic performances, the Newport Music Festival, the Providence Philharmonic Orchestra, and the Irish Music Festival.

Utah appropriated $17,500 in a recent budget for the Utah State Institute of Fine Arts, an arts contest, a writing contest, crafts, and the Utah Symphony Orchestra. In addition, the Utah State Fair Association was given $2,000 for a fine arts contest, ceramics contest, and music contest. Vermont supports the Vermont Symphony Orchestra with $5,000. Virginia, the only state which makes a major appropriation to a theater, in a recent state budget appropriated $15,000 to the Barter Theatre, as well as $271,000 to the Virginia Museum of Fine Arts. Washington State appropriated $14,633 to the Henry Art Gallery.

Table VIII-1 shows the amount of city support for the arts as compiled from the results of a questionnaire sent to forty-six city governments by the Library of Congress. The total for each city shows that the amount appropriated varied from very little in some cities to over $4 million for New York City. In general, most of the funds support art museums, but some of these funds are channeled into other activities by the museums themselves. For example, the Art Institute of Chicago supports the Goodman Theatre, a school for dramatic arts.

Table VIII–1 Subsidies for the arts by selected cities for operating expenditures[a]

	Museums[b]	Music, opera, ballet	Theater	Total subsidy
New York City	$2,526,224	$95,866		$4,718,824[c]
Chicago	697,181			697,181
Los Angeles				196,988
Philadelphia	764,760	25,000		789,760
Detroit	543,081			543,081
Baltimore	40,594	119,994		448,588[d]
Houston	39,500	25,000	$3,000	67,500
St. Louis	320,008			320,008
San Francisco	778,706			817,006[e]
Dallas	80,000			80,000
New Orleans	40,000	8,275		48,275
Pittsburgh	25,000	55,000		80,000
San Antonio	81,000		1,500	163,500
San Diego	171,112			171,112
Seattle	115,075			115,075
Buffalo	73,430	57,300		130,730
Atlanta	10,000	13,500	5,000	28,500
Kansas City, Mo.	97,034	9,925	42,830	149,789
Newark	525,426			525,426
Oakland, Calif.	159,166			159,166
Birmingham	90,000			90,000
St. Paul	13,500	10,000		23,500
Norfolk	69,083	2,000		71,083
Providence, R.I.	24,877	1,500		26,377
Richmond	5,000			5,000
Sacramento	66,866	25,500		92,366
Scranton, Pa.	28,740			28,740
Springfield, Mass.	83,648			83,648
Syracuse, N.Y.	25,000			25,000

a. Operating expenditures may include capital costs.
b. Some part of funds allocated to museums may go, in a few cases, to the other arts when the museum supports such activity.
c. Includes $2,096,734 capital expenditures.
d. Includes $288,000 from gifts and endowment funds.
e. Includes $38,300 from gifts and endowment funds.
Source: Library of Congress survey conducted by Legislative Reference Service, 1959.

It is difficult to compare the government support to the arts in the United States with what is done in Europe. In the United States, state and city governments do support the arts with increasing amounts, although undoubtedly support of music and theater at all levels in Europe is relatively greater than it is in the United States. It seems likely, however, that the art museums in Europe that normally charge admission are more self-supporting than their counterparts in the United States.

Reasons for subsidization

In our economy, under a free market system, we normally assume that the best allocation of resources is determined by the free market. The price of goods and services reflects the cost to society of these services, and the consumer purchases them on the basis of what they are worth to him.

Every dollar spent on the arts represents a dollar of resources which has been transferred from some other use. Normally, therefore, we would believe that a dollar's worth of arts should be equal in subjective value to a dollar's worth of other goods and services. If we lower the price of theater tickets or opera tickets through a subsidy, consumers will normally buy more. The value to a consumer of the marginal purchase of tickets will be equal to the price of the tickets, which in fact is lower than the cost of producing that additional service. Hence, one would normally argue that it would be a waste of resources to subsidize the arts or any other such field.

Social benefits exceed private benefits

Thus, to maximize economic welfare, the price of any good or service should be equal to the marginal social cost of supplying the good or service. However, economic welfare is only a part of total welfare. As A. C. Pigou noted,

> On the one hand, a man who is attuned to the beautiful in nature or in art, whose character is simple and sincere, whose passions are controlled and sympathies developed, is in himself an important element in the ethical value of the world; the way in which he feels and thinks actually constitutes a part of welfare. On the other hand, a man who can perform complicated industrial operations, sift difficult evidence, or advance some branch of practical activity, is an instrument well fitted to produce things whose use yields welfare. The welfare to which the former of these men contributes directly is non-economic; that to which the latter contributes indirectly is economic. The fact we have to face is that, in some measure, it is open to the community to choose between these two sorts of men, and that by concentrating its efforts upon the economic welfare embodied in the second, it may unconsciously sacrifice the non-economic welfare embodied in the first.[14]

Two points are involved in Pigou's statement. One is that there may be social benefits or social costs, which in theory are subject to monetary

14. A. C. Pigou, *The Economics of Welfare* (4th ed.; London: Macmillan, 1938), pp. 12–13.

measurement but which are not equal to the private benefits or private costs. That this leads to a misallocation of resources has long been recognized by economists. Pigou, however, is saying something else. He is suggesting that a certain type of society or of man or of consumption may be *ethically* better than another. Pigou brings this out clearly when he writes,

> Of different acts of consumption that yield equal satisfaction, one may exercise a debasing, and another an elevating influence. The reflex effect upon the quality of people produced by public museums, or even by municipal baths, is very different from the reflex effect of equal satisfactions in a public bar. The coarsening and brutalizing influence of bad housing accommodations is an incident not less important than the direct dissatisfaction involved in it.[15]

Essentially he is claiming that there is a hierarchy of values; some things are better in some non-economic sense than others. To the extent that people agree that values can be ranked and to the extent that they agree on the ranking, citizens may desire to subsidize and promote those values which generally have been agreed upon as the most desirable.

A closely parallel argument rests on the proposition that the social benefits from the arts are greater than the private benefits. Attending an opera, the theater, or going to a museum, it is alleged, leads a consumer to be a better citizen. This rationale appears to be based on the proposition that the arts are educational, that they improve the quality of citizenship, that they make the citizen more thoughtful, and that they teach him about the world. It is undoubtedly true that there is something to this position—that attending a good play or a good opera may in fact improve the quality of citizens. For example, the arts undoubtedly improve conversation. By attending a play or an opera, going to a concert, or visiting an art gallery, an individual learns more, becomes exposed to more ideas, and as a result can talk more fluently about more subjects. To the extent that other individuals' pleasure is increased because there are more people they can converse with, the arts benefit people other than those who pay for tickets.

While it is true that some theater is educational, it is less obvious that the best way to achieve these benefits is to establish resident companies in major cities. Such companies will benefit only a minority of the population, a group which by most standards least needs its education and recreation subsidized. A more practical approach would be to finance a traveling company to tour the public schools. Such a company could tour

15. *Ibid.*, p. 17.

all the high schools in a state, thus bringing live drama to those who most need it.

Prestige

Another reason advanced for aiding cultural activity is that it raises the prestige of an area. Again, social benefits are greater than private benefits. The more arts, the more vigorous the arts, the better developed the arts, the more prestige any one country has with the citizens of other countries. This has been generally recognized, both in the United States and elsewhere. France, by subsidizing any company that wants to present French plays or music outside the boundaries of the country, admits its force. The American Department of State, when it subsidizes the export of American cultural attractions, is acknowledging its effect. Russia also subsidizes the export of some of its cultural attractions. At heart, this argument is based on national defense: subsidizing the arts is an attempt to attract the minds and allegiance of people beyond the borders of a country by exhibiting a vigorous cultural life.

Attraction of business and tourism

In any city, a thriving cultural life may be a great attraction. On balance, it may make the difference in determining whether some company establishes a new plant or research office in that city. It can lead to the attraction of better men for universities located in the area. It is clear that a thriving cultural life makes it easier for colleges and universities to attract faculty members and graduate students. It therefore becomes very much in the interest of large companies and institutions of higher learning to support the arts in their communities. Furthermore, it is in the interest of the whole city to aid the arts, at least in some small way. A few thousand dollars a year spent to maintain a fine symphony orchestra may lead to the influx of thousands of dollars in business. The same argument, of course, can be applied to the maintenance of a major league baseball or football team. In fact, many cities have subsidized major league sports by building stadiums and renting them to the team at low rates. The justification of this procedure is normally that it will attract more business to the city.

Certainly part of the attraction of New York City is its thriving theater district, its great museums, its opera houses, its ballets, and its symphony orchestras. Many tourists come to New York City just for the theater. Some businesses locate there because it is an area with a large supply of highly trained labor, labor which has migrated to New York at least in part because of its cultural advantages.

Income redistribution

Another argument takes two forms: first, since the arts are too expensive for the poor to afford, admission prices should be lowered through government aid; second, since the performers in the arts are inadequately paid, we should subsidize the performers. If it is the patrons who are to be subsidized, then it would appear that, rather than cut the price of all theater, opera, and concert tickets, it would be preferable to issue discount tickets to those in reduced circumstances, such as students and the poor. In fact, we do find such discounts being offered. In many cities, provision is made for free concerts for children, and in New York, cut-rate tickets are sold, in effect, to students and employees of large institutions to attend the Broadway theater. The justification for subsidizing the performers appears somewhat tenuous, to say the least. It is on a par with subsidizing farmers and merchant seamen. If it is rational to subsidize performers because they are poor, then by implication it must be more rational to subsidize all people who are poor, regardless of their occupations.

The "income redistribution" argument for subsidy to the arts, then, indicates a policy of selected aid, with the government supplying the difference between the list price and a low price for the poor. It does not justify a blanket outlay for the performance of art works.

Subsidies for opera and for the theater can be intended to stimulate the creation of new operas and new plays. In fact, in Canada and France, as we have seen, such subsidies are given directly to playwrights and composers. The National Endowment for the Arts allocated $150,000 in its first year to commission new works and to defray the cost of copying scores and parts. If the intent is to encourage the writing of new plays, operas, or musical compositions, such direct aid is more efficacious than subsidizing the performance of established works.

Income distribution

Another criticism of the market mechanism is based on income distribution. The market reflects the desires of individuals as weighted by their purchases. Since their purchases depend on their income, the rich have more to say about the allocation of resources than the poor. This, of course, is true and applies to all products, not only the arts. However, it is probably true that if the allocation were determined by equally weighting all individuals, less rather than more art would be produced, since people with low educational attainments usually do not appreciate or desire the arts and since these people are normally also the ones with small incomes. Hence, the current allocation of resources, as determined by the current income distribution, leads to more art than would exist with a more equal distribution of income.

Price discrimination

There is a further rationale for aiding the performing arts. It is clear that if the public is willing to pay the cost for opera, ballet, or any other art form (or for that matter any product or service), the value of the art form must be greater than what the public is foregoing, so that consumers will be better off with the opera than without. For some consumers the value of the opera is very great and they might be willing to pay $100 to see a performance; for others the value is lower and they would be willing to pay no more than $5. If the opera house charges a single price it might not be able to pay for the cost of the opera. At $100 only a few buy tickets; at $5 the house is sold out, but $95 in potential revenue is lost from the would-be $100 buyers. If the management could charge $100 to the real lover of opera and $5 to the less enthusiastic devotee, it could collect more revenue per performance and, by assumption, pay the cost of the opera. However, if it must charge the same price per seat to all patrons irrespective of the intensity of their love for opera, costs will not be covered. This may easily be the situation of many of our opera houses today. A more desirable allocation of resources—that is, a longer season —could be achieved if all the intensely interested people could be made to pay higher prices.

In other words, the opera house must practice price discrimination; it must charge those with an intense liking for opera more for a seat than those who are less enthusiastic. To discriminate successfully is not easy. In order to do so, one must be able to differentiate the market and keep the people with strong demand for opera from purchasing tickets at the lower price which is being charged others.

Consider the Metropolitan Opera in New York, which practices price discrimination. Those who purchase season tickets are asked to contribute to the opera. In fact, in some cases the Metropolitan Opera Society "suggests" how much should be contributed for each price range of tickets. Thus, those who have season tickets pay a considerably higher price per seat than those who buy individual tickets. But part of the cost of the price discrimination is borne by the non-theatergoing taxpayers, since such contributions are tax-deductible.

Purchasers of season tickets cannot, though, be made to contribute. Pressure can be applied by withholding better seats for successive seasons, but this is the only pressure available to the Opera Society. In principle, if the benefit from a longer opera season that goes to each individual were taxed and given to the opera company to extend the season, society would be better off. This is not practical. But, on the basis of the compensation principle,[16] a subsidy from general tax revenue might be justified.

It should be borne in mind, though, that since gifts to non-profit organizations such as opera are tax deductible, more funds are forthcoming than would be in a completely free market with no government. Hence, even though some individuals do not give, in the aggregate enough resources may be devoted.

Infant industry

It has been claimed that with more information and more exposure to the arts, people would participate in them more frequently, and that what is needed is to bring the arts to the people to develop the demand. For the theater this argument is weak. At one time the legitimate stage was widespread; since then it has been replaced by other forms of amusement. The Federal Theatre Project, while bringing drama to millions, had no measurable long-run effect on playgoing.[17] Many people have experience with the theater at some point in life, and yet they reject it. The only new art forms are motion pictures and television, and neither is an infant industry. Like the argument for tariffs, the argument for stimulating an infant industry appears at best to be a temporary expedient. Thus, it would seem that the infant industry argument does not have a great deal of validity, either empirically or theoretically.

Innovation and the arts

By one definition, great art must be innovative. New ways of saying old things must be developed, or new ideas must be expressed in new ways. A new painting resembling technically the style of Rembrandt is worth little and would usually not be considered great art. A well-composed play that dealt with a hackneyed theme and treated it in a commonplace fashion would be unlikely to win for its author the Nobel Prize for Literature. To survive the test of time, to win the plaudits of the public, and to add luster to contemporary art, a work must be novel.

The importance of new processes and products is not confined to the world of art. If an electronics manufacturer or a drug company tries to survive merely by imitating what others have developed, it is unlikely to be successful. But one important difference exists: in manufacturing, if a

16. The compensation principle states that if in theory, the people who benefit could be taxed to compensate those that lose and still be better off, then the change should take place.
17. The companies organized under the Federal Theatre Project disappeared without a trace as soon as federal funds were withdrawn. In 1940 and 1941, after the project was abandoned, there were fewer resident companies in existence than in 1935 when it started. See Chapter VII.

new product is developed or a new process invented, it can be patented and the developer can reap the benefits.[18] In the world of arts no such protection exists. When the Theatre Guild launched *Oklahoma!,* a musical which integrated story, song, and dance, there was no way to prevent imitation. And in fact all successful musicals since have been built on the innovations of *Oklahoma!*

Thus the returns from new approaches in art may be great but do not accrue entirely to the innovator. In technical economic terms, the social gains exceed the private gains. Whenever the entrepreneur cannot capture the entire benefit from his action, he will devote few resources to it. As a consequence entrepreneurs will do less innovating than is desirable, since there will be some experimentation in which the gain to society is greater than its cost but the gain to the producer is less than its cost. In such a situation a subsidy would produce a more efficient use of resources.

Summary of reasons for subsidization

The most common arguments for subsidization are based on educational advantages: social benefits exceed private benefits. The benefits are hard to measure and depend largely on subjective views of welfare— a more cultivated society benefits all members. A second argument is based on the proposition that there is an economic benefit to be derived from more art; for example, additional business will be attracted to the area. The income redistribution contentions do not stand up under careful consideration, but the price discrimination argument, while rather technical and of dubious practical significance, has theoretical justification. The final argument deals with the benefits from innovation. Since great art, by some peoples' definition, must be innovative art and since the benefits (from innovating) to society exceed those to the innovator, subsidies are called for.

Who should subsidize?

In the section above we have considered the reasons for aiding art forms. We have ignored in general the question of who should do the aiding, whether it should be done by the city government, the state government, or the federal government. Who should do it depends in part on why it is being done. In general, the arguments about attracting more business to a community would seem to lead to the city government's being the source of revenue, since a federal government subsidy for all cities would defeat the objective of attracting more business to any one of them.

18. In some areas, e.g., basic research, developments are not patentable; hence the same problem arises.

In general, subsidization by the local government may be preferred, since the city is interested in making the area a better place to live. At the city level there is more local control.[19] Each area provides the amount of culture its citizens desire. In the United States, as we have seen, it is the city governments which have been the primary sources of government aid.

The best argument for state help would seem to be that states have better tax sources and, consequently, can more easily allocate funds to the arts. People who live outside the city limits benefit from the arts; yet, if the city government does the subsidizing, they do not bear the cost. City councils, being generally interested only in the benefits received by city voters, will ignore the improvement in the well-being of suburbanites when appropriating funds for the arts. Hence, they will tend to under-invest in culture. The same argument applies, but to a weaker extent, to state subsidies: individuals residing outside the state may benefit without paying any of the taxes used to support the arts. However, since almost all beneficiaries are state residents, the problem is probably negligible at the state level.

The same reasoning applicable to state governments would apply to the federal government. The federal government has the largest tax re-sources. People cannot avoid federal taxes easily by moving out of the area. In addition, a federal subsidy for the arts would allow an orchestra to travel widely, not just through one state but throughout the country. Because everybody would be paying, such art groups would be ex-pected to travel widely, even to some of the sparsely populated areas of the United States.[20] Much of the recent controversy over subsidizing the arts has been concerned with obtaining federal funds. State and local tax revenues are allegedly being strained already. Consequently, it is felt that the federal government, with its greater tax resources, can more easily aid the arts.

The prime argument against the federal government as a source for subsidies is based on an objection to federal control. The arts would un-doubtedly be hampered by more control. It seems likely that the federal government would want a voice in determining the allocation of its re-sources. For example, during the thirties, under the auspices of the Works Progress Administration, the federal government undertook to sponsor various arts. Even though Harry Hopkins, head of the WPA, believed in a

19. There also may be more corruption and fewer able administrators. Hence, many might prefer that most functions be handled by the national government. The problem here is outside the scope of this book and deals with the whole issue of a federal system.

20. The Arts Council of Great Britain has practically abandoned any effort to bring the arts to the people in sparsely populated areas. See W. E. Williams, "The Arts and Public Patronage."

"free, uncensored, adult theatre,"[21] the problem of political control grew with the project. Practically at the very start in 1936, Elmer Rice resigned because of an administration ruling that no ruler or cabinet officer of any foreign nation could be portrayed on a Federal Theatre stage. One production, *The Cradle Will Rock,* was prevented from opening by federal government authorities. In Chicago, the play *Model Tenement,* which dealt with a rent strike, was banned, reportedly on order of the mayor.[22] The state WPA leaders in Illinois also prevented the local opening of *Hymn to the Rising Sun* because it "was of such a moral character that I can't even discuss it with a member of the press."[23] (The play later opened in New York where the critics praised it.) In Massachusetts there was opposition to the production of *Valley Forge* by Maxwell Anderson; and in Connecticut, citizens of New Britain protested that Shakespeare's *Merchant of Venice* was anti-Semitic.

The WPA officials in California canceled *Judgment Day* by Elmer Rice. David Niles, who was head of the WPA information service, said that the cancellation of *Judgment Day* was not censorship, which as a known liberal he opposed, but merely "selection."[24] But, of course, "selection" is the nub of the problem; someone has to do the selecting. A subsidized theater is left with the choice of a safe program which no one will criticize or a program that may win critical acclaim but will also produce opposition. As Hallie Flanagan puts it, "If you are playing safe you depend upon old plays which have had safe receptions or you imitate the formulas as closely as you dare. Every time you open a new play, or an old play in a new way, you run the risk of failure—and at the same time, the only chance of a creative success."[25] Inasmuch as almost no one desires to subsidize a theater of pap, the issue becomes a matter of deciding "whether it [the body subsidizing] wants plays chosen by non-political people, in which case some will probably be politically unwise; or by political people, in which case either caution or party politics will rule."[26]

The Federal Theatre Project attempted valiantly to steer clear of partisan politics and yet put on stimulating drama concerned with current problems. Such an attempt was, as would be any such effort, doomed to failure. In the case of this project, the program itself was supported and owed its very existence to one party, for the Republicans opposed subsidized drama. No matter how good the intentions of the administrators,

21. Hallie Flanagan, *Arena* (New York: Duell, Sloan and Pearce, 1940), p. 67.
22. *Ibid.,* pp. 135–136. The mayor later denied all knowledge of the production.
23. *Ibid.,* p. 136.
24. *Ibid.,* p. 287.
25. *Ibid.,* p. 226.
26. *Ibid.,* p. 288.

they were more likely to reflect the opinions of the New Deal than of Herbert Hoover. The very people attracted to the project would, of course, favor the programs of the administration, and what to them was an unbiased presentation of the facts would appear to the opposition as wilful omission or misrepresentation of the vital arguments against Roosevelt's programs. For example, the Living Newspaper productions, such as *Power* (an inquiry into the use of power), *One-Third of a Nation* (a history of slum housing), and *Triple-A Plowed Under* (the farming problem in America) dealt with governmental solutions to social issues that the Republicans felt were better left in the hands of private enterprise. Undoubtedly, had conservatives been running the program, the Living Newspaper productions would have been concerned with the growth of government in Washington and the "destruction" of free enterprise.

While there is general agreement that there was considerable governmental pressure involved in the Federal Theatre Project, it is argued that a national arts foundation could avoid the problem of governmental control. The Rockefeller Panel Report on the performing arts, after admitting "the problem of protecting artistic freedom,"[27] suggests that the European experience and the National Science Foundation show that the arts can be aided without impairing artistic freedom. While the National Science Foundation certainly does not censor research, it is all too apparent from public complaints that the direction of research is being influenced. Those fields and those types of projects that are believed by NSF to be productive are favored. Hence, the direction of research is diverted from what it might have been. This is inescapable when large funds must be allocated among competing ends.

Frederick Dorian, in his book *Commitment to Culture,* attempts to document the freedom from control of the arts under subsidy in Europe. Yet he writes that "censorship in Austria applies to the entire scope of the performing arts,"[28] and "in the patterns of art support [in Italy] there is a constant give and take. . . . The overall result has in recent years inclined to the liberal side."[29] "In the fall of 1960 this play [*Arialda* by Giovanni Testori] was removed from a Milan theater because it 'offended the public morale.' "[30] Also in 1960, the Archbishop of Naples objected to and succeeded in halting the performance (in opera form) of *Le Martyre de St. Sébastien* by Debussy at a state-supported opera.[31] In France, "art patronage has been an exponent of the power in charge."[32]

27. *The Performing Arts: Problems and Prospects* (New York: McGraw-Hill, 1965), p. 145.
28. *Commitment to Culture,* p. 45.
29. *Ibid.,* p. 67.
30. *Ibid.,* p. 106.
31. *Ibid.*
32. *Ibid.,* p. 191.

"The Fifth Republic has, if anything, reinforced the role of government art support and, there can be no mistake about it, imposed a more rigid supervision of the national art institutes."[33]

The British Arts Council seems, however, to have escaped the problems of most of its Continental neighbors, since there have been few complaints about governmental control. Yet it should be noted that the stage is censored in England by the Lord Chamberlain, and in 1962 "a Parliamentary committee decided that while ideas on the printed page provided 'little mischief,' the same ideas on the stage were a 'stimulation' to vice."[34]

The relative rareness of examples of censorship in Europe are not proof of the freedom of the arts. Examples of censorship in Russia are even rarer. Few would argue, however, that the arts are free behind the Iron Curtain. Artists know what will be supported and what will not and tend to produce that which is approved. In Europe writers and performers know what will be aided and what will be censored, and in Great Britain few scriptwriters satirize the Queen since they know it will not be permitted.

After reading Dorian's book, this author was struck by the relative freedom of the arts in the United States. Censorship is rarer and tends to happen at the local level. What is banned in Boston may flourish in Connecticut. No monolithic organization directs the arts into approved channels. The very diversity of sources of revenue for the arts guarantees that variety will exist. If an artist cannot receive support for his work from one source, countless others exist, and if his work has any merit he is almost sure to find a patron or an audience.

The new federal program does not seem to present much danger to the arts yet. The small size of the appropriations means that the National Endowment for the Arts cannot affect the direction of the arts. Only if the funds grow to such a size that they begin to dominate a substantial portion of the activity would there be much danger. Moreover, part of the funds must be turned over to the states for administration, a limitation which reduces the power of the federal government to channel the arts.

Two avenues are available to aid the arts without central control. The government can grant tax concessions to theater projects without regard for their content—in which case no politician or government official can be involved in the selection of plays—or the subsidy programs can be administered by the states.

The route that would lead to the most vigorous and enterprising theater would be the route of tax exemption. If the federal government

33. *Ibid.,* p. 205.
34. New York *Times,* December 6, 1962, p. 53.

eliminated all taxes—admission and income—on playhouses and legitimate stage productions and if states and cities eliminated all real estate and admission taxes, the free drama would be greatly stimulated without the problem of "selection."[35] Any state or federal program of cash aid to the theater would tend to degenerate into support for companies which concentrated on the classics—the safe ones—and light comedies and musicals.

If the states or cities did the subsidizing, the problem of political control would be less. Since party control is divided among the states, there would be more diversity in the type of programs presented. Yet even state-administered programs would be likely to lapse into dullness since the subsidies would probably be controlled by civil service personnel anxious to maintain their jobs in spite of changes in administration. Therefore, they would opt for the safe but mundane and revive already-established pieces.

The arguments presented above for subsidizing the stage do not give an unambiguous answer to the question of how much aid there should be. The answer clearly depends on how much theater is desired. Nationwide, however, an increase in funds devoted to drama may lead to no increase in the production of good plays if all the available talents are already involved in the theater. Certainly any large federal program would encounter this problem. True, playwrights could be lured from motion pictures, directors from television, and actors from both. But such a shift would be to the detriment of films and broadcasting. In the long run more skilled people might be drawn into the performing arts, but as was suggested in Chapter II, it appears that the talents necessary to write a good play are scarce, and it might take huge sums to increase the number of good playwrights even modestly.

On the other hand, as Chapter II also showed, plays of limited appeal have been squeezed out of the commercial market. A national program of aid to the theater would probably result in a larger market for such works and hence entice some writers back to the stage from other media. An increase in the number of plays of limited appeal could only benefit the stage in the long run. While few might be masterpieces, more experimentation would be encouraged and this might lead to new approaches in drama. Even if these innovations benefited the entire theater, the producer or author who experimented might reap few of the gains. As was argued above, there may be too little investment in this area, and a national subsidy might stimulate the theater and have total benefits greater than total costs. Yet a policy of cash grants could have the wrong

35. Exempting income earned in backing a theatrical production from federal income taxes would amount to a huge subsidy.

effect; rather than stimulating innovation, it might discourage it. Groups producing safe and non-controversial theater would in all likelihood get the funds and be better able to compete with the innovators. Tax exemption, however, would benefit the theater as a whole and would lead to more innovation.

How much aid?

To achieve the desired results both of freedom for the theater and more theatrical activity, tax relief appears to be the appropriate means. The removal of the admission tax is a step in the right direction, for there are good reasons why drama ought to be helped and no reasons why it should be harmed. The excise tax on tickets seems both inexplicable and undesirable, and its repeal at the federal level is to be commended. Yet many states and municipalities still tax tickets. The abolition of the federal tax on tickets, as Chapter VI showed, will probably expand theatrical activity on Broadway by approximately 10 per cent. The effect outside New York cannot be predicted from the data at hand, but the removal of the tax will certainly lead to more summer stock, more touring, and maybe more resident companies.

The federal government could go further; federal income taxes on the profits of theatrical enterprises could be removed. While this action would have no effect on non-profit repertory companies, it would stimulate summer stock, touring companies, and Broadway productions. Non-profit organizations, such as repertory companies, opera houses, and ballet groups, would be unaffected by such tax exemption. But an income tax exemption for earnings from the performing arts would invigorate all branches of the arts.

A city or state wishing to stimulate drama could waive real estate taxes and remove any taxes on admission, but these items would have only a small effect. Cash grants are required if it is desired to give more substantial help to the performing arts. The amount of aid would depend on the size of the city and the amount of theater, opera, and ballet the community wanted. Let us imagine, for example, a city of moderate size with no professional repertory company, which wishes to establish one that will operate from thirty to thirty-six weeks a year in a five-hundred-seat house. Such a theater could be supported at the box office if the population over fourteen years old in the area were greater than 750,000.[36] If the area has less than that, the city could expect the box office to contribute toward costs the ratio of the total population in the area (over fourteen) to 750,000. That is, a metropolitan area with a

36. Cities below 750,000 generally do not have such an establishment, while those with larger populations usually do.

population of 500,000 (over fourteen) could expect two-thirds (500,000/750,000) of total costs to be covered by the box office. Hence, if a resident company in a five-hundred-seat theater with total costs of $300,000 per year is to exist, a subsidy of $100,000 a year must be forthcoming.

Unfortunately, even if a city is willing to spend the money, it may still be unable to establish a viable repertory company. As noted in the previous chapter, the presence and success of a resident theater has usually depended on the efforts of one or more dedicated and talented individuals. A city may be anxious to establish such a theater, yet have difficulty in attracting the talent. Assuming that a talented director can be found, the desirability of a subsidy will depend on the value of the stage to the community. The city should ask: "Will the theater attract enough new business to the area to compensate for the subsidy, or would business prefer the cash?" If businessmen would prefer lower taxes to a subsidized theater (i.e., new business will not compensate for higher taxes), then is the value to the community in terms of an improved cultural climate great enough to make it worthwhile? It should be borne in mind that the chief beneficiaries of the theater (besides those who work there) will be the better-educated, wealthier portion of the population.

To subsidize or not to subsidize?

A partial list of areas subsidized by the federal government would include agriculture, education, research, mining, shipbuilding, the merchant marine, aviation, and motor transportation. Most economists will agree that certain of these subsidies are unjustified and distort the allocation of resources in our society. In other cases, such as education and research, advocates point to the social benefits from these activities and claim that if unsubsidized the market would produce too little research and too little investment in education. The argument for subsidizing the theater is akin to the one for subsidizing education; if higher education should be subsidized, then by the same token the performing arts (which are educational) should be aided. Note, however, that aid to higher education and aid to the arts are subsidies which benefit chiefly the well-to-do. Thus they can be considered to be regressive in their effect on income.

Unfortunately, there has been little rational discussion of the issue. Most arguments for aiding the performing arts have amounted to asserting either that the arts cannot survive without help—which is clearly untrue for the theater—or that "I like the arts, I think there should be more of them, and therefore everyone should be taxed to help them." On economic grounds, neither of these arguments justifies governmental aid.

The chief argument against subsidy is that such aid distorts the allocation of resources. With aid, box office earnings will not cover total costs, and the value consumers put on the company will be less than the total cost to society of having it. It follows therefore that the total welfare of society will be less than if there had been no subsidy. In addition, an unsubsidized theater will be freer than a subsidized one.

In the end, whether one believes in subsidies for the theater or not depends on one's taste for the theater and one's beliefs concerning the external social benefits of having a large and active theater. In any case, the best method of furnishing such aid for the sake of a free, unfettered theater would be tax exemption.

IX | Remedies and suggestions

The stage is an anachronism. Once the only form of dramatic entertainment, it survives as a handicraft industry in a mechanized world. What the garment industry did for clothing, motion pictures and television have done for drama. Those desiring humor or an emotional catharsis can obtain them from their neighborhood cinema or their television sets more cheaply than through the theater. Yet, as something is lost when the craftsman is replaced by the machine, something is lost when motion pictures and television replace live actors. The silver screen and television are not inferior, for they offer products that on occasion achieve brilliance. Nevertheless, for those who can afford it and for those with wit enough to appreciate it, the legitimate stage survives.

Over forty million homes view television each week;[1] more than forty million people visit film houses each seven days;[2] but less than eight million tickets are sold to Broadway shows each year. Total attendance at professional live theatrical performances in one year is smaller than weekly attendance for motion pictures. In spite of being dwarfed by other entertainment media, the theater remains the artistic core of the world of drama, and Broadway remains the quintessence of the stage. Yet as we have seen, Broadway is only one part of the world of the stage; the road and summer stock serve larger audiences. On the other hand, even though the audience and the receipts of summer and winter stock companies, as Table IX-1 shows, are insignificant, more new scripts are done by those companies than see an opening on Broadway. Each part of the universe of the theater forms an essential element in the whole, has its own problems, and needs its own solutions.

Broadway

The Broadway theater is the heartbeat of the theater world. Much maligned and criticized, it still fashions the most polished productions,

1. Conversation with Mr. Colman of the Public Relations department of the A. C. Nielsen Co., May 18, 1967.
2. Department of Commerce, *Statistical Abstract of the United States, 1963*, p. 210, Table 275. In 1961 average attendance was forty-two million.

earns the most money, attracts a large audience, and charges the highest prices. Its future depends partially on whether the spiraling expenses of mounting a Broadway production can be kept within reason.

In recent years, the multiplication of paper work, incidental expenses, and legal requirements have pushed production costs to new heights. In 1964, the New York State Legislature enacted new legislation requiring producers to file more reports and to keep more records. Notwithstanding the good intentions behind this law, one major effect has been an increase in paper work. New secretaries had to be hired, more legal fees were engendered, and accounting expenses rose. The purpose of the new statutes is to protect innocent investors from rapacious producers. In an investigation of theatrical practices, the attorney general of New York found that "kickbacks" from costumers, scenery suppliers, and advertising often remained in producers' pockets and were not reported to investors. In a number of cases it was found that the reports to backers were inaccurate. There is little doubt that, as in many other fields, unscrupulous promoters have milked unwary investors.

Legislation to protect investors has not been notably successful in other fields. For example, George J. Stigler, a well-known economist, studied the effect of the Securities and Exchange Commission's regulations on investors' profits from corporate securities. He found that the average rate of return and the percentage of defaults was the same in the fifties as it had been during the twenties before the formation of the commission.[3] It seems uncertain, by analogy, whether the new laws of New York State will protect backers better than the SEC has protected investors in public securities. Inasmuch as almost all financial losses on Broadway stem from the failure of new productions, saddling the theater entrepreneur with additional red tape may add to the woes of Broadway rather than contribute to its prosperity.

Regulation begets more regulation. In the late forties the Securities and Exchange Commission ruled that the limited partnership agreement used on Broadway was a sale of securities to the general public and subject to regulation. The commission assured Broadway entrepreneurs that only a short set of papers would be required and that five days after filing, unless the commission objected, backers could be accepted. In practice, five days grew to six or seven weeks and the short set of papers multiplied endlessly. At one time the SEC proposed that a synopsis of the plot be included with the material filed. Since timing may be all important

---

3. George J. Stigler, "Public Regulation of the Securities Markets," *Journal of Business,* XXXVII (April, 1964), 117. See also Irwin Friend and Edward S. Herman, "The S.E.C. through a Glass Darkly," *ibid.* (October, 1964), pp. 382–405, and Sidney Robbins and Walter Werner, "Professor Stigler Revisited," *ibid.,* pp. 406–413. Both articles dispute Stigler's findings.

Table IX–1 Estimated gross receipts and attendance at various types of theater, 1962/63

Type	Gross receipts ($millions)	Attendance (millions)	Period
Broadway	$43.5	7.6	1962/63 season
Road	31.5	7.8	1962/63 season
Summer stock	22.6–30.6	8.8–10.2	Summer of 1962
Off-Broadway (New York)	3.0	0.7–1.1	1962/63 season
Permanent resident company	1.5–6.0	0.5–2.0	1962/63 season

Note: Summer stock receipts are estimated on the basis of capacity gross as reported in a survey; we assume that the theaters operate at 60–70 per cent of capacity on the average (see Chapter VII). Off-Broadway is estimated by assuming that the estimated average receipts for one week in February (see Chapter I) are typical of forty weeks of the year, and two-thirds of that amount for twelve weeks. The figures for permanent resident companies are based on fragmentary data from a survey (see Chapter VII). The lower figure assumes average total receipts of about $100,000 for fifteen companies—approximately the median figure in the survey; the higher number assumes average receipts at $400,000, the highest estimate received in the survey (see Chapter VII for more details). Broadway and road grosses are taken from *Variety*, June 26, 1963, p. 70.

Attendance figures are estimated by dividing gross by estimated average prices—weekly capacity gross divided by the number of performances per week and by the number of seats in the house equals price (for Broadway, off-Broadway, and the road, the number of performances per week is eight; for stock theaters it is assumed to be seven).

in securing the right star, director, and theater, the delays have contributed enormously to the difficulties of mounting a Broadway production. The net result of these rules is that the producer who once could and often did direct his production, who once could handle all paper work with the aid of a single secretary, now must employ lawyers, accountants, and business managers and can only rarely find time and energy actually to direct the show.

Those concerned with the plight of the New York theater often point to "featherbedding" and union demands as major contributors to higher costs. As Chapter IV shows, only a small part of the rise in opening expenses can be attributed to unions. While there is little doubt that make-work rules do exist, and that stagehands and musicians have been paid for doing no work, theatrical costs would be lower by only 4 per cent at most if expenses of the crew had remained unchanged in real terms from the twenties. Musicians are normally neither used nor paid for in most straight shows. Thus, even if producers refused to pay for work not done, only a very minor portion of expenses could be reduced—the problems of Broadway originate with factors other than unions.

Climbing advertising expenditures have, on the other hand, led to noticeably higher production and operating costs. Newspaper linage rates are not the prime cause, nor is increased publicity in the dailies. The rise in outlays for publicity stems apparently from higher expenditures on non-newspaper advertising. Since theatergoers claim to be rarely influenced by radio, television, billboards, and magazine advertising, Broadway manager might try reducing their expenses on such paid publicity.

Even if restrictive regulation were repealed and even if producers contracted advertising, costs would continue to mount on Broadway. The stage, as has been mentioned, is primarily a handicraft industry. Live actors must appear in front of a small live audience. As wages and salaries continue to rise in the United States, so wages and salaries of performers will advance. Higher expenses therefore seem inevitable.

Growing production costs force producers to concentrate on fewer and longer-running plays and musicals. For the last thirty-five years this process has been continuing and appears likely to be maintained. If the operating surplus—the difference between receipts and operating costs—remains unchanged while the expense of mounting a production grows, the producer has no choice. He must be more selective, choosing for presentation only those scripts with the prospect of substantial runs. Since other branches of the theater—such as summer stock, amateur theater, and university players—depend on Broadway-certified shows for their fare, the decline in new openings on Broadway will adversely affect these sectors. In addition, the motion picture industry depends on Broadway for many of its better scripts; it too will suffer.

In the past, prices have risen with operating costs. The operating surplus has therefore been maintained but not argumented. If there is to be any expansion in the number of shows launched on Broadway or even if the number of openings is to be maintained, the operating surplus must advance. Prices, in other words, will have to go up faster than operating costs. Higher ticket tariffs will naturally lead to a reduction in attendance, but as was found in Chapter VI, a rise in prices will lead to a less than proportional fall in attendance. In the end the only way to prevent a further abatement of activity on Broadway is for theater owners and producers to insist on higher house scales.

Not only should ticket prices be hiked, but the structure of tariffs needs overhauling. That seats for weekend performances are generally considerably more difficult to obtain than tickets for weekdays indicates that prices for Saturday nights are too low. With an appropriate scale, theatergoers would find it no more difficult but more expensive to visit the theater at a popular time than at an unpopular time. Moreover, higher prices for weekend seats would lead to improved operating surpluses and consequently more openings. In the end both Broadway and New York theatergoers would benefit. The former would be able to repay backers sooner and the latter would find, if they were willing to pay the price, that securing a seat for the weekend was no more difficult than purchasing one for any other time.

In addition to having forced higher costs on Broadway managements, the laws of the land have almost eliminated any flexibility in the pricing of seats. If demand increases, both the statutes of New York State and those of the federal government have effectively prevented the producer from raising ticket prices.[4] If demand falls, only through the clumsy device of "two-fers" can the tariff be cut. Such rigidity is undesirable and harmful. The federal law, however, has been repealed and more flexibility in ticket prices is now possible than in previous years. Yet the state statutes still encumber the theater.

Before 1938, Leblang's ticket agency often purchased large sections of tottering shows to market the seats at a discount—often as much as 50 per cent—from list. Students, elderly people, and those who were careful with their money haunted the lobby of Leblang's looking for bargains. Many young people, introduced to Broadway through Leblang's, developed a taste for the legitimate stage which later led them to become faithful playgoers. Subsequent to the prohibition against selling tickets for any price other than the one printed on them, the only practical means of reducing prices has been to issue "two-fers," the distribution of which is spotty, since they tend to go to large organizations. The previous system was more flexible and more interesting for the would-be playgoer, who could wander into a cut-rate ticket agency and choose among the shows that were reducing prices.

Furthermore, the law prohibits all but licensed ticket brokers from retailing tickets at more than the prices printed on them. Licensed agencies may charge as much as $1.50 commission plus tax. Price ceilings have never worked well, nor do they in this case. When seats are in short supply, the value of tickets is bound to appreciate. The conversion of the sale of a ticket at the market price from an innocent business practice into a criminal act will cause the guileless, the pure, and those fearful of the law to shun the brokerage business. Because anyone caught scalping tickets may go to jail, pay a heavy fine, or—if he is a broker—lose his license, the rewards must be substantial for the practice to flourish. The net result is that fewer tickets are sold at what the market will bring than if there were no law. As a consequence, the tariff for those who want their seats immediately is forced higher.

For theatergoers, then, the repeal of the restrictions on pricing would

4. The federal law required that the price be printed on the ticket, and that the box office cannot deviate from the established list. It had also been ruled that all tickets in a certain section must be sold at the same price. Therefore a producer cannot raise prices for a performance after he has begun to market tickets. Conversely, to lower prices would involve giving rebates to all who had purchased seats for the performance in question. In effect, if seats have been sold much in advance, prices cannot be quickly raised; once raised, they also cannot be lowered without involving the production in considerable expense. The New York State law prohibits brokers from raising prices above the list plus the legal commission.

be beneficial: net costs of attending the theater would decline. Weak productions could and would market their seats at reduced prices through discount houses. More tickets would be available without a long wait for hit shows, with the result that the cost of buying a seat on short notice would be reduced. Those who do not object to waiting would be able eventually to secure seats at list price or, if they waited longer, less. With no legislation, prices would be high in the beginning and slowly decline as demand was satisfied. The theater industry would also benefit. A long wait to see a play is a cost to consumers, yet the theater does not benefit from the wait. Broadway could increase its total revenue by selling tickets at the market price, thereby eliminating the long wait.

Dramatists, stars, and backers would benefit as well from the repeal of the restrictions. Since gross receipts as measured at the box office would include premiums for purchasing on short notice, those who receive a share of the gross would earn more—at least in the short run.

Why then have such restrictions been instituted? Many people prefer queues over prices as a means of distributing scarce goods, and those who believe in this approach contend that the wealthy should have no greater claim on tickets to hit shows than the poor. Waiving the ethical problems involved, it seems only necessary to point out that if one individual has a ticket that another wants and they voluntarily make a bargain, both individuals are better off than if the law prohibited the transaction.

Some people do benefit from the present law. The lower the prices to shows, the more people will visit Broadway and the more actors will be employed.[5] Consequently, Equity has been a strong supporter of attempts to prohibit scalping. Theater owners and producers tend generally to favor the legal restrictions even though superficially they are harmed by the law. Many undoubtedly support the regulations from a belief in the fairness of the queue, and some genuinely believe the public would object to a free market in tickets. A few may actually profit from the law, since "ice" often makes its way back to the box office. The New York State investigation found that payoffs were made to managers of theaters and to box office personnel. Theater owners and producers often can control these people and always have ultimate supervision of ticket distribution. Therefore, owners and entrepreneurs can, if they wish, receive "ice." Any such income does not have to be split with authors, stars, backers, or tax collectors as it would if there were no restrictions. Thus, it is very possible for a producer or theater owner to earn more from illegal premiums than he could by open sale of tickets for what the market would bring.

Three solutions to the problems of "ice" have been voluminously discussed; the author will offer a fourth. Let us consider them.

5. Assuming the supply of shows is unaffected.

Rigid enforcement. The reaction of government officials to disclosures of scalping has been to insist on more enforcement. New York State passed new legislation in 1964 to prevent charges above the legal minimum; the attorney general of New York has requested even more stringent licensing of box office personnel. Such an approach is not only ineffectual but harmful, for costs of marketing tickets rise, red tape grows, and the cost of scalped seats climbs.

The central ticket agency. Another approach has been to attempt to channel all tickets through a central agency, which would sell some at prices above the list. The funds generated would then be kept within the theater, and flexibility in pricing would be possible. Skeptical producers and theater owners have been reluctant to lose control over their seats. From the point of view of the audience such a system would be unfortunate, since the agency would monopolize ticket sales and consequently would inflate prices. Moreover, a central ticket agency that handled all the seats for Broadway shows would almost inevitably be considered a violation of antitrust laws.

The twenty-five-dollar-ticket proposal. The attorney general of the state of New York, Louis J. Lefkowitz, proposed that a limited number of seats for hit shows be set aside, to be sold by brokers at up to twenty-five dollars per seat, plus 20 per cent commission. In this way much of what is now "ice" would be returned to the production. No provision is made for lowering tariffs, although he does suggest that the last three or four rows in the orchestra be sold at less than one dollar to attract impecunious Broadway devotees. Except for the seats to be sold at high prices, there is little flexibility in the system. There would be ample opportunity to earn large sums by redistributing the one-dollar seats at fifteen dollars or more. The twenty-five-dollar limit also is unrealistic. While few seats sell for more than thirty dollars, any limitation can produce the same problems that currently plague Broadway. The proposal would lead to legal "ice" and illegal "ice."

The flexible price solution. Why not sell seats like other products? Allow the management to alter the scale frequently to meet changing conditions. For example, suppose no price was printed on the ticket, although a suggested list could be indicated. Before the opening, the producer and the theater owner decide what the market will bear. The objective is to have tickets available at the box office up to at least a week prior to the performance. After the show opens, tickets are marked down if demand has been overestimated. If, on the other hand, demand has been underestimated, the scale is raised for future sales. From then on managers might find it inexpedient to alter the scale more often than once a month. Prices would be advertised in the daily newspapers, and tickets could normally be bought at the box office for the next week. Theater-goers wishing seats for the next night would patronize a broker who, having bought his tickets from the box office, would receive a premium for the service of making seats available at very short notice. For a new hit, box office prices for the best seats might be as high as twenty-five dollars, but after several years they might fall to five dollars.

The advantages of such a system are manifold: prices would adjust to demand; the irritating waits for seats to Broadway shows would be shortened; all earnings from the sale of tickets would accrue to the pro-duction and to the theater; many shows would have seats available at low prices for those who were young and wished to experiment with the theater. Competition between shows could be counted on to prevent average ticket prices from rising "too high." Inasmuch as there would always be some shows with low prices, theatergoers could always find fare within their budgets. Those desiring to see the latest hit could either pay the tariff or wait—a situation quite similar to the purchase of most prod-ucts.

The main disadvantage with the flexible price scheme is the possibility of offending playgoers. Theater people like to claim an indifference to monetary gain; they would be reluctant to be cast as Shylocks who exploited every shift in demand. Whether an open attempt to charge theatergoers as much as the market will bear would lead to the alienation of the audience, who might then give up Broadway, is uncertain. Certainly most producers of most products, including the theater, prefer to justify any price rise on the basis of increased costs. To counter unfavorable publicity that the solution might bring, it might be necessary to launch a publicity campaign designed to point out the advantages to the public—including faster payment to investors, which in turn could lead to the launching of more shows.

In any case, the laws preventing a flexible ticket price policy should be repealed. There is no justification for legislation aimed at scalping; the laws' main effects are harmful. With more freedom in pricing, tickets would cost both more and less than they do now, the theater would be more profitable, and playgoers would benefit from greater choice of productions, shorter waits for seats, and the increased possibility of finding less ex-pensive seats for Broadway shows.

Off-Broadway

Off-Broadway operations seem to be slumping. Although the number of performances may be staying the same, the number of productions appears to have reached a peak. The consequent advancement in average length of run suggests that production costs in the little theaters may be on the upswing. Nevertheless, the proliferation of small houses proves that the theater in New York is far from dying.

Besides exhibiting esoteric and older dramas, off-Broadway serves as a vehicle for presenting the talents of new actors, directors, and authors. Mostly financed by wealthy relatives and friends, the small theaters may depend strongly on good times for continued success, and any serious drop in incomes and the stock market might lead to a drying up of backers' funds. The little houses also require for their existence actors, directors, authors, stagehands, box office personnel, and others who are willing to work for considerably less than their counterparts on Broadway. If the theatrical unions apply too much pressure on the managers of these small enterprises, off-Broadway may die.

Off-Broadway, like Broadway, utilizes the clumsy device of "two-fers" to reduce prices below list. Any change in the law which would permit managers to adapt tariffs to changes in demand would be desirable. However, the need in the small theaters is considerably less than uptown, since few downtown shows ever experience the heady sensation of having their seats scalped.

The road

The road plays the puppet to Broadway. The future of touring companies hinges on the future of the New York theater, and any diminution of openings along Broadway will eventually result in fewer shows on tour. The road has declined in recent years, primarily from the reduced availability of suitable scripts. As the number of new Broadway productions has waned, so has the touring business. Moreover, in the last few seasons, tryout cities have seen less activity because the practice of testing new shows through New York previews has been growing steadily. Improvements in transportation such as the jet plane have smoothed the way for theater lovers to splurge on Broadway. No longer must the out-of-town playgoer wait for stale crumbs to be cast in his direction. He can feast directly on the smorgasbord of Broadway. With continued progress in transportation, more and more devotees of drama will spurn the supposedly second-rate touring company for the best there is—Broadway.

The prospects of the road, in consequence, are grim. Unless the slippage in Broadway openings can be halted, future offerings on the road will be meager. To the extent that the proposals suggested above for revitalizing the New York theater are instituted and are successful, the road will gain. In addition, a more positive approach to theater in many communities could make much difference; the elimination of onerous local taxation, for example, would encourage Broadway impresarios to send their productions on tour. In the end, though, the road is probably dying, and while not likely to expire in the next decade, may easily be extinct by the twenty-first century.

Summer theater

Multiform and multifold, summer theaters teem like weeds for a season and then are gone. Spreading from the East, they seem destined to cover the face of the land. From the accomplished Stratford Shakespeare Festival to the boisterous Pittsburgh Light Opera to the gawky barn theater, summer stock is many things to many people.

In spite of the fact that the profitable musical tent theater has become big business, most operations remain small. Even though the practice of using packages will no doubt continue to grow, resident companies will endure. Cursed with incompetent managements, scorned by critics, and abhorred by performers, the little stages thrive by offering a simple and cheap product. Their salvation has lain in their diversity and anonymity, which has staved off attempts by most theatrical unions to organize their operations. To make their scenery, to work in the box office, and to maintain their theater, apprentices (almost all of whom desire an affiliation with Actors' Equity) are necessary. The reward for being an apprentice is the right to join Equity after participating in a minimum number of performances and seasons. Because of the dependence of these houses on the apprentice system, only Equity of all theatrical unions polices the industry. As long as Equity is free to strangle the summer theater by abolishing the apprentice system or by demanding exorbitant wages and working conditions, the continued prosperity of the "straw-hat trail" will lie with the performers' union.

As in most small enterprises, success depends primarily on the skill of the manager and secondarily on the location of the business. Theaters near large centers of population or located in resort areas have a better chance of prospering than others. A restaurant operated in conjunction with the house can be a lucrative investment and usually enhances the attractiveness of the operation.

Communities desiring to promote theater should look to their laws, many of which discriminate against the live stage. In one county, for example, where only one legitimate theater exists, taxes are placed on live performances from which motion pictures are exempt. In addition, many communities prohibit acting on Sunday, even though, with matinees usually unprofitable, summer theaters need to work seven days a week to make ends meet.

Two offsetting trends will probably continue to influence the growth of summer stock: the dispersion of the system into new areas of the country, and the improvement of roads, which will diminish the number of houses and upgrade the remainder. As summer stock spreads to parts of the Middle West, South, and Far West, more companies will come into existence. With improved transportation, theatergoers can travel farther to visit the theater; consequently, in the more densely settled parts of the country, a consolidation of summer theaters can be expected.

Winter stock and repertory companies

Permanent resident companies emphasize the intellect in their offerings. Nevertheless, since World War II, the number of cities housing such companies has multiplied. The increase is due to two factors: the audience required to break even is so much smaller than Broadway audiences, and the companies operate generally in a non-profit atmosphere which frees them from most taxes. As an appreciation of culture and its benefits grows, private and public encouragement will lead to more such companies. At the same time, as more and more people are exposed to Shaw, Miller, and Shakespeare in their literature courses, interest—and consequently patronage—will mount.

But do these companies supplement or compete with other local theater? That the development of the Arena Stage in Washington, for example, has not been matched by any reduction in patronage at the nearby National Theater, and that the birth of the New York Repertory Theater of Lincoln Center has also left attendance unaffected on Broadway indicates that these companies carved out their own audience. Yet, the Repertory Theater of Lincoln Center did Arthur Miller's *After the Fall* during the first season, a play that Broadway impresarios would have been eager to present. We can conclude, therefore, that most permanent resident companies outside New York do not compete with visiting road shows, but that New York repertory companies did in fact compete for scripts and certainly for the time and energy of veteran performers and directors. Broadway has been limited only by the supply of good scripts; therefore, the Lincoln Center company, to the extent that it produces new plays, reduces the number of productions on Broadway. If the new company continues to emphasize new plays—two out of three productions in the first season were world premieres—the achievement of the Lincoln Center group will be minor: a "new" form of production, the repertory system, will be substituted for the single production. Encouragingly, the new directors of the Lincoln Center company have apparently changed that orientation and no longer compete with Broadway.

Critics, actors, and directors like to point to repertory as a superior form of theater. They stress that a permanent repertory company learns to act together, achieves its own style, and is more stimulating for the performers. Certainly all these things are true, yet unsubsidized repertory companies have been notably unsuccessful. Part of the difficulty has been that since the show changes every night such companies must sell the public on the organization itself rather than on a particular show. Since the public has at best only an academic interest in the organization, but has a desire to see particular shows, repertory companies have never been popular. A company with a developed style and a limited group of actors is also limited in its repertoire, and this is one of the major drawbacks of repertory companies. For example, the Comédie Française, which does magnificent productions of Molière, is much less successful with Racine.

Nevertheless, this is not to gainsay the value to the American theater of an organization which will develop a unique native acting form and which will perpetuate the classics. To the extent that it concentrates on plays that would be done on Broadway, however, it adds little to the New York theater.

Pay television—help or harm?

If pay television becomes a reality in the next decade, it may have considerable effect on the world of live drama. Broadway productions brought instantaneously to millions at one dollar per set could turn the Broadway legitimate theater into a gold mine. Such a development, however, might easily kill the budding permanent companies, eliminate touring shows, and decimate summer theater. But these results are unlikely; what is good theater is not necessarily good television and vice versa. Pay television is most likely to lead to productions of scripts specifically for the television audience. The effect on Broadway may be catastrophic. First, a new demand for the scarce talented playwright will have been added, a demand which could diminish the number of scripts being written for the stage. Second, good drama will be available on television for a dollar or so, reducing the need for playgoers to spend fifteen dollars to see a show. In the end, the live spoken drama will survive, but it may do so on a reduced scale.

Taxes and subsidies

In the previous chapter, taxes and subsidies were discussed in detail. It is sufficient to note here only that the elimination of the federal excise tax of 10 per cent on admissions (motion pictures and the theater) will eventually be passed on in higher income to playwrights, directors, and stars and lead to only a small increase in Broadway output. The removal of the tax may, however, benefit summer stock theaters most. More barn theaters will spring up under the impetus of higher profitability. Permanent resident companies, such as the Lincoln Center, the Arena, the Alley, and so forth, will be unaffected by the change, since they have normally been exempt from taxation.

Although the commercial theater could be subsidized, the possibilities seem remote. Any government cash aid (not tax relief) to the stage will probably be channeled through the permanent resident companies as it already has been. The Lincoln Center, for example, is receiving help from both the city and the state. If a sufficient number of such theaters were generated, the rewards from writing plays of limited appeal, and thus unsuitable for Broadway, might induce writers to try such works. As we saw, many authors feel constrained by the limitations of writing for a large audience. If a nationwide market for scripts of more limited appeal were developed, more new plays might be created.

Conclusion

When the twenty-first century considers the achievements of the mid-twentieth-century American stage, it will weigh our playwrights. Great acting disappears before the very eyes of the audience; masterful direction lasts only as long as the production; but the written words live on. The importance of the actor and the director should not be disparaged, however, for no play can be produced without performers. Their abilities breathe life into a script. A fine production needs, as well, direction to define and distill the meaning of the dramatist. Yet the roles of both the actor and the director are interpretative: they are limited by the play.

Great playwrights are born, not made. Consequently, there seems little that can be done to stimulate masterpieces. But reduced costs on Broadway or a large market outside New York might lead to the creation of more intimate plays which, while excellent, might have limited appeal. Such theater is not to be scorned and in the end may produce great works.

In any case, the theater will be limited by a shortage of talent. It will always be dwarfed by television and motion pictures. Because of its handicraft nature, costs will always be higher and results more uncertain than in the other media. To expect the theater to compete for the affection of the general public is simply irrational, but to believe in the continued flourishing of the essence of Dionysus is simply—rational.

Appendixes

A | Tables relating to Broadway productions

Table A–1 Three-year moving average of total productions, 1919/20 to 1964/65

Season	Total productions	New straight shows	New musicals
1919/20	148	99	42
21	163	112	44
22	173	120	43
23	185	132	40
24	196	139	43
1924/25	223	157	45
26	249	176	48
27	261	183	50
28	251	178	48
29	241	170	44
1929/30	215	115	36
31	209	147	30
32	189	133	28
33	177	131	23
34	158	124	20
1934/35	145	118	16
36	134	108	15
37	121	95	14
38	109	81	15
39	100	71	17
1939/40	86	60	17
41	81	56	16
42	77	51	16
43	87	55	18
44	90	56	19
1944/45	88	56	18
46	82	53	16
47	77	47	14
48	75	45	15
49	68	38	16
1949/50	69	39	16
51	70	39	13
52	69	41	11
53	62	40	9
54	57	37	11
1954/55	58	37	10
56	59	35	10
57	58	36	10
58	58	37	11
59	57	37	13
1959/60	54	36	14
61	53	35	16
62	51	34	14
63	57	37	17
64	58	38	14
1964/65	66	38	16

Source: Variety, June 26, 1966, p. 64.

Table A-2 Number of shows playing during an average week in February, 1926/27 to 1965/66

Season	Total shows	Straight shows	Musicals
1926/27	46.8	26.8	17.2
28	44.8	26.8	16.2
29	37.0	22.0	12.8
1929/30	39.5	28.8	8.5
31	25.5	21.2	4.2
32	27.5	21.0	3.5
33	22.8	17.5	3.5
34	18.2	13.2	2.0
1934/35	19.2	15.2	2.0
36	24.8	19.8	2.0
37	20.2	16.2	3.0
38	23.2	19.2	4.0
39	24.0	16.2	4.5
1939/40	17.0	13.0	2.0
41	22.8	15.0	4.0
42	19.8	13.8	5.0
43	22.2	15.2	4.0
44	26.5	17.5	7.0
1944/45	28.8	17.2	9.5
46	24.8	13.8	11.0
47	22.5	14.0	7.5
48	18.0	10.0	7.0
49	24.0	14.2	5.8
1949/50	26.0	15.2	7.8
51	23.0	14.0	8.0
52	21.2	13.2	5.0
53	21.8	14.8	4.0
54	22.5	16.5	3.0
1954/55	23.8	13.8	6.0
56	25.2	19.2	4.0
57	21.0	14.0	6.0
58	22.5	13.5	7.0
59	25.8	16.8	7.0
1959/60	23.0	13.0	11.0
61	27.0	15.0	12.0
62	30.0	18.0	12.0
1962/63	22.0	13.0	9.0
64	23.0	13.5	9.5
65	22.5	11.0	11.5
66	24.3	15.5	8.8

Source: Variety, February issues, 1927–66.
Note: The figures are the sum of the number playing during each of four weeks divided by four.

Table A–3 Estimated average February weekly attendance, 1926/27 to 1965/66 (thousands)

Season	Total of straight shows and musicals	Straight shows	Musicals
1926/27	270.2	128.8	141.4
28	285.8	139.9	145.9
29	253.7	133.7	120.0
1929/30	233.9	155.1	78.8
31	151.0	122.1	28.9
32	144.6	117.2	27.4
33	127.7	97.6	30.1
34	87.2	69.8	18.4
1934/35	103.5	83.1	20.4
36	120.3	105.4	14.9
37	131.2	108.1	23.1
38	140.0	103.9	36.1
39	122.1	81.2	40.9
1939/40	103.7	82.9	20.8
41	127.5	89.1	38.4
42	110.9	66.5	44.4
43	136.5	93.0	43.5
44	201.3	123.1	78.2
1944/45	200.8	103.9	96.9
46	187.4	88.3	99.1
47	162.6	90.9	71.7
48	138.9	57.1	81.8
49	158.1	103.1	55.0
1949/50	165.3	83.5	81.8
51	171.5	94.0	77.5
52	176.3	91.8	84.5
53	118.3	66.7	51.6
54	170.3	108.5	61.8
1954/55	181.8	102.3	79.5
56	185.8	130.1	55.7
57	167.8	90.4	77.4
58	167.5	90.9	76.6
59	178.0	102.0	76.0
1959/60	183.6	77.5	106.1
61	181.4	70.0	111.4
62	175.1	77.2	97.9
63	153.9	68.4	85.5
64	148.2	70.9	77.3
1964/65	151.8	51.2	100.6
66	195.2	102.9	92.3

Note: See p. 170 in Appendix D for computation.

Table A–4 Box office receipts, four weeks in February, 1924/25 to 1965/66 (1966 $ thousands)

Season	Motion pictures	Total theater box office receipts	Straight shows	Musicals
1924/25	$1,458	$ n.a.	$ n.a.	$ n.a.
26	1,721	n.a.	n.a.	n.a.
27	2,697	5,643	2,126	3,029
28	3,502	6,328	2,377	3,741
29	3,604	5,535	2,126	3,044
1929/30	3,895	5,275	2,569	2,258
31	4,245	4,124	2,285	799
32	3,350	3,643	2,130	697
33	2,873	2,751	1,846	687
34	3,343	2,379	1,355	364
1934/35	2,906	2,566	1,654	459
36	n.a.	3,088	1,968	356
37	n.a.	2,834	1,982	547
38	n.a.	2,672	1,820	852
39	n.a.	3,169	1,504	978
1939/40	3,559	2,318	1,407	525
41	n.a.	2,965	1,566	865
42	n.a.	2,367	1,081	963
43	n.a.	2,699	1,426	835
44	n.a.	3,880	1,880	1,631
1944/45	n.a.	4,585	1,781	2,194
46	n.a.	3,685	1,528	2,158
47	n.a.	3,093	1,510	1,394
48	n.a.	2,525	872	1,507
49	n.a.	3,370	1,669	1,169
1949/50	n.a.	3,526	1,658	1,543
51	n.a.	3,168	1,317	1,707
52	n.a.	3,228	1,538	1,077
53	n.a.	2,630	1,312	949
54	n.a.	3,118	1,818	661
1954/55	n.a.	3,212	1,309	1,050
56	n.a.	3,519	2,246	804
57	n.a.	3,344	1,660	1,445
58	n.a.	3,795	1,649	1,716
59	n.a.	4,027	2,004	1,637
1959/60	n.a.	4,171	1,364	2,514
61	n.a.	4,413	1,540	2,629
62	n.a.	4,181	1,625	2,257
63	n.a.	4,289	1,652	2,487
64	n.a.	3,217	1,379	1,839
1964/65	n.a.	3,479	978	2,416
66	n.a.	4,019	1,860	2,159

Note: The figures are adjusted for changes in the price level as expressed in the Consumer Price Index.
n.a. Not available.
Source: Variety, February issues, 1927–66.

Table A–5 Top and average ticket prices, 1926/27 to 1965/66 (1966 dollars)

Season	Top straight shows[a]	Top musicals[a]	Average[b] straight show prices	Average[b] musical prices
1926/27	$6.60	$8.57	$n.a.	$n.a.
28	6.73	10.17	n.a.	n.a.
29	6.36	10.15	n.a.	n.a.
1929/30	6.63	11.46	n.a.	n.a.
31	7.48	11.06	n.a.	n.a.
32	7.27	10.19	n.a.	n.a.
33	7.56	9.13	n.a.	n.a.
34	7.76	7.93	n.a.	n.a.
1934/35	7.96	9.02	n.a.	n.a.
36	7.47	9.58	n.a.	n.a.
37	7.33	9.46	n.a.	n.a.
38	7.01	9.43	n.a.	n.a.
39	7.41	9.56	n.a.	n.a.
1939/40	6.79	10.09	n.a.	n.a.
41	7.03	9.02	n.a.	n.a.
42	6.51	8.68	n.a.	n.a.
43	6.13	7.68	n.a.	n.a.
44	6.14	8.34	n.a.	n.a.
1944/45	6.86	9.05	n.a.	n.a.
46	6.92	8.71	n.a.	n.a.
47	6.65	7.77	n.a.	n.a.
48	6.12	7.37	n.a.	n.a.
49	6.48	8.50	n.a.	n.a.
1949/50	6.72	8.02	4.70	5.76
51	5.79	7.34	4.99	6.20
52	6.51	8.67	4.79	5.90
53	6.25	8.38	4.51	6.19
54	6.89	8.61	4.63	6.09
1954/55	7.05	8.21	4.61	6.34
56	6.95	8.16	4.87	6.81
57	7.51	8.99	5.05	7.43
58	7.67	9.05	5.33	6.89
59	7.75	9.38	5.55	7.09
1959/60	7.84	9.66	5.82	7.53
61	7.59	9.78	5.69	7.39
62	7.97	9.85	6.09	7.12
63	7.88	9.15	5.20	6.55
64	7.77	9.51	6.01	7.36
1964/65	7.65	9.94	5.87	7.62
66	7.23	9.18	5.46	7.07

a. Average of the highest-priced seats for each for four weeks in February.
b. Capacity gross divided by total seats available divided by eight performances and averaged for straight shows opening September through December and for all openings of musicals.
n.a. Not available.
Source: Variety, various issues, 1927–66.

Table A–6 Average run for shows opening during season, 1927/28 to 1961/
62

Season	Musicals	Plays	Three-year moving average	
			Musicals	Plays
1927/28	143.5	68.8		
29	124.8	75.4	114.7	70.1
30	75.7	67.0	93.4	66.9
1930/31	79.7	58.4	74.5	56.5
32	68.1	44.1	96.3	51.1
33	141.1	50.8	90.2	54.4
34	61.3	68.3	106.6	60.5
35	117.6	62.6	112.1	67.2
1935/36	157.6	70.8	130.9	69.2
37	117.6	74.4	169.6	67.9
38	236.1	58.5	155.1	67.5
39	111.7	69.5	166.1	68.2
40	150.4	76.6	156.4	88.9
1940/41	208.0	120.5	192.1	95.9
42	218.0	90.6	230.4	111.7
43	265.2	123.9	232.0	97.2
44	212.8	77.1	214.4	100.6
45	165.3	101.0	200.8	98.1
1945/46	224.3	116.1	158.2	98.3
47	85.1	77.7	163.3	101.7
48	180.5	111.3	228.8	97.5
49	420.9	103.6	268.3	111.4
50	203.5	119.4	282.4	115.6
1950/51	222.8	93.8	190.2	95.4
52	114.3	72.9	214.5	97.1
53	276.4	124.5	260.3	116.4
54	360.3	150.7	302.8	142.1
55	271.6	151.1	482.0	152.4
1955/56	814.0	155.4	451.8	135.7
57	269.9	106.7	424.1	132.4
58	188.4	135.3	252.0	130.4
59	297.9	149.4	289.3	128.8
60	381.7	101.8	336.9	149.1
1960/61	331.0	196.0	349.6	142.3
62	336.0	129.1		

Sources: Computed from *Best Plays* volumes and *Variety*, various issues, 1927–61.
The total length of run for each play that opened during a season was computed, and
then all were averaged.

Table A–7 Total Broadway shows and performances playing during season, 1927/28 to 1963/64

Season	Number of shows playing	Performances		
		Total	Plays	Musicals
1927/28	242	17,055	10,089	5,171
29	231	17,529	9,872	5,356
30	233	16,363	11,252	3,132
1930/31	188	12,639	8,778	2,190
32	175	8,901	6,054	1,267
33	124	8,257	4,783	2,347
34	149	8,130	5,911	1,233
35	155	9,141	6,871	2,347
1935/36	119	8,649	7,155	1,035
37	121	8,172	6,722	954
38	111	8,128	6,551	1,151
39	100	8,309	5,465	1,529
40	96	7,916	5,041	1,041
1940/41	81	7,704	5,085	1,717
42	86	7,240	4,561	1,748
43	93	9,707	5,451	2,361
44	96	8,889	4,957	3,057
45	96	11,666	6,922	3,238
1945/46	99	11,328	6,311	4,612
47	103	11,235	6,960	3,096
48	89	10,254	6,003	2,984
49	89	9,673	5,592	2,253
50	69	8,983	5,056	2,825
1950/51	92	8,446	4,975	2,808
52	89	8,614	4,589	3,257
53	65	7,571	4,391	2,655
54	66	8,485	5,098	2,317
55	72	8,917	5,503	2,860
1955/56	70	9,390	6,439	2,781
57	78	8,973	5,736	2,828
58	85	8,247	4,782	3,320
59	73	8,943	6,222	2,414
60	76	9,214	4,606	3,805
1960/61	70	9,445	4,493	4,140
62	73	9,055	4,262	4,587
63	71	8,954	4,466	4,007
64	82	7,975	4,494	3,368

Note: "Number of shows playing" is total number of openings plus holdovers. "Total performances" is total number of performances of holdovers and openings during season. Data are computed from season data compiled by the author from the *Best Plays* volumes and *Variety*. They exclude City Center productions, off-Broadway productions, and visiting limited-run companies such as the Comédie Française.

Table A–8   Theaters and performances per theater, 1928/29 to 1944/45

Season	Theaters	Performances per theater	Season	Theater	Performances per theater
1928/29	66–80[a]	221–267[a]	1945/46	36	315
30			47	35	321
			48	35	293
1930/31	66	192	49	31	312
32	64	139	50	30	299
33	59	140			
34	56	145	1950/51	31	272
35	56	163	52	30	296
			53	33	232
1935/36	53	163	54	33	257
37	50	163	55	31	288
38	48	169			
39	47	177	1955/56	30	313
40	43	184	57	31	289
			58	32	257
1940/41	43	179	59	31	288
42	43	168	60	33	279
43	41	237			
44	39	228	1960/61	33[b]	287
45	36	324	62	n.a.	n.a.
			63	n.a.	n.a.
			64	36[c]	223

a. The number of theaters is unknown; however, it could not be smaller than 66. The New York *Evening World*, January 15, 1929, put the number at 80, which was the highest estimate the author found.

b. The figures were computed by Robert A. Baron in his study of Broadway for the League of New York Theatres.

c. Number of theaters listed in *Variety* for June 17, 1964, p. 59.

Sources: The number of theaters is taken from Wharton, *Crisis in the Free World Theatre.* The listing of theaters is by year in Wharton's report. It is assumed that the "66 theaters" in the listing for 1931 is applicable to the 1930/31 season. The total number of performances is taken from Table A-7.

Table A–9 Average total costs of major items for plays opening during selected seasons (1966 dollars)

	1927/28 1928/29	1939/40 1940/41 1941/42	1949/50 1950/51	1954/55 1955/56	1960/61
Average weeks run[a]	8.66	11.75	13.02	18.98	19.00
Box office receipts	$162,349	$302,104	$292,338	$490,785	$554,230
Company income	91,683	214,884	197,891	350,864	409,089
Theater income	70,666	87,220	94,447	139,921	145,141
Total costs	127,528	234,659	247,134	348,153	485,152
Playwrights	12,748	24,487	27,069	41,149	44,346
Crew	7,195	n.a.	17,305	26,268	29,957
Directors	3,047	n.a.	10,160	11,394	16,059
Scenery designers	2,089	4,415	4,398	4,987	6,541
Cast salaries	51,573	n.a.	76,697	107,382	145,304
Managers	1,637[b]	3,102[b]	12,488	18,771	23,093
Advertising	19,861	n.a.	28,047	36,090	71,268
Scenery	10,414	n.a.	19,860	16,506	25,243
Props	4,945	n.a.	2,836	2,499	5,213
Costumes	3,312	n.a.	7,980	5,557	10,247
Electrical and sound	3,397	n.a.	3,406	4,620	5,661
Total itemized costs	115,655	n.a.	203,867	271,334	382,226
Remainder	16,533	n.a.	41,839	77,459	102,256

a. Total number of performances by all shows opening in a season divided by the number of such shows.

b. Only stage and company managers; other years include general managers as well.

Note: Computed by adding total production costs to the product of weeks run and operating costs. See Tables III-2 and III-3 for the data and for the reason the sums of the items do not equal the totals.

n.a. Not available.

B | Sources and biases of the cost data

The Theatre Guild data,[1] especially for the early period of the twenties, are probably unrepresentative, at least in part. Some overhead and administrative costs appear to have absorbed into the general administration of the Guild. In the financial statements, no mention is made of, nor expense listed for, the stage manager, general manager, or office. For the same period, Bernheim has entries for these items.[2] The Theatre Guild papers, however, list Board of Managers' royalties, which undoubtedly cover these expenses.

The plays organized by the Theatre Guild during this period were more successful than the average; of the six presented, none operated at a deficit and most showed a substantial profit. On the other hand, over half of the nine Bernheim productions operated at a loss. While the box office grosses of the Bernheim sample averaged less than those of the more successful Guild plays, the difference was within expected normal sampling variation. And the grosses from both sources do not differ significantly from the average gross of all Broadway plays during the first week of February, 1928.[3] While the average gross reported in *The Business of the Theatre* is lower than this figure, the mean of the Theatre Guild box office receipts is higher.

This suggests that the figures in Bernheim are biased downward. Still, we cannot be sure, since it is reasonable to assume that the mean box office gross for a week in February—one of the best theater months—is higher than the average for the whole year. Bernheim neglects to mention the date of his survey; the chances are, however, that it was taken during a poorer theater month. Nevertheless, the survey data appear to be low; the Theatre Guild figures definitely are too high; the mean gross of all fifteen, therefore, may be just about right.

Other differences appear between the two sources: the greater profitability of Guild productions naturally produced higher royalty payments to authors; the house took a smaller share of the gross of Theatre Guild shows than of the survey plays. Better theater terms may be attributable partly to the Theatre Guild's reputation for successful shows. But with these exceptions the data from the two sources appear to be reasonably comparable. Average production costs were almost exactly the same, $17,569 (Bernheim) and $17,471. Total operating costs were also remarkably similar, $5,618 (Bernheim) and $6,009, especially considering the large difference in weekly gross, $8,314 (Bernheim) and $12,368.

1. Data collected from the Yale University Library collection of Theatre Guild papers.
2. Bernheim, *The Business of the Theatre,* pp. 176–180.
3. Computed from grosses reported in four issues of *Variety,* February 8, 15, 22, and 29, 1928.

Just what time period the data presented in *The Business of the Theatre* represent is unclear. The gross is apparently an average of weekly grosses from the premiere to the date of the survey, a period that varies from four weeks to twenty-two. Whether the figures on costs are an average of the expenses for the run up to the time of the survey, represent a "typical" week, or stand for the week of the survey is uncertain.

The Theatre Guild records show the total box office income, the total operating expenses, and each individual item's cost for the entire season. To get weekly figures the costs and income were divided by the number of weeks of operation. Averages from the more recent seasons represent, as often as possible, the mean for the third, fourth, and fifth weeks of operation. When the show closed before the fifth full week, the figures are an average of the last three full weeks. If the show ran for less than three weeks, the last two full weeks were averaged; for a run of less than two weeks, the total for the one full week was taken. Shows shuttering within a week were disregarded.

In general, both the take at the box office and the cost of operation decline over time. The average for a whole season will be less than the average for the third, fourth, and fifth weeks alone. As a consequence, the box office figures and those based on the gross—such as the share of the theater, stars, and authors—are undoubtedly lower for the 1927/28 and 1928/29 seasons than they would be if it had been possible to follow the procedure used in later seasons.

Two offsetting biases, then, affect operating costs. Because Theatre Guild shows were more successful than the norm, the mean box office income and the mean total costs are probably higher than the population parameter; on the other hand, since the averages represent either a whole season or a run of more than five weeks, they are undoubtedly lower than they would be for the third, fourth, and fifth weeks. Thus the figures shown may be close to those desired.

To a lesser extent, some of the same biases exist for the 1940/41 and 1941/42 seasons and for the 1949/50 and 1950/51 seasons. The size of the samples, eight and eleven, is rather small, especially for the earlier period. The figures come from three producing organizations, all of which are more successful than the average. While flops are included in the sample they are probably underrepresented. Nevertheless, the average gross of the sample was $11,672, well within expected sampling variation of the mean gross ($11,256) of straight shows in February of 1940, 1941, and 1942. Certainly, whatever bias may arise from the sources is not large enough to raise the average gross significantly.

A priori, there seems little reason to believe that costs of successful producers would differ significantly from those of unsuccessful or new producers. While novice impresarios, being unfamiliar with short cuts, may spend more for some items than established entrepreneurs would, they may also have a more difficult time raising capital and consequently operate on a stricter budget. These two tendencies may offset each other; total production costs are probably affected only slightly by the experience or inexperience of the entrepreneur; the expense of particular items in the total, however, may be influenced by the producer's knowledge.

For the 1939/40 and 1940/41 seasons, production cost data were poor or unavailable. It was possible to obtain information only on payment to scenery designers and total production expenses.

Estimates of operating costs for the 1939/40, 1940/41, and 1941/42 seasons do appear to be biased. In all eight shows of the sample, stars received a share of the box office ranging from 7.5 per cent to 20 per cent of the gross. Fragmentary data from the early fifties indicate that a leading actor secured a share of the box office in only about half the productions.[4] It therefore seems unlikely that major performers received a percentage of the gross in all plays of the late thirties and early forties while a decade later a substantial number did not; it is more probable that the sample is biased.

While the major effect of this bias is to inflate the salaries of actors, it will also—if the stars have the drawing power credited to them by the management—swell box office receipts. A look at Charts III-1 and III-4 suggests that actors' salaries are overestimated in 1939/40, 1940/41, and 1941/42, that operating costs in general have been affected, and that box office gross does seem a little high when compared to other seasons. We can conclude that there is probably little bias in the sample data on total production costs for the periods around 1940 and around 1950, but that the sample operating costs and the sample grosses are somewhat exaggerated for the seasons just before World War II.

The most reliable figures are from the 1954/55 and 1955/56 seasons and from the 1960/61 season. The data from the latter season included figures from new producers as well as established ones, and the data from the mid-fifties also seem reasonably unbiased. Most of the information on the latter period comes from the records that Hobe Morrison, drama editor of *Variety*, turned over to the New York Public Library; Morrison had received the statements from backers. A bias, either upward or downward, may come from the self selection involved in voluntarily sending *Variety* financial statements. It may be that only investors in successful plays wish to publicize these statements; on the other hand, it may be that the backers of the most profitable shows prefer to keep their good fortune to themselves. But failures and successes are both included in the sample. Thus it is impossible to tell whether or not the Public Library data can be considered a random sample of the 1954/55 and 1955/56 seasons.

Between September 1, 1960, and June 1, 1961, twenty-nine straight shows opened on Broadway. Robert A. Baron, in his study for the League of New York Theatres, presents data on total production costs for twenty-five of these plays. The average production cost for the twenty-five shows was $92,158; the mean cost in the sample of fifteen which remained in the League files at the time of this study was $102,063. The difference is not significant. However, the average outlay on the productions whose records had been recalled from the files of the League of New York Theatres by their producers was $77,076. While the difference can still be attributed to chance because of the large variation in costs from show to show, it suggests that the average of the figures on costs in the sample remaining in the League's files is higher than the true average for all the shows of the season.

It should also be noted that the mean length of run during the season of

4. The Playwrights' Company records and the Kermit Bloomgarden records indicate that for three of five plays given during 1949/50 and 1950/51 and for four of seven plays given during the 1954/55 and 1955/56 seasons, stars received some percentage of the gross.

Table B–1   Comparison of Baron's data with fifteen-play sample

	Baron's data		Fifteen plays		Percentage of Baron's mean costs
	Mean costs	Size of sample	Mean costs	Size of sample	
Total production costs	$92,158	25	$102,063	15	111
Scenery (building and painting)	20,560	23	24,119	13	117
Directors' fees	4,075	23	4,381	14	108
Set designers' fees	3,235	22	4,060	13	126

Source: Data in the files of the League of New York Theatres, which also contained an unpublished, untitled study by Robert A. Baron.

shows included in the sample was 138 performances, while the average for those recalled was only 58 performances and, for those on which Baron had no data, 4. It appears, therefore, that the less successful productions are underrepresented here as well as in earlier years. No correlation can be found, though, between length of run and average production costs; some of the most expensive shows are failures, while some low-budget productions become great successes. Table B-1 above presents averages of a few items from Baron's sample and from the sample of fifteen; the size of the sample is given in each case.

The sample of approximately fifteen shows exhibits an average figure which is roughly 11 per cent higher than Baron's larger sample. His data, though, are still only a sample of the population; the universe is an infinite number of shows produced under the identical conditions existing during the 1960/61 season.

In order to measure real changes in operating and production expenses, the population must be defined as including all plays which might have been produced under the same circumstances. For if the population consists of only the plays actually produced, a change in the type of production might lead to a rise in expenditures while underlying cost conditions remained unchanged. For example, one season might see an increase in the number of costume plays that would raise average production costs above previous years. But the outlays necessary to launch shows of the type exhibited the year before would be the same. Therefore, we must consider the universe to be all shows that could be produced under identical conditions.

From Baron's data, we can estimate that the probability is less than 5 per cent that the true population mean lies outside the $78,500 to $105,816 range. The detailed sample data are for fifteen plays. Can we consider these to be a random selection of productions? If the fifteen shows were picked at random from Baron's data there would be less than a 5 per cent probability of the mean's differing from Baron's by as much as it does. It thus appears that the fifteen plays we have to work with are probably *not* a random sample of the twenty-five. We must therefore conclude that the production figures for the sample of fifteen shows are too high; the best guess is that they are inflated by about 11 per cent. It is possible that Baron's sample of twenty-five is biased by the exclusion of four shows that folded quickly. The direction in which this affects our estimates, however, is uncertain. The data in the text have been adjusted downward by 11 per cent except where Baron gave estimates for all twenty-five.

C | The audience survey: how it was conducted and possible biases

The survey

In April of 1962, a survey was conducted by the author in seven theaters for a total of eighteen performances. The shows included in the sample were designed to be a representative sample of Broadway productions. Three musicals and four straight shows were selected. Two of the straight shows were comedies. One of these, *A Thousand Clowns,* had just opened and been widely acclaimed; another, *A Shot in the Dark,* had been running for about six months. *Gideon,* one of the straight shows, was on cut-rate tickets—"two-fers"— while *A Man for All Seasons* was universally acclaimed and a sellout. One of the musicals was a very, very long run—*My Fair Lady. How to Succeed in Business Without Really Trying* was the biggest success of the season. The third and final musical *Milk and Honey,* was chosen to represent the average good musical.

Two trial surveys were made initially. On Tuesday, April 10, 1962, questionnaires were distributed at the performance of *A Shot in the Dark.* Included with each questionnaire were a business reply envelope and instructions to mail the questionnaire back to the author. Two days later a somewhat different approach was used. Questionnaires were again distributed; the instructions this time, however, were to drop the completed questionnaires in boxes that were placed around the theater near exits. As was expected, the proportion of response was considerably better when people were asked to fill out the questionnaires immediately and drop them into boxes. In the trial run, 50 per cent of the audience was represented in the responses to the questionnaire when they were collected by boxes, while 32 per cent of the audience was represented when they were collected by mail. The instructions for filling out the questionnaires requested that only one member of the family respond.

Question seven in the questionnaire asked the cost of the evening's entertainment and the number of individuals covered by this amount. Each response was weighted by the number of people indicated in question seven. Anyone who checked that he was a guest was excluded. Dividing this sum by the number of people in the audience, an estimate of the proportion of people who responded was computed.

While over 50 per cent of the audience was represented in the test run with boxes for the questionnaires, the response in subsequent runs was considerably less. Thirty-one per cent of the audience was represented in the straight-shows survey, and only 17 per cent of the audience at musicals responded. There was considerable variation from performance to performance for a given show, but there was even more variation between shows. There

Audience questionnaire

Please check or fill in the blank:

1. Male ___ Female ___ Married ___ Single ___

2. In what age group do you belong?
   Under 18 ___
   18 to 25 ___
   26 to 35 ___
   36 to 45 ___
   46 to 60 ___
   Over 60 ___

3. Are you a guest? Yes ___ No ___

4. How much did you pay for each ticket? ___ per ticket.
   (a) How many tickets did you buy at this price? ___
   (b) Where did you buy your tickets:
   Box Office ___   Ticket Agent ___
   By Mail ___   Hotel ___
   Theatre Party ___ Other ___
   (c) What is the price printed on your ticket? ___

5. Are you on an expense account? Yes ___ No ___

6. Did you go to a restaurant before the show? Yes ___ No ___

7. Approximately how much do you expect this evening's entertainment to cost? (including the price of the tickets, dinner out, drinks, transportation, parking, baby-sitting, etc.?) ___

   How many individuals (including yourself) does this cover? ___

8. Do you live in New York City or within commuting distance? Yes ___ No ___

9. If yes, how long will it take you to go home tonight? ___

10. If no, why did you come to New York? Business ___ Both ___ Pleasure ___ Other ___

11. How did you happen to pick this show?
    Word of mouth ___
    Advertising: TV ___ Radio ___ Newspaper ___ Other ___
    Critics: Newspaper ___ Magazine ___

12. What curtain time would you prefer?
    7:30 . . . . ___
    8:00 . . . . ___
    8:30 or 8:40 . . . ___
    9:00 . . . . ___

13. When did you see your last Broadway show?
    Within the last week ___
    1 to 2 weeks ago ___
    2 to 4 weeks ago ___
    1 to 2 months ago ___
    2 to 4 months ago ___
    4 to 8 months ago ___
    Over 8 months ago ___
    This is my first Broadway show ___

14. When did you see your last off-Broadway show?
    Within the last week ___
    1 to 2 weeks ago ___
    2 to 4 weeks ago ___
    1 to 2 months ago ___
    2 to 4 months ago ___
    4 to 8 months ago ___
    Over 8 months ago ___
    I have never seen an off-Broadway show ___

15. When did you see your last motion picture?
    Within the last week ___
    1 to 2 weeks ago ___
    2 to 4 weeks ago ___
    1 to 2 months ago ___
    2 to 4 months ago ___
    4 to 8 months ago ___
    Over 8 months ago ___
    I have never seen a motion picture ___

16. How many hours did you watch television last night?
    Not at all ___
    Less than an hour ___
    1 to 2 hours ___
    2 to 4 hours ___
    Over 4 hours ___

17. Approximately what was your family income last year?
    Up to $ 4,000 ___
    $ 4,001 to $ 7,000 ___
    $ 7,001 to $10,000 ___
    $10,001 to $20,000 ___
    $20,001 to $50,000 ___
    above $50,000 ___

appear to be two good explanations for the much smaller response in the later survey than in the test survey. Of course, it might be that the test-run audience for *A Shot in the Dark* was unique; there is, however, no particular reason to believe so. In the later test, the physical size of the questionnaire was reduced considerably; this was done at the suggestion of the usherettes, who had found that the large questionnaires inside the programs tended to be awkward and bulky. The smaller size, though, had less visual effect. Moreover, since the questionnaire was smaller, it was less visible and may have gone unnoticed by anyone who did not open his *Playbill*. Reducing the size of the questionnaire, therefore, seems to have been a mistake. Also lowering the rate of response was the fact that the smaller questionnaire contained more questions. Nevertheless, the change in format should not have biased the results.

The large variation between shows in the rate of response may be largely due to the different physical characteristics of the theater. Some theaters were laid out in such a manner that boxes could easily be placed near exits without blocking them. In other theaters there was no way to place a box near exits without obstructing them—the fire laws prohibit anything blocking an exit. In a few cases the initial survey in a particular theater resulted in a very poor response rate, since it was not realized ahead of time that a large proportion of the audience left by way of ground floor fire exits. Since most respondents dropped their questionnaires in the boxes on their way out of the theater, large portions of the audience were unrepresented if no box was handy.

There did not appear to be any distinct pattern in rate of response by the day of the week. Weekdays tended to be slightly better than weekends, although the difference does not appear significant. Saturday night was generally poorer than Friday night. The response on Friday night for the straight shows was the best of any day of the week. Week-nights, on the other hand, appeared to be best for musicals. Most of the variation from day to day was probably due to chance fluctuations and to the location of the boxes.

In the whole sample, 24 per cent of the audience was represented. If this is a random sample of those in the theater, we can draw meaningful conclusions about theatergoers.

Biases

The basic problem in any survey is whether those who respond are a random sample of the population. For some reason people in the balcony and in the cheaper seats tended to respond more frequently to the questionnaire than those sitting in the orchestra. This reaction may be due to the location of the collection boxes. All individuals in the balcony had to pass a box when exiting, but some in the orchestra did not. Yet even in the balcony there is an inverse relationship between ticket price and rate of response. The rate of response in the cheapest seats was 40 per cent, while that in the most expensive seats was only 9 per cent. For the results to mean anything, we must assume that there is no bias introduced by non-respondents. That is, while people in the orchestra and the balcony clearly differ as to rate of response to questionnaires, we must assume that a random group in each price category responded.

Did the respondents answer the questions accurately? Some questionnaires were clearly incorrect. "Humorous" individuals took extreme positions on all questions. A respondent who said that he had never seen a motion picture, that his income was either zero or above $50,000, that he had paid $100 for a

Table C–1   Comparison of data from various sources

	A Shot in the Dark (1962) (Boxes)	A Shot in the Dark (1962) (Mail)	*All evening performances* (1962)	Playbill (1960)	Playbill (1963)
Percentage responding	50.1	31.7	23.6	n.a.	n.a.
Percentage out-of-town	34.4	51.4	34.2	26.8	31.3
Median age	40.4	44.8	38.9	42.4	39.5
Median income	n.c.	n.c.	$13,200	$9,650	$11,011
Travel time one way (minutes)	48.1	49.6	51.6	n.a.	n.a.

n.c.: Not computed.
n.a. Not available.

ticket, and that he expected to take six hours to go home, could be easily weeded out. More bothersome is subtle dissembling on a single question. One question deals with income, an extremely sensitive matter. Two offsetting tendencies might be expected: some individuals might be inclined to underestimate their income, because of the fear of tax authorities or because they wish to hide the amount from theater companions; others might tend to overestimate their income as a form of bragging. Pride might also affect answers to the question on Broadway show attendance, how many hours weekly they watch television, when they saw their last motion picture, how much the evening cost, and whether they are on an expense account.[1]

The data may not be representative of the entire season since the whole survey was conducted, except for the trial, during the week after Easter, which is usually one of the best weeks of the year for the theater. Many individuals who give up the theater during Lent attend the week after. Also, college students are often in town for that week on Easter vacation. Such factors as these may consequently bias the results.

Table C-1 compares a few of the relevant attributes of theatergoers. *Playbill* figures are given for the period from October, 1959, to October, 1960, and for the calendar year 1963. Total figures for the audience survey and for the two experimental surveys at *A Shot in the Dark* are listed as well. Considerable variation appears from column to column. Compare the data for *A Shot in the Dark* for the two trial performances. A very large proportion of the respondents to the questionnaires collected by mail claimed to be from out of town. The difference in proportion from the New York City area suggests either that there had been a convention from which a large group decided to see *A Shot in the Dark* or that visitors respond better to mail questionnaires than to those collected on the spot. Alternatively, local people may be more reluctant to fill out questionnaires at home to be returned by mail than to do it immediately. The last two hypotheses, however, seem unlikely. Tourists may simply have more free time to fill out the form in their hotels; hence, a larger proportion of respondents may be from out of town. But the percentage of visitors to New York on expense accounts was much higher for

1. See Chapter V for a discussion.

the performance at which the audience was asked to mail back the form than for any other. While it is plausible that the proportion of responses from out of town is affected by how the forms are collected, it seems less likely that this would bias visitors' responses to the question dealing with expense accounts. Note that for local people there was no difference in the proportion on expense accounts between the two trial surveys. In fact, for New Yorkers there seemed to be no significant difference between the responses for any question. Thus the significant variation between the questionnaires collected in boxes and those collected by mail seems to be primarily due to differences in reported number of visitors to New York and differences in the porportion of visitors on expense accounts. The reasons for the variation in response for visitors can only be speculated about, but in any case, there appears to be no bias for local playgoers.

Other differences that are notable are in the reported income of individuals. It should be noted that the median income as reported in the *Playbill* survey of theatergoers was only $9,650 in 1960 and $11,011 in 1963, while the survey median was $13,000. However, on the basis of unpublished *Playbill* figures furnished by John Enders, who conducted the study, the author computed a median income of $12,791 for theatergoers in 1961. This figure is almost a $3,000 rise in the median income from 1960. Thus there appears to be a good deal of variation from year to year in the *Playbill* results. Moreover, the *Playbill* figures may be biased, since they were based on interviews. Individuals are very probably less liable to reveal their true income in an interview than in an anonymous questionnaire. Fear of tax authorities could bias their responses downward. Hence, the *Playbill* figures are probably more unreliable than the audience survey figures.

Moreover, the survey figure may be higher than *Playbill*'s because of the methods of calculation. Each respondent in the survey was weighted by the number of individuals in his party. If, as seems likely, those with high incomes had more than the average number of people in their party while those with low incomes a less than average number, then the median calculated would be higher than the one calculated by just counting each respondent once (the *Playbill* method). Moreover, Baumol and Bowen report a median income of $14,087 for Broadway for 1963–65, not much higher than the survey figure.[2] The unpublished *Playbill* figures for 1961 ($12,791), the survey data for 1962 ($13,-000), and the Baumol and Bowen median for 1963–65 ($14,087) are all consistent, considering that incomes have generally been rising. The other published median income data from *Playbill* all appear to be too low.

In conclusion, we can say that there easily may be biases in our data. However, comparing our data with that collected in different ways or by different people does not lead us to strongly suspect our results; differences are explicable.

2. William J. Baumol and William G. Bowen, *Performing Arts—The Economic Dilemma* (New York: Twentieth Century Fund, 1966), p. 458, Table IV-G.

D | Statistical analysis of the demand for and supply of Broadway shows[1]

The purpose of this appendix is to estimate elasticities between income-quantity, income-quality, price-quantity, and cash cost-quantity. From these figures, computed from the cross-sectional data discussed above, and from time series data, a reasonably clear understanding of the theater's problems emerges.

One problem with the audience survey data must be stressed. The questionnaires were returned by people in audiences; they did not represent a random sample of the population in the New York area or even of theatergoers and potential theatergoers. To generalize about the effects on theatergoing of variables such as income, one must say something about the whole population. It is only possible to generalize from a selective sample of people to the whole population if the differences between the population in the sample and the general population are known.

The ratio of the proportion of individuals in the audience in each income class to the proportion for the population as a whole measures relative frequency of attendance by income for the population. For example, if 10 per cent of the audience earned over $20,000 a year and 10 per cent of the audience made under $5,000 a year, and these same proportions held for the total population, then income would clearly be unrelated to attendance. On the other hand, a finding that 5 per cent of the audience earned under $10,000, whereas 50 per cent of the population received under $10,000, and that 50 per cent of the audience made over $20,000 would indicate a strong income effect. The measure of relative frequency is, then, the proportion of individuals in an income class in the theater divided by the proportion of people in that income class in the total population. The total population is assumed to be the total number of families and unrelated individuals in 1960 in the New York–Northeastern New Jersey Standard Consolidated Area.[2] Correlating relative frequency and income, the income elasticity of demand for theater tickets at the mean is 1.135; the regression explains 98 per cent of the variance, and the F statistic is 107.2. The same regression in logarithms produces a slightly better result; 98.6 per cent of the variance is explained, the F statistic is 142.3, and the income elasticity of demand is 1.03. Both regressions are significant at the 1 per cent level; in neither case is the income elasticity of demand —computed at the mean—significantly different from 1. Roughly, therefore, an improvement in income will lead to a proportional growth in theatergoing.

Per capita earnings influence more than just the frequency of trips to Broadway; higher incomes can be presumed to lead to greater expenditures on theatergoing. As incomes advance, individuals will buy a higher "quality"

1. Part of this appendix appeared as "The Demand for Broadway Theatre Tickets," in *Review of Economics and Statistics*, XLVIII (February, 1966), 79–87.
2. Bureau of the Census, *U.S. Census of Population, 1960.*

night at the theater by paying more for the tickets, dining at more expensive and presumably better restaurants, and transporting themselves to the theater in more agreeable ways. Simply correlating income and cost of evening will measure the effect of income on quality; because our concern is with the expenditures of Broadway playgoers as a function of income, the proportion of the population who are theatergoers need not involve us.

From Table D-1, which presents the results of these regressions in logarithms, it can be seen that income is positively related to expenditures per evening.[3] The time required to go home is included in the regression so that the cost of traveling to the theater for any income group can be held constant. A 1 per cent rise in income would lead to a 0.2 per cent increase in the average price of tickets bought, a 0.35 per cent increase in expenditures on other items per person, and a 0.41 per cent increase in total outlays for the group as a whole. The results are hardly encouraging for the legitimate stage: when earnings expand, expenditures on non-theater activities—such as dining out, transportation, and baby-sitters—increase noticeably, but spending on tickets goes up by less. Higher incomes lead individuals to buy only slightly better seats.

As total and per capita wealth continue to rise and are reflected in increased income, we can predict a proportionate growth of attendance on Broadway, a smaller jump in the amount spent on complementary goods, and a still smaller rise in the price of tickets bought. One result of the increased desire to buy better-quality seats as people become richer is that the higher-priced tickets become relatively more popular. Greater dispersion in prices should have occurred, but we have no data to check this hypothesis.

Time series results

Without a knowledge of how price and cost affect theatergoing, a full understanding of the forces at work is impossible. Since ticket prices are fixed, price-quantity and cost-quantity elasticities cannot be derived from the audience survey. It is necessary, therefore, to consider a more explicit time series model in which ticket charges vary. Our model will be as follows:[4]

$$(1) \qquad A_i = f(Y_i, C_i, S_i);$$

$$(2) \qquad S_i = g(A_i, P_i, M_i);$$

$$(3) \qquad C_i = h(P_i, T_i, O_i).$$

Where A_i is attendance in the ith period, Y is income, C is the cost of attending the theater, S is the number of shows (musicals and plays on Broadway), P is ticket prices, M is the dummy variable for sound motion pictures, T is transportation cost to the theater, and O is other costs of attending a Broadway show. Function (1), simply stated, says that attendance in any period is a function of income in that period, costs of attending the theater in

3. A semi-logarithmic formulation gives almost identical results with slightly lower R^2's.

4. An alternative model would have the supply of shows in one period a function of price and attendance the previous year. Such a model was tested and found to have substantially the same coefficients for the demand variables except for the shows coefficients. The elasticity of attendance with respect to the number of shows was computed from the coefficient and was considerably above 1. This indicates that the addition of another show leads to an *increase* in *average* attendance—hardly plausible.

Table D–1 Survey regression coefficients of income and travel time one way on selected cost items (in logarithms)

| | Income | Travel time one way | |
Dependent variable	Regression coefficient	Regression coefficient	F statistic
Cost of evening	.408	.120	133.1
	(.026)	(.033)	
Cost of evening per person	.258	.114	100.8
	(.019)	(.025)	
Cost of tickets	.191	−.005[a]	88.2
	(.014)	(.019[a])	
Cost of everything but tickets per person	.345	.229	59.5
	(.036)	(.046)	

a. Travel time one way was included in this regression to test the hypothesis that higher costs of travel might lead to lower expenditures for tickets—a trade-off. While the sign is right, the variable is not significant.

Note: All data are from audience survey for the evening performances and for respondents who were not guests and were from New York City and the surrounding area. There were 1,228 questionnaires in this category with all the relevant data filled out. The midpoint of each income category except the highest—$50,000 and over—was used as the income observation; those checking $50,000 and over were excluded; also excluded were those under 18 or over 60 or on expense accounts. The numbers in parentheses are the standard errors.

that period, and the number of shows playing. Function (2) says that the number of shows playing in any period is a function of attendance in that period, ticket prices at that time, and the length of time since sound motion pictures were introduced. Function (3) expresses the relationship between the cost of attending the theater in any period, ticket prices, travel costs, opportunity costs,[5] and other costs (baby-sitting, dining out, etc.).

Attendance is clearly a function of income and prices. In addition, the number of different shows playing will affect theatergoing. The greater the number, the greater the possibility that individuals will find something that interests them.

Population clearly affects theatergoing. The greater the population in the New York area, ceteris paribus, the more tickets will be sold. Unfortunately, accurate annual data on the population of the area are unobtainable. Even if such statistics were available, the appropriate area to include would be uncertain. In the late twenties, Broadway undoubtedly drew from a smaller region than in the sixties. The New York City population has shown little tendency to increase since 1930 and is uncorrelated with attendance. If the population of the appropriate area has grown steadily as seems likely, then the coefficient of the income variable will be too large; this follows since income has also

5. Opportunity costs of theatergoing should be included in any measure of total expenses. See Jacob Mincer, "Market Prices, Opportunity Costs, and Income Effects," in Measurement in Economics: Studies in Mathematical Economics and Econometrics in Memory of Yehuda Grunfeld (Stanford, Calif.: Stanford University Press, 1963). Unfortunately we have no data from which to estimate opportunity cost.

had an upward trend. In interpreting our results, we must keep this factor in mind.

While seats are being demanded, shows are being supplied. The number of theaters with shows playing during a week depends on the overall demand for theater tickets—if demand is high, some shows will remain in operation that would have closed when conditions were bad—and on the number that opened recently. The former factor is reflected in price and attendance, while the latter depends at least in part on the availability of factors of production.[6] Normally, if factors of production are scarce, costs and prices will rise. In the late twenties and early thirties after sound was developed, the expansion of the motion picture industry was phenomenal; motion picture receipts of downtown New York film houses doubled between February, 1925, and February, 1928, and tripled between 1925 and 1931.[7] Actors who could talk, singers, and directors who could deal with the spoken word were avidly sought. Hollywood bid them away from Broadway. Performances per theater fell from between 221 and 267 for the 1928/29 season to 139 for the 1931/32 season; theater rent fell from about 45 per cent of the gross to 30 per cent or less.[8] Note that the top ticket price of straight shows, after adjusting for price changes, increased each year, with the exception of 1932, from 1927 through 1935 when it reached $5.80 in 1947–49 dollars—two cents more than in February, 1963. Musical prices also increased rapidly: in 1927 the average price of the best seat was $6.23; the next year it jumped to $7.39; by February, 1930, it had risen to $8.33; in 1963 it was $7.06 in 1947–49 dollars.[9] In Chapter III we found that production and operating costs rose considerably more rapidly during the thirties than during any other period. In fact, operating costs in the 1960/61 season were not appreciably higher than operating costs in the 1939–42 seasons, yet they were considerably higher than they had been during the 1927–29 period. Production costs tripled between 1927–29 and 1939–42. In the face of the Great Depression, therefore, production and operating costs increased and prices rose, even though many theaters were dark. Something must have been affecting supply: that something, it seems most likely, was that film producers were bidding artists away from Broadway. Our supply function will therefore include a dummy variable for sound movies. Since the introduction of sound motion pictures would most likely have the greatest effect the first year, a smaller effect the second, and so on, the variable will be $1/t$, where t is the number of years since 1928; before 1929, the value of the dummy variable will be 1.[10]

6. See Chapters I and II for a complete discussion of this point.
7. Computed from various issues of *Variety*.
8. Performances per theater were computed by dividing the total number of performances during the season by the number of theaters on Broadway; total performances were computed by adding the total for each show as given in *Best Plays* volumes and supplemented by *Variety*. The number of theaters was taken from John F. Wharton, *Crisis in the Free World Theatre*, p. 18.
9. Computed from various issues of *Variety*.
10. Sound motion pictures were first introduced in October, 1927, with *The Jazz Singer*. The value of the dummy in 1928 = 1, 1929 = 1, 1930 = ½, 1931 = ⅓, and so forth. The dummy variable lags the introduction of sound by two years since it must have taken some time for the effect to be felt. Ideally the number of sound films should be used, but unfortunately it is unavailable on an annual basis. Other dummy variables were tried, such as holding the value of the dummy at 1/10 after year eleven and of having two price variables—before and after sound. The former

While attendance must have been reduced somewhat with the introduction of sound, its effect on supply appears dominant. Prices rose rather than fell. Inserting a dummy variable for motion pictures in the demand equation adds nothing to explained variances and has no affect on the other coefficients.[11]

Although in most expositions price is an endogenous variable, ticket prices in this model are assumed to be a function of costs and a random element. This approach is not unreasonable. The house scale is usually established weeks before opening by considering the cost of the show, the prices charged by previous productions in that theater, and by expectations concerning the probable success of the venture. The price variable is an average of the cost of the most expensive seats for a regular performance of each production playing during the month of February. Since the house scale normally remains unchanged throughout the run whether tickets are being scalped or discounted, list prices fail to reflect demand. Unfortunately, the top ticket price may be a poor estimate of the average ticket price. We will assume, however, that our measure of ticket prices is an unbiased index of the average over a period of time.[12] The measure, therefore, while reflecting costs, expectations, and other elements, is probably reasonably independent of demand and can therefore be treated as exogenous.

In the long run, average attendance per show is probably a constant. If so, the long-run equilibrium condition for our model can be expressed as: $A = \alpha S$. With the addition of this equilibrium condition there are four endogenous variables—A, S, P, and C—and four equations. But in the model tested, it is assumed that the market is not necessarily ever in long-run equilibrium; price must therefore be taken as exogenous.

Unfortunately no data or insufficient data on travel expenses and on other expenses of attending the theater exist for the entire period. This lack, however, may be tolerable: even though the population has been moving to the suburbs, with improved transportation, the real cost in time and money may have remained approximately the same. Assuming that travel costs and other expenses of theatergoing have no trend in time and are uncorrelated with the other variables, there would be no harm in excluding them. To the extent that they may have had an upward trend, they would be reflected in the income coefficient and would tend to lower it. Consequently, Function (3) has been dropped from the model and P_t has been substituted for C_t in Equation (1). The model is now:

$$(4) \qquad A_i = f^*(Y_i, P_i, S_i);$$

$$(5) \qquad S_i = g(A_i, P_i, M_i).$$

Attendance, therefore, will be considered as a function of income, the supply of shows, and the real price of tickets; later the total cost of attending the theater will be reintroduced.

---

dummy gave values virtually indistinguishable from the ones reported. The latter approach produced poor results.

11. Television apparently has had no effect on either supply or demand. The coefficient of a dummy variable for television was insignificantly different from zero.

12. The evidence suggests that this is a reasonable assumption: the ratio of the highest ticket price for a regular performance and the average list price from 1950 to 1963 remained almost constant; there was no noticeable trend.

The data

The basic data for testing the model extend from 1928 to 1963 for the month of February, a period which covers basic shifts in the pattern of theater-going. In the 1927/28 season, both attendance and openings on Broadway reached an all-time high. With the advent of hard times, attendance dropped to half its former level and the number of new productions sank even further.

Attendance for an average week in February was estimated by dividing the total gross receipts for musicals and for straight shows separately by the average top ticket price; the quotient was then multiplied by 1.6—the mean ratio of the price of the best seats to the average list price of all seats during the fifties. The result was an estimate of attendance at straight shows and at musicals; the two numbers were summed to get the total. It should be noted that the average list price of seats may easily differ from the average paid price if tickets are scalped or discounted, if brokerage fees are charged, or if seats at some price sell slower than others. We presume, however, that no bias is introduced by this method.

The number of shows is the total of straight shows plus the total of musicals playing each week during February of each year divided by four. Ticket prices are a weighted average of the prices of the best seats for straight shows and for musicals: since musicals have nearly 35 per cent more seats available than do straight shows,[13] musical ticket prices were weighted by 1.3475 and straight shows by 1; an average was then computed—in actual practice it makes little difference whether the average was weighted or not. The change in excise taxes during this period resulted in a divergence between the price the theater received and the price the playgoer paid. An adjustment was made in the price variable in the supply equation. Hence two price variables, P_d and P_s, were used in the model.

If published per capita GNP figures were used in testing the model, considerable variation in income would exist because of transitory factors. Since deriving the long-run effects of income and price is our aim, a measure of permanent income was employed. The model for permanent income is a common one: permanent income in period i is a weighted average of actual income in period i and permanent income in period $i - 1$. Thus, if permanent income is called y^* and actual income is y, we can write $y^*_i = \beta y_i + (1 - \beta) y^*_{i-1}$. Our only problem is to estimate β and y^*_{i-1}. Clearly, we can write $y^*_{i-1} = \beta y_{i-1} + (1 - \beta) Y^*_{i-2}$ and by substitution: $y^*_i = \beta y_i + \beta(1 - \beta) y_{i-1} + (1 - \beta)^2 Y^*_{i-2}$.

This substitution can be extended indefinitely, but it will always involve on the right-hand side a y^* term. As more terms are added, the importance of the value of y^* diminishes. Per capita income in 1919 was chosen as the original y^* to compute permanent income in the years between 1927 and 1962. The model was tested using various β's; the best fit was for β's from .3 to .5. For the results in this chapter, permanent income was computed with a β at .4. A different β would make only a small change in the results.

Testing the model

This appendix is primarily concerned with the factors affecting attendance. Three ways of estimating the parameters of the demand equation will be

13. Computed from a sample of all the productions on Broadway in the fall of 1962.

considered. First is the naive approach: attendance is regressed on price, income, and number of shows; a dummy variable for motion pictures can be added. This approach hypothesizes that the supply of shows is determined outside the system, a dubious conjecture; if false—that is, if the number of shows is a function of attendance—then the naive estimates will be biased.

One method of dealing with this bias is a two-stage-least-squares.[14] Briefly, the problem with the naive approach is that the size of the residuals of the demand equation is not independent of the number of shows—a variable that appears in the demand equation; consequently, the coefficients will be biased. The two-stage-least-squares approach circumvents this difficulty by using the reduced-form equations to predict the number of shows. The resulting predicted values will be an exact function of the exogenous variables. Hence, these values are independent of the residuals and, when used in the demand equation, will give consistent estimates.

As mentioned above, two variables, population and travel expenses, which are left out of the model, are likely to be correlated with income and hence bias its coefficient. Therefore, we can have little faith in its magnitude. We will test the effects, on all other coefficients, of forcing the income coefficient to be the same as that computed in the cross-sectional part of this appendix. To do this, it is only necessary to remove the effect of income from our dependent variable and then use the same two-stage-least-squares approach discussed above.

There are several problems involved in using cross-sectional figures on the relationship between income and attendance in the time series data.[15] Time series income data may be measuring a shorter or longer run than do cross-sectional data; hence, it may be incorrect to use the cross-sectional coefficient. Kuh and Meyer have shown that the introduction of extraneous estimates tends to bias the coefficients upward.[16] In interpreting our results, this must be considered.

Table D-2 presents the results of these tests. The most interesting rows of the table are those listing the elasticities: the price elasticity estimates are very similar; they vary from −.48 to −.64. The naive tests—in which attendance is run on price, income, and number of shows—result in the lowest price elasticities and the highest multiple R^2's. The two-stage-least-squares tests probably reflect more accurately the demand for theater tickets, but the results differ little from the naive approach. Note that when the income elasticity is forced to 1, the price elasticity rises only slightly to −.64, it is still rather inelastic. As was mentioned above, slightly higher coefficients can be expected when extraneous estimates are used; thus the results seem consistent with each other.

The elasticity for the number of shows measures the effect of a change in number of shows on attendance; these elasticities are all approximately 1, suggesting that a change in the number of shows leads to a proportional

14. See J. Johnston, *Econometric Methods* (New York: McGraw-Hill, 1963), chap. ix. Since our model is exactly identified, two-stage least squares is equivalent to indirect least squares.
15. See L. R. Klein, *An Introduction to Econometrics* (Englewood Cliffs, N.J.: Prentice-Hall, 1962), chap. ii, and Edwin Kuh and John R. Meyer, "How Extraneous Are Extraneous Estimates?" *Review of Economics and Statistics,* XXXIX (November, 1957), 380–393.
16. *Ibid.*

Table D–2 Various formulations of the demand model of theatergoing

	Naive linear	Two-stage-least-squares linear	Naive multiplicative	Two-stage-least-squares multiplicative	Two-stage with income forced to cross sectional[a] (multiplicative)
Price coefficient	−14.057	−15.585	−.453	−.563	−.643
	(6.390)	(9.601)	(.228)	(.306)	(.512)
Income coefficient	.053	0.54	.364	.371	
	(.010)	(.015)	(.064)	(.084)	
Number of shows coefficient	6.440	6.755	.973	1.075	1.153
	(.433)	(.738)	(.074)	(.115)	(.191)
Price elasticity	−.482	−.534	−.453	−.563	−.643
Income elasticity	.348	.357	.364	.371	1.030[b]
Shows elasticity	.917	.962	.973	1.075	1.153
Total R^2	.878	.735	.862	.762	.528[c]
Durbin-Watson	1.989	1.239	1.844	1.381	.469

a. Income coefficient forced to 1.030 as given in Table D-1 from the cross section study.
b. Taken from cross section study, Table D-1.
c. Computed on basis of attendance with income removed.

change in attendance. An elasticity of 1 would indicate that producers face an infinitely elastic demand for their product; that is, within the range of 18 to 30, the addition of another show, if it is of average quality, will increase the total number of theatergoers sufficiently to sustain the new show. The theater, therefore, appears to have the characteristics of a perfectly competitive industry; while the industry demand curve is inelastic, any firm (producer) can sell as much as he wishes (mount as many productions as he wishes and market their seats) without reducing prices. As long as the marginal cost of a new average-quality show is less than the expected revenue, it will premiere. As producers bid for the scarce supply of good scripts, fine actors, and knowledgeable directors, marginal costs increase. In the end, the supply of talent determines how many shows will open.

The industry supply schedule, however, is inelastic in the short run. As can be seen from Table D-3, an increase in price leads to a less than proportional growth in the number of shows. This result is not surprising; the problem with the theater has been a shortage of trained and talented writers, players, and directors. Any increase in Broadway activity requires drawing scarce talent away from motion pictures and from television.

The results turn on the specification of the model: another specification, such as excluding price from the supply function of shows, might make two-stage-least-squares inappropriate; in that case three-stage-least-squares would be required.[17] A three-stage approach was tried, but the results were unimpressive: the price coefficient in the demand function turned out to be positive but insignificantly different from zero.

17. See Arnold Zellner and H. Theil, "Three-Stage Least Squares: Simultaneous Estimation of Simultaneous Equations," *Econometrica*, XXX (January, 1962), 54–78.

Table D–3 Various formulations of the supply model of theatergoing

	Naive linear	Two-stage-least-squares linear	Naive multiplicative	Two-stage-least-squares multiplicative
Price coefficient	2.479	2.352	.445	.426
	(.748)	(1.116)	(.157)	(.222)
Attendance coefficient	.090	.074	.610	.564
	(.012)	(.026)	(.073)	(.126)
Motion picture dummy coefficient	11.234	13.663	.133	.145
	(2.587)	(4.797)	(.034)	(.052)
Price elasticity	.516	.489	.445	.426
Attendance elasticity	.629	.518	.610	.564
Motion picture elasticity	.085	.103	.133	.145
Total R^2	.899	.779	.869	.743
Durbin-Watson	2.043	1.522	1.990	1.682

The model above is predicated on the assumption that the introduction of sound motion pictures affected the supply of factors of production more than it affected attendance. While undoubtedly it had some effect on demand, there are reasons to believe that the major effects—several of which were discussed above—were on supply. In addition, the dummy variable for motion pictures is more highly correlated with number of shows than it is with attendance: the simple correlation coefficient between the dummy motion picture variable and attendance is .66, and between it and the number of shows playing, .82.

The findings depend also on the assumption that estimated attendance and the price variable are, at least, unbiased indexes of theatergoing and ticket tariffs; moreover, the outcome hangs on the truth of the premise that all relevant variables are included and that the excluded ones are uncorrelated with those in the model. Since the price of tickets is only part of the cost of attending the theater, we know that important factors are left out: the outlay for transportation, travel time to the theater, the expense of dinner in a restaurant, and the cost of baby-sitters, all of which should be taken into account but are ignored because of inadequate data. We assumed that this exclusion would have little effect. But if the price variable is correlated with other costs, the estimated elasticity would be too high, since it would be reflecting the effect of these other items. The crucial proposition is that the items left out are uncorrelated with the exogenous variables.

We know from the audience survey data that in 1962 the cost of theatergoing averaged $16.37 per person, of which $7.99 was spent on a seat. A 10 per cent rise in price of tickets would lead, therefore, to a 4.88 per cent rise in the cash cost of theatergoing and a 5 per cent fall in frequency of attendance. It follows, that the cash cost-quantity elasticity is about −1.[18]

The time series data suggest an income-quantity elasticity considerably

18. Costs of theatergoing undoubtedly include the time spent in travel and in the theater. A simple correlation in logarithms of travel time to the theater with relative attendance produced a regression coefficient of −1.82, suggesting that time in transit does affect frequency of playgoing. This is consistent with the Mincer article cited above.

smaller than was computed in the cross-section. It is possible that income, which at least since the early thirties has had a fairly steady upward trend, is correlated with other variables excluded from the model, such as travel expenses of visiting Broadway and restaurant costs. If so, measured income elasticity is too small. Since the population has moved steadily to the suburbs, travel time and/or cash costs may have risen. Moreover, restaurant prices reflect labor costs, which have climbed since the thirties. Therefore, there is a good a priori reason to believe that these variables are correlated with income and thus that the time series income elasticity is underestimated.

Eliminating the federal excise tax

What do these figures tell us about the effect of eliminating the 10 per cent tax on tickets? The abolition of the federal admissions tax on December 31, 1965, may be expected to expand attendance and the number of shows playing by about 10 per cent. The growth stems from an increase in shows playing when the tax is removed; with an expansion in number of shows, attendance rises; with higher attendance, more shows will be presented; and so forth.

Formally, this result derives from solving the original equations for the percentage change. Thus:

$$(7) \qquad A = a_1 P_d^{b_1} Y^{b_2} S^{b_3};$$

$$(8) \qquad S = a_2 P_s^{b_4} A^{b_5} M^{b_6}.$$

Then by substitution of (8) in (7) and solving for A,

$$A = a_1^{1/(1-b_3 b_5)} a_2^{b_3/(1-b_3 b_5)} P_d^{b_1/(1-b_3 b_5)} P_s^{b_4 b_3/(1-b_3 b_5)} M^{b_3 b_6/(1-b_3 b_5)} Y^{b_2/(1-b_3 b_5)}.$$

Call the situation before the tax is removed 1, and afterward 2. Then the relative change in attendance A_2/A_1 is:

$$(9) \qquad A_2/A_1 = \left(\frac{P_{d2}}{P_{d1}}\right)^{b_1/(1-b_3 b_5)} \left(\frac{P_{s2}}{P_{s1}}\right)^{b_4 b_3/(1-b_3 b_5)}$$

and similarly for shows:

$$(10) \qquad S_2/S_1 = \left(\frac{P_{d2}}{P_{d1}}\right)^{b_1 b_5/(1-b_3 b_5)} \left(\frac{P_{s2}}{P_{s1}}\right)^{b_4/(1-b_3 b_5)}.$$

Now by assumption, in the long run $A = \alpha S$; that is, average attendance is constant.

Hence: $A_2/A_1 = S_2/S_1$.

Therefore:

$$(11) \qquad \left(\frac{P_{d2}}{P_{d1}}\right)^{b_1/(1-b_3 b_5)} \left(\frac{P_{s2}}{P_{s1}}\right)^{b_4 b_3/(1-b_3 b_5)} = \left(\frac{P_{d2}}{P_{d1}}\right)^{b_1 b_5/(1-b_3 b_5)} \left(\frac{P_{s2}}{P_{s1}}\right)^{b_4/(1-b_3 b_5)}.$$

If we assume $b_3 = 1$ since our estimate of it is not significantly different from 1, then the two forms dealing with the ratio of supply prices are equal. Consequently, for Equation (11) to hold, $P_{d2}/P_{d1} = 1$, or in words, the price to the consumer remains unchanged. The removal of the tax is reflected entirely in more revenue for the production. Thus $P_{s2}/P_{s1} = 1.10$. Using the two-stage-least-squares multiplicative coefficients (Table D-3, Column 4):

$$S_2/S_1 = A_2/A_1 = (P_{s2}/P_{s1})^{b_4/(1-b_5)} = 1.075.$$

It seems reasonable, however, to claim that an increase in average revenue would stimulate or maintain the same number of productions on Broadway irrespective of whether it originated with higher attendance or from higher ticket prices. That is, if ticket prices changed by β per cent, the effect on the number of shows should be no different than if attendance changed by β per cent. Hence b_4 should be equal to b_5. In fact they are not significantly different; their mean is 4.95 or approximately .5. Assuming $b_4 = b_5 = .5$, the abolition of the 10 per cent ticket tax will lead to a 10 per cent increase in shows and attendance. Dropping the tax will therefore aid the theater but not revolutionize it.

Conclusion

The low income elasticity of demand for playgoing seems surprising; a figure considerably greater than 1 was expected by the author for such a luxury good as playgoing. The explanation may lie in the fact that theatergoing in New York requires considerable time—about two and a half hours inside the theater and, for the average commuter to Manhattan, about 140 minutes round trip.[19] Inasmuch as higher income people tend to place a greater value on their time, including that spent in consumption, than do lower income people,[20] they will substitute in consumption those goods which use relatively little time for those that use a great deal. Playgoing obviously falls in the latter category. Opportunity costs of theatergoing go up with a rise in income. Hence, advances in earnings lead to a desire to spend more on theatergoing (income effect) and to an appreciation in the opportunity costs of doing so. The measured income elasticity only reflects, therefore, the net effect income has on consumption.

The slow growth in the Broadway audience appears to be a result of a modest net income elasticity, an increase in ticket prices, and possibly the flight to the suburbs which has increased travel time and opportunity costs. Fears that the theater is pricing itself out of the market seem unfounded, but higher prices may well have reduced playgoing a little.

Operating expenses largely reflect wages since the theater is not subject to important productivity gains. Therefore, in the long run we can expect the climb in costs and ticket prices to parallel the movement in personal income. As incomes advance, so will the cost of attending the theater. Luckily for Broadway, the income elasticity is higher than the price elasticity and theatergoing should grow, albeit slowly. But if transportation costs, baby-sitting fees, and restaurant prices also climb, the effect of advancing incomes may be almost completely offset by the higher costs of attending the theater.

19. New York—New Jersey Transportation Agency, *Journey to Work* (New York: New York-New Jersey Transportation Agency, 1963). Average travel time to work is about 70 minutes one way. At times other than rush hour it will be less for some individuals and more for those depending on public transportation. The average, then, for off hours may not differ greatly from 70 minutes.
20. Mincer, "Market Prices, Opportunity Costs, and Income Effects."

Selected bibliography

Books

Anderson, John. *The American Theatre*. New York: Dial Press, 1938.

Baumol, William J., and Bowen, William G. *Performing Arts—The Economic Dilemma*. New York: Twentieth Century Fund, 1966.

Beckhard, Richard, and Effrat, John. *Blueprint for Summer Theatre*. New York: J. Richard Press, 1948.

Bernheim, Alfred L. *The Business of the Theatre: An Economic History of the American Theatre*. New York: Actors' Equity Association, 1932; reissued, New York: Benjamin Blom, 1964.

The Best Plays of [1927–1928]——, ed. Burns Mantle, John Chapman, Louis Kronenberger, and Henry Hewes. New York: Dodd, Mead, 1928——.

Cullman, Marguerite. *Occupation: Angel*. New York: W. W. Norton, 1963.

Dewhurst, J. Frederic, and associates. *America's Needs and Resources*. New York: Twentieth Century Fund, 1955.

Dorian, Frederick. *Commitment to Culture*. Pittsburgh: University of Pittsburgh Press, 1964.

Enders, John. *Survey of New York Theatre*. New York: Playbill, 1959.

Eustis, Morton, *B'way, Inc! The Theatre as a Business*. New York: Dodd, Mead, 1934.

Flanagan, Hallie. *Arena*. New York: Duell, Sloan and Pearce, 1940.

Freedley, George. *Broadway Playhouses*. New York: New York Public Library, 1943.

Hornblow, Arthur. *A History of the Theatre in America*. 2 vols. Philadelphia: Lippincott, 1919.

Houghton, Norris. *Advance from Broadway: 19,000 Miles of American Theatre*. New York: Harcourt, Brace, 1941.

Hughes, Glenn. *A History of the American Theatre, 1700–1950*. New York: Samuel French, 1951.

Landstone, Charles. *Off-Stage: A Personal Record of the First Twelve Years of State Sponsored Drama in Great Britain*. London: Elek, 1953.

Lichtenberg, Robert M. *One Tenth of a Nation*. Cambridge, Mass.: Harvard University Press, 1960.

Lord, William J., Jr. *How Authors Make a Living*. New York: Scarecrow Press, 1962.

Purcell, Ralph. *Government and Art*. Washington, D. C.: Public Affairs Press, 1953.

Quinn, Arthur Hobson. *A History of American Drama, from the Beginning to the Civil War*. New York: Appleton-Century-Crofts, 1951.

Rockefeller Brothers Fund. *The Performing Arts: Problems and Prospects.* New York: McGraw-Hill, 1965.

Shaw, George Bernard. *Advice to a Young Critic and Other Letters.* New York: Crown Publishers, 1955.

Winter, William. *The Wallet of Time.* 2 vols. New York: Moffat, Yard, 1913.

Magazines and journals

Barnett, William. "Auditing a Limited Partnership in the Theatre," *Journal of Accountancy,* XCVII (May, 1954), 593–602.

Bernnys, Edward L. "Theatre Survey," *Theatre Arts,* XXXIII (December, 1949), 17.

"Broadway Has a New Angel—the Theatre Party," *Business Week,* December 8, 1956, pp. 110–114.

"The Disintegration of the Road," *Literary Digest,* XC (September 4, 1926), 27–28.

"Effects of Technological Changes on Employment in the Amusement Industry," *Monthly Labor Review,* XXXII (August, 1931), 261–267.

Equity (various issues).

French, H. "British Film Production," *Banca Nazionale del Lavoro Quarterly Review,* IX (September, 1956), 124–131.

"Getting Them Back to the Movies," *Business Week,* October 22, 1955, pp. 58–63.

Hamilton, Clayton. "The Long Run in the Theatre," *Bookman,* XLII (February, 1916), 643–652.

Heffner, Hurbert C. "The Decline of the Professional Theatre in America," *Quarterly Journal of Speech,* XXXV (April, 1949), 170–177.

Helburn, Theresa. "What's Right with the Theater," *New Republic,* LVIII (April 10, 1929), 226–227.

Kerr, Walter. "Killing Off the Theater," *Harper's,* CCX (April, 1955), 55–62.

Lippman, Monroe. "The Effect of the Theatrical Syndicate on Theatrical Art in America," *Quarterly Journal of Speech,* XXVI (April, 1940), 275–282.

Maney, Richard. "Advice to Those Who Want Two on the Aisle," *New York Times Magazine,* June 5, 1949, pp. 19–22.

Mills, G. "Public Expenditure on the Arts in Great Britain," *Yorkshire Bulletin of Economics and Social Research,* XI (December, 1959), 86–99.

Millstein, Gilbert M. "The City—A Love Letter," *New York Times Magazine,* June 7, 1959, pp. 16–17, 44–50.

"Money Behind the Scenes," *Economist,* CXCVI (August 6, 1960), 540–541.

Murdoch, Lawrence C. "S.R.O. and SOS: The Performing Arts Paradox," *Business Review,* Federal Reserve Bank of Philadelphia (March, 1962), 3–14.

"Regional Theatre: U.S.A.," *Theatre Arts,* XXXIII (August, 1949), 17–56.

"Report on Theatre in New York," *Billboard* (various issues).

Scitovsky, Tibor and Ann. "What Price Economic Progress," *Yale Review,* XLIX (September, 1959), 95–110.

Shaffer, Helen B. "Government and the Arts," *Editorial Research Reports,* II (August 2, 1961), 561–578.

———. "Movie-TV Competition," *Editorial Research Reports,* I (January 18, 1957), 43–61.

Simonson, Lee. "Theatre: Gamblers' Paradise," *New Republic,* LXXII (September 7, 1932), 93–96.

Sobel, Bernard. "Musical Comedy: From Florodora to Hazel Flagg," *Theatre Arts,* XXXVII (February, 1953), 18–23, 84.

Starr, Isidore. "Recent Supreme Court Decisions: Baseball, Boxing and Show Business," *Social Education,* XIX (December, 1955), 357–362.

Stubs (various issues).

"Study Blames Television for Theatre Drop," *Broadcasting Magazine,* February 3, 1958, p. 58.

"Theatre-Business," *Fortune,* XVII (February, 1938), 66–72, 102–106.

Variety (various issues).

Williams, W. E. "The Arts and Public Patronage," *Lloyds Bank Review,* XLIX (July, 1958), 18–29.

Winston, Clement, and Smith, Mabel A., "Income Sensitivity of Consumption Expenditures," *Survey of Current Business,* XXX (January, 1950), 17–20.

Pamphlets

Enders, John W. *Who's Who in the Audience.* New York: Playbill, annually since 1955.

Findlater, Richard. *The Future of the Theatre,* Fabian Tract 317. London: Fabian Society, May, 1959.

———. *What Are Writers Worth?* London: Society of Authors, 1963.

Middleton, George. *The Dramatists Guild.* New York: Dramatists Guild, 1959.

Stage & Screen: Interviews by Donald McDonald with Walter Kerr, Drama Critic, New York Herald-Tribune, *and Stanley Kramer, Film Producer and Director, with a Comment by Edward Reed.* One of Series of Interviews on the American Character. Center for the Study of Democratic Institutions, 1962.

Wharton, John F. *Crisis in the Free World Theatre.* New York: League of New York Theatres, 1961.

Public documents

Commission of Fine Arts. *Report to the President on Art and Government.* Washington, D. C.: Government Printing Office, 1953.

Great Britain. Arts Council of Great Britain. *20th Annual Report, 1964/65.* London, n.d.

New York State. *Inquiry by Hon. Louis J. Lefkowitz, Attorney General of New York State, into Financing and Ticket Distribution Practices in the New York Legitimate Theatre.* 2 vols. December, 1963.

United States. Bureau of the Census. *United States Census of Business, 1958,*

Vol. V: *Selected Service Trades, Summary of Statistics*. Washington, D.C.: Government Printing Office, 1961.

———. Federal Works Agency. *Final Report on the WPA Program, 1935–1943*. Washington, D.C.: Government Printing Office, [1947].

———. House of Representatives. Committee on Education and Labor. *Hearings on the Federal Advisory Council on Arts*. 86th Cong., 1st Sess., 1959.

———. ———. *Hearings on Aid to Fine Arts*. 87th Cong., 1st Sess., 1961.

———. ———. *Hearings on Economic Conditions in the Performing Arts*. 87th Cong., 1st and 2nd Sess., 1961.

———. ———. *National Foundation on Arts and Humanities, Questions and Answers*. 89th Cong., 1st Sess., 1965.

———. House of Representatives. House Appropriations Committee. *Hearings on Department of Interior and Related Agencies Appropriations for 1967*. Part III, 267–353. 89th Cong., 2nd Sess., 1966.

Unpublished material

Barr, Richard. "Off-Broadway Theatre." Prepared for the Special Studies Project, Rockefeller Brothers Fund. Mimeographed, May 17, 1963.

Birkenhead, Thomas Bruce. "Economics of the Broadway Theatre." Unpublished Ph.D. dissertation, New School for Social Research, 1963.

Fichandler, Zelda. "A Permanent Classical Repertory Theatre in the Nation's Capital." Mimeographed, June, 1959.

Little, Stuart W. "The Broadway Producer." A report for the Rockefeller Brothers Fund. Typewritten, May 20, 1963.

Watts, John Gaydon. "Economics of the New York Legitimate Theater, 1948–1958." Unfinished Ph.D. dissertation, Columbia University, n.d.

Weiss and Geller Research. "An Exploratory Study of Theatre Audiences, Present and Future." Chicago: Mimeographed, March, 1956.

———. "Angels Without Wings: An Exploratory Study of Investors in the Living Theatre." Chicago: Mimeographed, March, 1956.

Index